NO PLACE LIKE MURDER

JANIS THORNTON

NO PLACE LIKE MURDER

TRUE CRIME IN THE MIDWEST

Forewords by Larry Sweazy and Ray E. Boomhower

AN IMPRINT OF
INDIANA UNIVERSITY PRESS

This book is a publication of

Quarry Books
an imprint of
INDIANA UNIVERSITY PRESS

Office of Scholarly Publishing
Herman B Wells Library 350
1320 East 10th Street
Bloomington, Indiana 47405 USA

iupress.org

© 2020 by Janis Thornton
All rights reserved

No part of this book may be reproduced or utilized in any form or by any means, electronic or mechanical, including photocopying and recording, or by any information storage and retrieval system, without permission in writing from the publisher.

The paper used in this publication meets the minimum requirements of the American National Standard for Information Sciences—Permanence of Paper for Printed Library Materials, ANSI Z39.48–1992.

Manufactured in the United States of America

Cataloging information is available from the Library of Congress.

ISBN 978-0-253-05277-3 (hardback)
ISBN 978-0-253-05278-0 (paperback)
ISBN 978-0-253-05279-7 (ebook)

First printing 2020

This collection of stories is a tribute to the innocent victims whose time on earth was deliberately and viciously cut short. Among them, and most heartbreaking, are four children: Dee McClure, age two, and his brother Homer, age three; eight-year-old Mollie King; and eleven-year-old Mary Elizabeth Breeden. Their precious lives were stolen from them almost before they began; and even worse, they were taken by someone they had trusted and loved. Rest in peace, sweet angels.

CONTENTS

	Foreword by Larry D. Sweazy	ix
	Foreword by Ray E. Boomhower	xiii
	Acknowledgments	xv
	Introduction	xvii

PART I: All in the Family

1	The Mysterious Death of Belle Shenkenberger	3
2	The Liberation of Nora Coleman	14
3	"Sweet Dreams, Mother"	23

PART II: Wife Killers

4	Dan Snider and the Strychnine Solution	35
5	The Case of the Drowsy Uxoricide	44
6	Death on Maish Road	54
7	Chirka and Rasico	66

PART III: To Err Can Be Murder

| 8 | Manhunt for the In-Law Outlaws | 79 |
| 9 | The Black Sheep of Goldsmith | 88 |

PART IV: Loved to Death

| 10 | He Was Her Man, but He Done Her Wrong | 105 |
| 11 | Fairy's Grim Tale of Murder on LaFountain | 119 |

PART V: Deadly Decisions

12	Murder on Anderson and Main	131
13	The Strawtown Murders	141
14	Murder Unbecoming a Hero	151

PART VI: Worst of the Worst

| 15 | The Awful Crime of Jesse McClure | 163 |
| 16 | Massacre on Laughery Creek | 173 |

PART VII: Local Legends

| 17 | The Legend of Kokomo Mayor H. C. Cole | 189 |
| 18 | Gun Girl | 199 |

PART VIII: Unsolved but Unforgotten

19	Murder Most Foul	211
20	The Strange Death of Garnet Ginn	222
	Bibliography	233

FOREWORD

WHEN I WAS FOURTEEN, I CAME DOWN WITH MONONUCLEOSIS. IT was the spring of 1974—that perfect time of the year when the grass is starting to turn green, the robins are nesting, and the mundane gloominess of winter begins to wash away with the fortuitous rains. It was time to get outside, hang out with my friends, and get as far away from my parents as I could. Instead, I was confined to bed for a month. Doctor's orders. No ifs, ands, or buts. Televisions were a luxury, and we had only one in the house. It was in the living room, and it was one of those twenty-inch screens set inside a wood cabinet that took up half of the wall. If I wanted to watch TV, I'd have to lie on the couch (called a davenport by my mom). That wasn't practical when everyone else was home, which meant I was left to watch game shows in the morning—great for a day or two—and soap operas in the afternoon. Boredom set in fast. Lucky for me, my mom borrowed a Time-Life encyclopedia from one of her friends, hoping it would take me a while to read as I recuperated. The encyclopedia wasn't one of those twenty- or thirty-volume sets but rather three thick volumes dedicated to the most notorious criminals of the twentieth century. Before long, I was immersed in the horrible deeds perpetrated by Lizzie Borden, Leopold and Loeb, and the Boston Strangler—and my love of true crime was born.

I would go on to read *Helter Skelter*, by Vincent Bugliosi and Curt Gentry, which was published in 1974, and instead of being afraid of the bogeyman, I feared Charles Manson and his followers. Then in the 1980s, I discovered Ann Rule, another vaunted contributor to the true crime genre. As much as I enjoyed those books, my own path to becoming a writer followed the fiction path, a mystery and crime fiction path. It's little surprise that one of my books, *A Thousand Falling Crows*, follows the aftermath of a shootout with Bonnie and Clyde—an idea born, no doubt, while I suffered from mono and read that encyclopedia from cover to cover. I read a lot of those stories three and four times.

This book reaffirms my appreciation for true crime writing in an unexpected way. Lizzie Borden, Leopold and Loeb, and the Boston Strangler are legendary; they have received the Hollywood treatment (more than once) and are forever imprinted in our popular culture. Janis Thornton, on the other hand, brings us stories that are mostly unknown outside the small towns where the crimes occurred.

I grew up in the small two-stoplight town of Chesterfield, Indiana (Madison County), so the sense of place of these stories feels familiar. And so do the people. I discovered stories of events that took place outside my back door in this wonderfully informative and entertaining volume of local true crime—stories I had never heard of before. I was introduced to fifteen-year-old Isabelle Messmer, the "Gun Girl" from Elwood, who, starting in 1933, went on a decade-long crime spree from Pittsburgh, Pennsylvania, to Texas, and back to Indiana. She was Indiana's own Bonnie Harper before anybody had heard of Bonnie and Clyde. And I learned about Grover Blake, who murdered his mother in 1908, in Anderson, Indiana (where I was born), for reasons I'll let you discover on your own.

To say *No Place Like Murder* reignited my interest in local true crime stories is an understatement. Each story was a revelation, new to me, which, of course, made me wonder why I hadn't heard of these stories before now. Thankfully, the author has painstakingly put together a collection that informs readers about the heinous crimes and goes the extra mile to honor the victims. As sad as "The Awful Crime of Jesse McClure" is, Thornton humanizes the tale as the murderer, sentenced to life in prison, meets his maker sooner than planned. A similar outcome is revealed in the story of "Dan Snider and the Strychnine Solution." Justice is served long after the law had delivered and executed its sentence. Both of these stories involve the murder of children—crimes so horrible that one would think the stories would endure forever. But they haven't, until now, until a memory monument was built of words and pages by the author.

I feel lucky to have grown up when I did, where I did, with parents who were readers and who did not censor the books that passed through my hands, my heart, and my mind. I wholeheartedly believe that those weeks spent in bed with mono were some of the most formative of my early creative life. Not only did I discover true crime fiction, but I also encountered interesting characters, sadness and triumph, and a sense of justice that I didn't know existed. I hope you, dear reader, will experience some of the same emotions in *No Place Like Murder* that I did. Janis Thornton has performed a wonderful service bringing these lesser-known stories to our attention.

Sadly, crime can occur anywhere, anytime—next door, to people we love, or to friends of friends. But time after time, in story after story, justice usually finds a way to be served. Or it doesn't. Which means the story is not yet over. Even a hundred years later. We may hope that the memory of the crime will live on until the final truth is known, just as it is in these stories.

Larry D. Sweazy
Noblesville, Indiana
March 16, 2019

FOREWORD

On January 15, 1951, in Ann Arbor, Michigan, an unknown assailant crept up behind Pauline Campbell, a thirty-four-year-old nurse on her way home from work, and viciously smashed her in the skull with a heavy rubber mallet. The murder sent shock waves through the quiet college town (home to the University of Michigan campus), with police believing the crime had been committed by "a maniac."

Residents were stunned when, a few days after the murder, police were tipped off that three young men from the nearby town of Ypsilanti—Bill Morey Jr., Max Pell, and Dave Royal—had committed the crime, with Morey doing the actual killing. A jury found Morey and Pell guilty of first-degree murder and sentenced them to life in prison (Michigan did not have the death penalty at the time) without the chance for parole, and Royal was convicted of second-degree murder and received a jail sentence of twenty-two years to life. Morey's father's reaction to the news—"I can't believe it; I just can't believe it"—reflected what many parents in the community were thinking.

To most, it seems that little could be learned from such a heinous crime. The case, however, soon drew the attention of a dogged freelance writer, John Bartlow Martin, who had not consciously set out to specialize in the subject but saw that "a criminal case offers an opportunity to write about people in crisis, and their problems." He realized that crimes did not happen by "blind chance—that something causes them. Sometimes the matrix is social, sometimes psychological, most often both." Writing about an individual criminal case, then, he noted, offered an "opportunity to write about a whole society. Crime in context."

In a four-part series published in the *Saturday Evening Post*, one of the most difficult pieces he had ever worked on, Martin, in talking with those involved, realized that when he was the same age as Morey, he and his friends had done some of the stupid and dangerous things Morey had done: drink alcohol before they legally could, drive around recklessly in cars looking for excitement, and base their actions on the opinions of their peers. Martin attempted to write not a sensational story but rather "a thoroughgoing study for a serious magazine [the *Post*] that would try to discover *why* it had happened." Although no final answer might be found for the question of why they killed, perhaps an understanding could be reached by getting at the facts of the case. "All is not," Martin added, "cannot be, darkness and mystification."

Martin, lauded by his contemporaries as "the ablest crime reporter in America," would be proud of the work done by Janis Thornton in her new collection *No Place Like Murder*, in which she presents twenty historic murders that, like the Morey case in Ann Arbor, shocked those in the Indiana communities where they occurred. Both the victims and the perpetrators in these cases would be recognizable today—a jilted lover, a couple stuck in an unhappy marriage, a soldier trying to adjust to civilian life, a crooked politician, an alcoholic, and other troubled souls. As Thornton has discovered, those who have come before us were not so different from us today. "We have all experienced," she notes, "the same range of human conditions—from joyful and wonderful to tragic and heartbreaking—regardless of the century we traverse."

As Martin discovered in his work, the reportorial question almost everybody finds hardest to answer is why. Why did you do this instead of that? Why did it happen just that way and no other? We may never know the final answer in the cases featured in this book, but at least, as Martin and Thornton discovered, there is something honorable in trying.

Ray E. Boomhower
Indianapolis, Indiana
June 25, 2019

ACKNOWLEDGMENTS

A JOURNEY OF 150 YEARS BACK THROUGH TIME IS ALL BUT impossible to accomplish alone, and fortunately I have many friends willing to help me along the way. Whether it was a wise foreword from a guest author or two, court transcripts, genealogical records, newspaper reports, photographs, prison mug shots and records, editorial advice, proofreaders, or simply encouragement, I am rich in wonderful, giving friends and professional acquaintances. This book has been a labor of love for quite a while, but it would never have been completed without them.

To the following people, I extend my deep and sincere appreciation:

- Aubrey Writers: Tim Byers, Bob Beilouny, Tom Kohlmeier, Mary Marlow, Sandra Miller, Chip Mann, Margie Porter, Larry Sells, and Kathy Smith
- Jenny Awad of the Dearborn County Historical Society
- Troy Bacon, chief of the Frankfort Police Department
- Michael Belis, historian, Twenty-Second Infantry Regiment Society, Lafayette, Louisiana
- Sherri Bonham of the Hamilton East Public Library in Noblesville
- Ray Boomhower
- Jim Bush
- Sharon Cowen
- Matt Geas
- Leroy Good
- Nancy Hart of the Clinton County Historical Society

- Jill Howerton and Carla Mullins of the Tipton County Historical Society
- Ruth Illges
- Linda Kelsay of Paxton Media Group
- Stewart Lauterbach of the Howard County Historical Society
- Christina Kennedy Nixon
- Mary Patchett
- Marjorie Pierce and Ranny Simmons of the Pipe Creek Historical Society (Madison County)
- Ashley Runyon of Indiana University Press
- Larry Sweazy
- William E. Tidler II
- Michael Vetman of the Indiana State Archives

Thank you, all! You're the best.

INTRODUCTION

WHO DOESN'T HARBOR A MORBID CURIOSITY ABOUT MURDER? WHO hasn't succumbed to the allure of a sensational crime and taken a peek behind the headlines? While many readers revel in crime fiction, it's true crime that reigns supreme among hard-core armchair detectives.

Hours of TV time are dedicated to it. The internet abounds with it. Hundreds of books flaunting every salacious true crime detail fill the shelves of bookstores everywhere. Even an annual CrimeCon was launched in 2017, drawing fifteen hundred true crime fans to the inaugural event in Indianapolis.

True crime aficionados are fascinated by the havoc their fellow humans are capable of wreaking. For them, learning details of the victims' worst nightmares is not only tantalizing; in a perverse way, it's almost comforting because it happened to someone else. In a sense, true crime offers its readers a "there but for the grace of God" revelation that allows them to vicariously experience unimaginable horrors behind a safety buffer of time and space.

No Place Like Murder emerged as the manifestation of my love for local history and my fascination with mysteries and true crime.

The former is a passion that developed as I researched and wrote a history book about my hometown of Tipton, Indiana, in 2012. Delving into the past introduced me to many intriguing people who, decades before, spent their entire lives in the same corner of the world I occupied. The project convinced me that the challenges our ancestors experienced a hundred or more years ago were not so very different from our challenges of today. People encounter the same range of human conditions—from joyful and magic to heartbreaking and tragic—regardless of the century they traverse.

The latter, my fascination for true crime, developed as an offshoot of my love for mysteries, which I have consumed for years in all forms—books, movies, and TV—as well as making up my own. Nothing gets my curiosity churning like trying to figure out why two plus two equals five.

This book examines the underbelly of our history through the retelling of twenty criminal incidents that ripped apart small-town Indiana between 1869 and 1950. As I scoured old court records and vintage newspapers, gleaning story material, I discovered that crimes committed a century ago were no less harrowing than any perpetrated during this century. Conventional wisdom tends to float the belief that horrific incidents didn't happen in the "good old days." But that's the thing about conventional wisdom: it's a belief, not science. One of the truths behind true crime is that a crime-riddled society is not unique to modern times.

Reams have been written about the likes of Belle Gunness and H. H. Holmes, two of Indiana's most infamous serial killers; and, of course, celebrated Depression-era Hoosier gangster John Dillinger has captured the public's fascination since 1933. But who else, I wondered, had been largely overlooked by biographers and true crime documentarians, and were they ink-worthy?

Combing through old Indiana newspapers, I quickly discovered the answer. The terrible crimes of passion committed by people such as Grover Blake, Virginius "Dink" Carter, John Chirka, Nora Coleman, and Harry Rasico more than confirm that evil lurks in the most innocuous places, often around the corner, and sometimes, even more frighteningly, under one's own roof. The stories in this book paint portraits of these and other homegrown killers, depicting them as ruthless opportunists whose selfish ambitions and vain conceit pushed them over the edge.

More importantly, the stories are intended as tributes to the innocent victims whose lives were stolen—Garnet Ginn, Amos Hamilton, Nellie Hiatt, Leland Holliday, Fairy McClain-Miller, Belle Shenkenberger, and Hannah King Snider among them. In a sense, recording their stories brings them back to life and embeds their memories in readers' hearts and minds.

No Place Like Murder also reveals how communities responded to losing one of their own to a soulless killer. Often the public's first response was the threat of a lynch mob, although one rarely materialized. Conversely, once the suspect's trial resulted in a guilty verdict, the jury often—though not always—showed mercy and tended to give the convicted killer life in prison rather than the death penalty. The way the killers chose to respond to the juries' leniency provides yet another layer to the story. Some of them stubbornly maintained their innocent plea, while others deeply regretted their murderous deed; a few turned their lives around and won a pardon, while others lost the will to live and died in prison.

All the stories told on the pages that follow dominated the newspaper headlines of their day, and some even gained national attention. Retelling them today allows readers to learn aspects of their past that they might never have known. Most importantly, *No Place Like Murder* provides a mirror that reflects a time and place not so very different from our own. I hope you find these stories as fascinating and unforgettable as I do.

Janis Thornton
Tipton, Indiana
May 1, 2019

NO PLACE LIKE MURDER

PART I
ALL IN THE FAMILY

1
THE MYSTERIOUS DEATH OF BELLE SHENKENBERGER

FRANKFORT, 1898

State vs. Sarah Shenkenberger was the trial of the century for Clinton County. For the first time in the county's sixty-eight-year history, a woman was to be tried for murder. If the jury found her guilty, she would surely face life behind bars or worse—the hangman's noose. After Sarah Shenkenberger had been arrested and charged with the murder of her daughter-in-law, Belle Sheridan Shenkenberger, Frankfort's *Daily Crescent* gleefully wrote: "The murder, if murder it proves to be, was one of the foulest, blackest and most diabolical ever conceived and carried out by the mind of a woman. To do such a deed, Sarah Shenkenberger must be a veritable Lucretia Borgia, and no punishment could be too severe."

Belle

A few hours before Belle Shenkenberger drew her last breath early Saturday, August 27, 1898, she sent for her three brothers. There was something she needed them to know.

Over the past month, her health had deteriorated at an alarming rate, while the doctor who tried to stop the encroachment of her mysterious malady couldn't even diagnose it. Belle was only twenty-three, and until this illness had taken hold, she had been a strong, vibrant wife and mother with a future full of potential.

Her brothers, Harry, Squire, and Elmer Sheridan, had a hunch the end was near when Belle summoned them from their beds at one o'clock that morning. While Frankfort slept, they tore into the hot August night, traversing the desolate city streets, rushing to their beloved sister's bedside.

Belle's husband, Ed, was currently serving in the US Navy aboard the USS *Minneapolis*. While he was away, she and their two-year-old son, Donald, had been living with Ed's parents, Henry and Sarah Shenkenberger. In the short time Belle had been sick, her family had begun to question Sarah's caregiving skills as well as her moral character. Consequently, they moved Belle to the home of her sister, Kate Cohee, two days before her passing. They hoped Belle's health would return once she was plucked from her mother-in-law's grip. Unfortunately, Belle's decline persisted, and she grew even more frail.

When the Sheridan brothers reached Belle's bedside that Saturday morning, she could barely speak above a whisper. Harry positioned his ear over her colorless lips as she recited her dying wish for her son's welfare and accused her mother-in-law of murder. Harry repeated her words to Squire and Elmer, who scribbled them on a tablet.

"I realize I am dying," she said. "I know she has systematically poisoned me, and I know that she wants my child. Do not let her have him. This is my dying request and statement."

Too weak to hold the pen, Belle touched it as her brother signed her name.

Belle and Ed

Belle Sheridan and Ed Shenkenberger caused quite the scandal when they left Frankfort to elope in Chicago on December 1, 1894. An intelligent, introspective, pretty young woman, Belle was just nineteen when she gave up a promising career at the Frankfort library to marry Ed. He, on the other hand, hadn't yet found his niche. At age twenty-four, he had already worked a variety of jobs and liked none of them. A year later, when Belle became pregnant with their son, Ed took off. In May 1896, when the baby was five months old, Belle filed for divorce, citing her husband's laziness, abandonment, and cruelty.

The couple never finalized their divorce, and Belle returned to the marriage, following Ed back to Chicago. They rented a flat there and took in boarders to supplement Ed's income as a pressman. It was yet another job he couldn't stomach. Melancholy nearly consumed Belle. She told friends she had nothing to live for and wanted to die. In late 1896, Ed sent his wife and son back to Frankfort to stay with his parents, freeing him to seek work in Albuquerque, New Mexico, where he was promptly arrested for nonpayment of his debts. Belle met him in Albuquerque after he was released six months later, and they returned to Chicago.

Ed, ever one for a new adventure, joined the navy in July 1898, at the height of the Spanish-American War, and sent Belle and little Donald back to Frankfort to live with his parents once more. It was at this point that the final events of Belle's life fell into place, like a line of dominoes waiting for the first to topple. Less than one month later, she would be dead of arsenic poisoning, and her mother-in-law would be charged with murder.

Sarah

Sarah McLaughlin was born in 1845 in Harmer, Ohio. She married fellow Ohioan Henry Shenkenberger, a shoemaker, in Lafayette, Indiana, in 1869. They settled in the Benton County town of Oxford, where Sarah kept house and raised her three children—Eddie, Laura, and Charlie. She was proud of her family and her home, cultivated many friendships, and seemed happy. In 1882, however, her even-tempered behavior underwent a change. As Henry later explained, she began to suffer "sick spells" that required medical treatment.

He called Dr. S. R. Roberts, who described Sarah as "peculiar." She would move about quickly while speaking alternately low and loud, Roberts said. She felt her life was a failure and feared someone would hurt her; at times, she wanted to die. Once, in the doctor's presence, Sarah pressed a revolver to her head and threatened to pull the trigger. The doctor diagnosed Sarah's erratic behavior as "woman trouble," a common malady of the day for which he had the perfect remedy. "I gave her a grain of morphine," he said. "Afterward, she became quiet and wanted more."

The use of addictive drugs such as morphine was common during the Victorian era. Access to drugs was unchecked. Opiates such as heroin, cocaine, and morphine were unregulated, misunderstood, and often misprescribed. Morphine in the late 1800s was considered a magical cure-all for a range of medical complaints, particularly among women.

Roberts said that over the next four years, he supplied Sarah with morphine at least a half dozen times. However, he likely had underestimated that number because after the Shenkenbergers moved to Frankfort in April 1896, Sarah became well known to all the local druggists. Her frequent purchases of morphine flagged her as a "known morphine eater."

The Murder

Belle and her two-year-old son moved into the Shenkenbergers' Frankfort home on West Wabash Street on Sunday, July 31, 1898. She agreed to pay twelve dollars each month for room and board but failed to mention that in seven or eight months, she would be giving birth to another child. Perhaps it was too early in the pregnancy for Belle to be certain, or perhaps she had other plans. Either way, her secret was exposed the very next day after she suffered a miscarriage.

Sarah had spent Monday afternoon at the Fuller farm picking fresh fruits and vegetables. When she arrived back home at five o'clock, she found Belle sick in bed, suffering from severe cramps in her lower abdomen. Electric heating pads had not yet been invented, so Sarah applied hot stove lids to Belle's belly to ease the pain. Sarah returned to Belle's room a couple of hours later and noticed something awful in her "slop jar."

"Belle's had a miscarriage!" Sarah shouted to her husband. "Call the doctor!"

By the time Dr. M. V. Young arrived, Belle had lost a considerable amount of blood. The heavy flow continued until Saturday, August 6, before it finally began to wane. But by then, Belle was almost too weak to get out of bed and had developed a fever and chills. Curiously, Young, who had known Belle her entire life, diagnosed her symptoms as malaria and left quinine and strychnine, a common treatment in those times.

The doctor returned every day that week. At first, he was encouraged by Belle's improvement, but by Thursday, August 11, her condition had taken a dive. She was nauseated, and her stomach hurt. By Saturday, August 13, she had developed an unquenchable thirst, her hands and feet were numb and cold, her body itched, her face was puffed, and her eyelids were swollen. She could not retain food or liquid and often vomited,

Belle Sheridan Shenkenberger of Frankfort was only twenty-three when, in 1898, she was poisoned by her mother-in-law, Sarah Shenkenberger. *Photo courtesy Sharon Cowen.*

purging a dark, coffee grounds–like substance. The doctor suspected she had overdosed on morphine, but Belle insisted she had not taken morphine. It was then that Young considered a more concerning possibility: poison. The Sheridan family was frantic.

All the while, Sarah dutifully tended to Belle, waiting on her hand and foot, preparing her meals, bathing her, helping her dress, cleaning up her messes. Sarah told Belle's family that she loved her daughter-in-law like her own flesh and blood, and she never missed an opportunity to demonstrate her selfless devotion. But to friends and neighbors, Sarah told a different tale.

"Sarah told me she couldn't stand her daughter-in-law," said Shenkenberger neighbor Minnie Steed. "Sarah called her 'lazy' and complained that instead of helping with housework, Belle spent all her time in her room reading novels."

One of Sarah's friends, Ella Campbell, confirmed Sarah's intense dislike for Belle. "After Belle's last visit about a year ago," Ella said, "Sarah told me that if 'that woman' ever came back to her house, she would scald her with a pot of boiling water and lock the door in her face."

On Thursday, August 25, Belle's mother, Mahala Sheridan, sat at her gravely ill daughter's bedside, feeding her spoonfuls from the glass of crushed ice Sarah had provided. After a few bites, Belle refused to take more, complaining of its bitterness.

"Mother, what's on that ice?" she said.

Mahala inspected the ice and noticed something odd: it was dusted with white powder. Mahala immediately hid the glass under the bureau and sneaked out of the house, heading to the next-door neighbor's to borrow an empty bottle. Later, Mahala poured the melted ice water into the bottle and gave it to her son Elmer, who delivered it to Dr. Young.

The doctor analyzed the liquid and was stunned by what he found—arsenic. He urged Elmer to get Belle out of the Shenkenberger house immediately. The Sheridan family acted without delay, moving Belle to her sister Kate's East Clinton Street home that very evening. For a few hopeful hours, Belle's outlook brightened, and she seemed to improve. However, any appearance of recovery was short-lived, and as her brother Elmer put it, "She began to sink."

By Friday morning, Belle's condition was alarming. She moaned continuously and weakly acknowledged imminent death. She could barely lift her head off her pillow when, shortly past 1:00 a.m. on Saturday, August 27, she asked Kate to fetch her brothers. Harry, Squire, and Elmer arrived within the hour. Belle drifted into a coma soon after and died at 4:35 a.m.

Young immediately conducted a postmortem with the help of Dr. William H. McGuire and the coroner, Dr. John M. Wise. They attributed Belle's death to arsenic poisoning and sent her stomach to Dr. John N. Hurty, secretary of the Indiana State Board of Health. On Thursday, September 1, Hurty sent his findings to town marshal George W. Bird. Hurty

Frankfort's police department of 1898 is shown in this photograph. Standing from left are Albert Nichols, Til Alford, Ed Miller, and Taylor Hill. Seated from left are Deputy John Denton, Mayor Barney Irwin, and Chief George Bird. Denton and Bird were the officers who arrested Sarah Shenkenberger and took her to jail, where she was charged with murder. Photo courtesy Frankfort, Indiana, Police Department.

had found more than enough arsenic in Belle's stomach to kill her. Bird read the report and went to find deputy John Denton, who already had the warrant for Sarah Shenkenberger's arrest.

Greeting Denton and Bird at her front door, Sarah remarked calmly, "I'm not surprised." She offered no resistance as they arrested her, charged her with murder, and locked her up in the city jail.

The Trial

Judge James V. Kent's Clinton circuit courtroom was packed from day one. Women, who far outnumbered the men, brought their dinners and ate them in the courtroom. Reporters from the Clinton County newspapers recorded every word of the drama. Their coverage dominated the front-page news, while banner headlines screamed each development, from "The Poisoning Case" to "Guilty as Charged."

The defense team's strategy was simple: they would prove Belle Shenkenberger committed suicide or that she died accidentally. As a backup, the defense team was prepared to plead that their client was insane.

Proving either of the first two scenarios was an uphill climb. Witness after witness took the stand relating the rapid decline of Belle's health, Sarah's overt contempt for her daughter-in-law, her addiction to morphine, and her recent purchase of arsenic. Proving Sarah was insane became problematic as well, particularly after the judge was quoted saying, "[Sarah's] own wonderful memory and intelligence upon the witness stand precluded the idea of insanity."

The trial lasted two weeks, while the jury heard testimony from some two dozen witnesses. The roster was composed of the Shenkenbergers' neighbors, Frankfort druggists, doctors, the coroner, an undertaker, expert witnesses, members of Sarah's and Belle's immediate families—including Edward Shenkenberger, on leave from his battleship after learning of his wife's death allegedly at the hands of his mother. Sarah, too, took the stand in her own defense.

The witnesses painted a picture of an unhappy social snob, resentful of the intellectually superior but sad young woman who ran away with her ne'er-do-well son and married him. In addition, druggist Charles Ashman swore that between August 15 and 20, he had sold Sarah two hundred grains of arsenic in powdered form. Sarah had claimed the arsenic was needed to kill a dog that had been killing chickens in her neighborhood. Apparently, the dog was the size of a house because, as Ashman said, less than five grains would kill a person.

Hurty, who made the chemical analysis of Belle's stomach, agreed that less than five grains would have proven fatal. In his testimony, perhaps the most damning for the defense, he said he had found 17.8 grains of arsenic in Belle's stomach.

Conversely, Dr. J. S. McMurray of Frankfort appeared on behalf of the defendant in exchange for a $100 stipend. It was McMurray's contention that Belle died not of arsenic poisoning but of Bright's disease, an acute kidney disorder. In response, a heated exchange between McMurray and prosecutor W. F. Palmer erupted, with Palmer berating McMurray as "a paid perjurer."

Closing arguments began after lunch on Friday, December 2, and continued until late the next afternoon. The jury began its deliberation shortly after. At about 9:00 p.m., word was spreading that the jury had reached its verdict.

"The courtroom, containing a half a hundred spectators, was quiet as a grave," the *Frankfort Crescent* reported.

Judge Kent was first to break the silence. Before signaling the bailiff to let the jury file in, Kent warned the courtroom that no demonstrations of approval or disapproval would be tolerated after the verdict was read.

"Have you agreed upon a verdict, gentlemen?" the judge asked the jury foreman.

"We have," the foreman said weakly.

"Then pass it to the clerk," the judge said.

The foreman walked slowly to the clerk and handed him the paper on which the verdict was written. The clerk gave it a quick look and read it out loud. "We the jury," he said in a strong voice, "find the defendant guilty of murder in the first degree and that she be imprisoned in the penal department of the Indiana Reformatory Institution for Women and Girls during the remainder of her natural life."

Henry Shenkenberger buried his head in his hands and gave a shriek of anguish. Ed stepped to his mother's side, while his sister, Laura, looked on in silence. Sarah sat through it all seemingly unfazed.

The *Frankfort Crescent* noted, "It was a most remarkable and never-to-be-forgotten scene."

Although the defense team immediately petitioned for a new trial based on a list of thirty-seven errors in the judge's rulings, the petition was denied.

The Monday following the trial, a *Frankfort Crescent* reporter visited Sarah in her jail cell. He reported that she was out of touch, irrational, and incoherent. Rambling, Sarah explained that she was merely boarding at the jail. She insisted Belle wasn't dead and was living with Edward and little Donald in Chicago.

"While she may not at this time be insane," the reporter wrote of Sarah, "there is good reason for thinking she soon will be."

Epilogue

On December 23, 1898, Sheriff Clark escorted Sarah Shenkenberger to Indianapolis, where she entered the women's prison to begin her life

On December 23, 1898, convicted murderer Sarah Shenkenberger entered the Indiana Women's Prison, where she spent fifteen years, until Indiana governor Samuel Ralston pardoned her. She was released on December 24, 1913. *Photo courtesy Indiana Historical Society, P0265.*

sentence. Thus began her family's relentless pursuits to get her paroled. Their final attempt, made in the summer of 1913, asserted that they wanted their mother home before she died in prison. Sarah's daughter, Laura, made an emotional plea to the parole board on June 24, 1913. With tears streaming down her face, she implored, "Gentleman, has not my mother already paid her price? Is it asking too much to allow her to be surrounded by loving hands and voices soft with sympathy during the period of life when the shadows each day grow longer and blacker?"

Indiana governor Samuel Ralston signed Sarah's parole on December 23, 1913. She was released from the Indiana Women's Prison the next day, fifteen years and one day after she had entered. Sarah was sixty-eight. From there, she and Laura traveled to Chicago, where she lived the remaining days of her life with her son Edward and his family.

Sarah's husband, Henry, died in early 1912 in Chicago. Sarah died in Chicago on February 12, 1930, at the age of eighty-four.

Why Sarah disliked her daughter-in-law enough to kill her was never understood. Could it have been that she blamed Belle for embarrassing the Shenkenberger family when the young couple ran off to Chicago to elope? Did she resent Belle for filing for divorce from Ed, or perhaps resent her for not going through with it? Was she trying to gain custody of her grandson, Donald? Or, as a *Frankfort Crescent* reporter asked shortly after her sentencing, was she simply insane?

"No!" she proclaimed. "I'm not crazy and never have been, and I'll not say I am. I'll tell the truth. I know I'm in my right mind. Belle killed herself, but I don't suppose the truth will ever be known."

2

THE LIBERATION OF NORA COLEMAN

ANGOLA, 1918

Every day of her twenty-nine years, Nora Coleman dutifully endured her neglectful mother's verbal and emotional abuse. She might have put up with it for twenty-nine more if, in those first few days of February 1918, she hadn't found herself in a "delicate condition." Her mother had no tolerance for children and frequently told anyone who would listen that if Nora should ever make her a grandmother, she would throw the child in the fire and watch it burn. Nora would not tolerate such threats against her unborn child. She instinctively knew not to wait too long before fixing the problem.

That day came on Wednesday, February 6. The temperature throughout the Angola, Indiana, countryside registered just below thirty-two degrees—cold enough to freeze a slab of beef but not too cold to keep a couple of sturdy farm women from performing their chores around the barnyard.

Shortly after Nora and her husband, Ward, had eaten supper, she strolled across the road to her in-laws' house and quietly entered through the kitchen, where a twelve-gauge shotgun leaned against a corner. Helping herself to the weapon, she plucked two shells from the cupboard and headed for her mother's farm. As Sepharna Gleason's only child, Nora had been raised on that farm, located three-quarters of a mile north on Angola Flint Road just west of Pigeon Creek Bridge.

Reaching the Gleason farm, Nora hid the weapon behind a hickory tree that stood between the house and the barn. And then, as was her custom, she helped her mother bring the livestock into the barn and milk the cows. Their work complete, Sepharna left the barn and walked briskly through the dark toward the back porch of the house. Nora retrieved the gun and took aim. The moment Sepharna reached the door, Nora fired. The full charge of the shot blew away the back of her mother's head, and she dropped instantly, landing facedown.

Nora returned to the barn, picked up the milk pail she and her mother had filled, and carried it into the house. She dutifully strained and stored the milk and finished the housework. When all the chores had been completed, Nora left the house, locking the door behind her. Stepping around her dead mother's body, she walked home.

"Oh, yes," she would tell her husband the next morning, "I knew Mother was dead. I wouldn't leave a cat in agony."

The Morning After

When Nora returned home at about 10:00 p.m., Ward was asleep. Too worked up to join him, she puttered around the house awhile and finally went to bed around midnight. She spent the next four hours tossing and turning. Finally, at dawn, she woke Ward and told him what she had done.

Reeling in confusion, shock, and disbelief, Ward dressed quickly and rushed across the road to tell his folks. Why Ward and his parents didn't report the shooting immediately was not publicly revealed, but when they finally did make the call, it was to their good friend, former Steuben County sheriff Austin Parsell.

Parsell counseled the Colemans and encouraged Nora to turn herself in. They agreed that being forthright was their only option, and Parsell drove the Colemans into town. On their arrival at Sheriff George W. DeLancey's office, Nora was presented with an arrest warrant and immediately placed in jail. Even then, her spirits remained high, and according to the February 13, 1918, *Steuben Republican*, she showed not an ounce of remorse.

The county coroner, Dr. G. N. Lake, arrived at the Gleason home around 11:30 a.m. By then, the news had spread through the county, and a horde of curiosity seekers beat him there, swarming the woman sprawled facedown on her porch, tramping through spattered blood and bits of brain, and tracking the mess into the house.

The coroner wrapped Sepharna's partially frozen body in a blanket and carried it to the bedroom, where he laid it on the floor. On examination, he determined that the wound on the back of her head measured nearly six inches. Inside her skull, he found remnants of buckshot. On closer look, he determined the impact of the shot had severed the head from the neck to above the ears. When he turned the body over, what was left of Sepharna's brain tumbled onto the floor. The undertaker, L. N. Klink, required a pound of cotton to fill the hole in her head.

Full Confession

As soon as Nora surrendered to the sheriff, she absolved her husband of any involvement. Her husband had not advised or encouraged her to murder her mother, she said, nor had he even known she had considered it. She told the sheriff that although she pitied her husband for the shame she had caused him, she doubted she would ever regret her act.

In her statement to Steuben County deputy prosecutor Thomas French, she explained why. "Since my earliest recollections," she said, "my life has been most unpleasant. I was an unwelcome child and have always been abused and nagged."

Following her marriage to Ward Coleman the year before, the relationship with her mother had only deteriorated, she explained, adding, "She seems angry all the time simply because Ward and I get along. Mother continuously said mean things about him, but I never told him. I shielded him always."

When French asked Nora if she realized what the penalty might be for her crime, she shrugged and said, "Why, I thought I would be able to cover it up some way."

The *Angola Herald* reported, "[Nora] talks freely, frankly and voluminously about her crime, but somehow does not seem to realize the enormity of her act. She says she does not believe there is anyone who would blame her if they knew of her provocation."

Later that day, the sheriff took Nora to the mortuary to make her mother's final arrangements and to pick out a coffin. The funeral would be Saturday at the Flint Methodist Church. Nora declined to attend. She had no interest.

After the reports of the sensational murder extended beyond the boundaries of the Angola community, newspapers throughout Indiana carried stories about Nora's sanity. Many of them included claims from people who had known the Gleason family for years. They said Nora was insane or at least mentally unbalanced. According to the *Fort Wayne Journal-Gazette*, "It is known that at least two members of her father's family have been insane." Her mother's cruelty was widely known too. And yet, regardless of Nora's intellectual acuity, the community's respect and sympathy were in her favor.

But that didn't spare her from an indictment. Within a week of the shooting, the Steuben County grand jury charged Nora with murder in the first degree. The trial was set for Monday, February 25, 1918.

Nora Goes to Court

Nora entered the courtroom wearing a plush winter coat over a simple blue dress. Her well-scrubbed face reflected the same expression it had displayed consistently since her arrest, the same one the papers described as "indifference."

Prosecuting attorney W. W. Ketcham made the opening statement, vowing to prove Mrs. Coleman had murdered her mother after "mature and careful deliberation." He reminded the jury that the defendant had been charged with murder in the first degree, and according to the law, the punishment must be either death or life imprisonment.

Defense attorney C. C. Carlin's lengthy statement laid out Nora's troubling upbringing, her family's history of mental illness, and her mother's bizarre behavior. When he finished, he told the court he intended to prove that his client could not be guilty because she was insane.

Over the next five days, witness after witness attested to Nora's mental challenges and the abhorrent circumstances of her life, from birth through the day of her marriage the year before. Witnesses revealed that she was born into a single-parent home in 1887, her father having deserted them after her mother became pregnant. They said that as a young girl, Nora had dressed strangely, tied her shoes onto her feet with rags, and often didn't bring lunch to school, mainly relying on the generosity of the other children. Everyone referred to her as slow, backward, dull, mentally deficient, unbalanced, or outright insane.

Many of Sepharna Gleason's neighbors answered questions about the family. They said Nora's grandfather was insane, as was one of her uncles, whom they called a "raving maniac." But her father, James Gleason, had earned the community's respect. Although her mother's "disagreeable disposition" had driven James away, he returned a few years later, paid off his debts, and accumulated a great deal of property, which he left to Nora when he died.

Almost all the neighbors spoke of Sepharna's hoarding—the crocks of spoiled meats and butter she had stashed in her cellar for years as well as more than two hundred pounds of sugar; the sand and ashes sprinkled throughout the house to cover up the "leavings" of the many cats that roamed freely; the barrel of hickory nuts in her bedroom alongside mounds of clothing, bedding, papers, and even piles of lard. Several talked about Sepharna's dislike of children. They recalled her saying that if Nora ever had a child, she would set it on fire and watch it burn. Birdie Kenyon, the dead woman's sister, told the jury that Sepharna had "despised" Nora since before she was born.

Husband Takes the Stand

On Wednesday, February 27, Ward Coleman testified for seventy-four minutes, revealing a sad picture of his wife. He had known Nora all his life and remembered her as a queer sort of girl, he said, who was often shunned by the other children. He began keeping company with her in 1905, when they were sixteen, and he married her January 1, 1917. Although Sepharna did not welcome a son-in-law, he said, she begged him and Nora to live with her because she did not want to be alone. "I told her I could not," he said with a shudder, "considering the way she lived."

Instead, the young couple bought a farm just three-quarters of a mile up the road from Sepharna's farm. And even though Nora had her own house to keep up, she continued to look after her mother and tend to her household and farm chores.

When Ward's testimony turned to the day of the murder, he swore he knew nothing of it until his wife woke him and confessed. "She got up early," he began. "When I asked her the time, she told me it was ten to four. She lit the lamp, fixed the fire, and got back into bed."

"That's when she broke the news?" the attorney asked.

"Yes," Ward replied, his tone dipping to barely a whisper. "She told me she would not be bothered with Mother anymore. Then she said, 'I took the shotgun last night and shot her.' I asked if she really meant it, and she assured me that she did. I asked her why she did it, and she said her mother had nagged, abused her, and drove her to it."

Defense Attorney Carlin turned toward his client seated at the table and fixed his gaze on her for a long moment. "What has been her demeanor since then?" he said, turning back to his witness on the stand. "Do you believe she understands the full depth and breadth of her act?"

Ward gave a barely discernible shake of the head. "She did not cry when we discussed it," he said. "Nor has she since."

Low Blood Pressure Defense vs. Proper Grammar Prosecution

To erase any doubt about Nora Coleman's sanity, five physicians tested and evaluated her. They were on the stand nearly all day February 28 and agreed there was no question of her mental deficiency. Dr. Peter N. Sutherland testified that when he examined Nora, she registered a blood pressure of 115. Because 128 was normal, she was clearly anemic, he said, adding that low blood pressure was a sign of insanity.

The physicians reminded the court of Sepharna Gleason's continual nagging and her threats about harming her grandchild. "These things," the doctors said, "coupled with the fact that Mrs. Coleman was in a 'delicate condition' the night of the murder, had preyed on her mind until she became insane."

In an effort to refute the insanity plea, the state introduced a letter into evidence that Nora Coleman wrote and sent to her friend Sue Alcott on February 11 from the Steuben County jail. In the letter, Nora admitted killing her mother because of her many threats, explaining, "Mother has told me repeatedly that if she could get a hold of my children ever, she would burn them at a stake." Sadly, she also wrote, "I have had a miscarriage which started Thursday aforenoon. I am very much weakened."

Although the letter contained Nora's confession, the state's larger point was the coherent way it was written, with proper grammar and accurate spelling. Could a mentally deficient woman have composed a handwritten message with such precision? The state thought not.

Saturday, March 2, was reserved for the final arguments. While the state insisted Nora Coleman had killed her mother to hasten her inheritance of the Gleason family farm, the defense maintained that the case they presented provided overwhelming evidence of his client's weakened mental state.

Carlin further used the case to exemplify the dangers of "indiscriminate marriages"—a term referring to an increasingly popular yet controversial belief at that time that states should prevent "feeble-minded and socially inadequate" people from marrying and reproducing. "This case might be worth its cost to Steuben County," Carlin said, "if, for no other reason, than to impress upon our citizens the danger of indiscriminate marriages and our duty to our mental defectives."

Reportedly, by the end of the defense team's closing argument, Ward Coleman was crying audibly, and not a dry eye could be found in the courtroom, except for Nora Coleman's. Her lack of emotion only reinforced her counsel's insanity theory.

And that's where the trial ended. Judge Daniel M. Link placed Nora Coleman's future in the hands of the twelve men on the jury at 6:10 p.m., just twenty-four days after she had aimed a gun at her mother's head and blew half of it away.

Not Guilty

The jury agreed on the second ballot that Nora Coleman was insane when she shot her mother and, therefore, should be acquitted.

At 8:13 p.m., the courtroom's maximum-capacity crowd watched the jurists march in and take their places.

"Gentlemen," said the judge, "have you reached a verdict?"

"We have, your honor," replied the foreman. "We, the jury, find the defendant not guilty."

Judge Link then called Nora to the bench and read her the conditions of the verdict: commitment to the East Haven Hospital for the Insane at Richmond. Hearing that, her indifference dissolved, and she finally displayed emotion. The papers interpreted the reaction as embarrassment.

"Thus closes one of the most distressing tragedies in the history of Steuben County," reported the March 6, 1918, edition of the *Steuben Republican*. "Mr. Coleman is considered a fine young man and had the sympathy of nearly everyone, and the young woman herself was of such a peaceful disposition that all who knew her are shocked by the tragic climax of her life."

The Matricide Returns

Nora Coleman returned to court in Steuben County on May 12, 1924, after more than nine hundred area residents signed a petition requesting her release from the asylum.

Evidence introduced at the hearing included statements from the previous and then current superintendents of the asylum. They asserted that although Nora would never exceed the intellect of a twelve-year-old, they had cured her of insanity, and she was no longer a threat to society.

Five physicians who had examined Nora prior to her murder trial agreed that she was now of sound mind and should be discharged.

Ward Coleman also testified to his wife's improvement and vowed that a fear of violence was no longer necessary.

Nora herself took the stand and spoke of her terrible deed. "It was dreadful," she said. "I am dreadful sorry. I could not realize it at first, but I do now." She explained that, at the time of the killing, she had been "scared beyond reason" that, if she had given birth, her mother would kill the child. But after receiving treatment for six years, she felt in control and ready to return home. "Furthermore," she declared, "if at any time, I find reason deserting me, I will certainly at once ask for help."

Although the judge professed admiration for Ward Coleman's desire to have his wife home so he could care for her, he refused to grant Nora's release, citing his concern for the community's safety and well-being.

The sheriff returned Nora to Richmond the next morning, and area papers were mum about her for another five years. Their silence was broken on March 22, 1929, when the *Angola Herald* ran a brief page-one story under the headline, "Nora Coleman Given Freedom." The story reported that Ward Coleman was the petitioner, the East Haven superintendent felt she was worthy of liberty, and her Angola neighbors agreed.

Surprise Reprise

Nora Coleman might have faded into obscurity after that had her husband's fifteen-year-old nephew, Paul, not stolen the Colemans' shotgun six months later. When the gun went missing, the Angola community worked itself into a frenzy, accusing Nora of taking it for another malicious purpose. Apparently their faith in her hadn't been as resolute as they had projected.

Nora was again locked up in the Steuben County jail to await a hearing and a possible return to East Haven. Surprising everyone except Nora, Ward's nephew confessed that he had initially "borrowed" the gun, but when the opportunity arose, he sold it to another boy for two dollars. Consequently, the gun was returned to the Coleman home.

And so was Nora.

Except for an occasional mention of who ate dinner with whom, Nora's name did not appear in the local papers for another two and a half years. But on February 26, 1932, the *Angola Herald* ran a five-line report reading, "Nora J. Coleman has filed suit for divorce from her husband, Ward Coleman. The plaintiff alleges cruel treatment." Four months later, in the real estate transfers column, the same paper reported that Ward had sold Nora their farm for one dollar. In May 1935, she sold it back to him and returned to the Gleason family farm, where she had been raised, where she had suffered nearly three decades of vile abuse from her mother, and where she had decided one cold February night that she'd had enough.

Why Nora chose to return to the source of her demons, no one could say, but she lived there until her death on September 25, 1957. She never remarried.

3

"SWEET DREAMS, MOTHER"

ANDERSON, 1908

The horse-drawn taxi rolled gently over the redbrick veneer of Walnut Street on Anderson, Indiana's, southeast side that Monday, March 23, 1908. While the warm sunshine ushered a welcome promise of spring to the city, a dark sadness enveloped the neighborhood. On reaching the William Blake residence, the hack stopped, and Grover Blake—a tall, broad-shouldered twenty-two-year-old—climbed out and gazed coldly at the only home he had ever known. Flanked by chief of police William E. Smith and Madison County sheriff Sol Smelser, Grover trudged toward the front door as if dragging a great weight, shoulders slumped, head down, eyes cast to infinity. If not for his father's leverage with the chief, Grover could have remained in his jail cell and avoided this humiliating spectacle.

Smith and Smelser gripped their prisoner's arms to nudge him across the threshold and into the east room, where they led him to the open casket. Grover reluctantly looked upon the disfigured face of the mother he cherished. After a long moment, his stone-like demeanor fractured, and his composure gave way to sobs. Burying his face in his hands, he leaned into the sheriff's shoulder and wailed without restraint. Only two people had known unequivocally the awful truth that led to this moment, and one of them lay in the coffin.

Although the last few brutal seconds of his mother's life would replay on a continuous loop in Grover's memory until the day he died, he never could recall exactly why he picked up the claw hammer and bashed in his mother's brains. He had only wanted a few bucks for a friendly game of cards. More recently, he had begun to wonder whether she would have given it to him, even somewhat reluctantly, had he merely thought to ask.

The Murder

Forty-six-year-old Louisa Blake made the short trip to the barn at the rear of her Walnut Street home shortly after eleven o'clock on Saturday morning, March 21, 1908. She thought she might find her son, Grover, nestled in the hay among the horses, sleeping off his latest drinking binge, but he wasn't there. For that she was grateful, although there was no telling where he had taken off to. It was almost noon, and she supposed he would have enough sense to come home once his stomach got to rumbling.

Grover was Louisa's only son. She loved him dearly and was proud of the close bond they shared. Despite the failed efforts of her husband, William, to engage Grover in the family horse-trading business, Louisa believed in their son. Grover had always been a good boy, and she was pleased with the bright young man he had become; although lately he had become unpredictable. The way she and William saw it, Grover hadn't been himself since the previous autumn, when he'd gotten arrested for forging his father's name on a fourteen-dollar check and passing it off at Druley's Grocery. Regardless, Louisa would do anything for Grover. In fact, with the forgery trial pending, she had called on the judge in his private office only two weeks before and begged him to be lenient with her son. A mother's love is unconditional.

With William in Wabash for the day buying horses, Louisa was alone in the house as she set about preparing a nice dinner for herself and Grover. Standing at the stove stirring a pot of potatoes, she heard the dining room door creak open, followed by the soft sweep of footsteps. Turning, she took in her son's disheveled appearance—his suit badly wrinkled, his handsome face sporting a day's growth of whiskers, and his blue eyes bloodshot and rimmed in red.

"I thought you promised not to do that," she said, referring to the liquor habit that had begun to dominate Grover's life. When he didn't answer, she asked, "Where have you been?"

Left: Twenty-two-year-old Grover Blake crushed his mother's skull with a claw hammer, killing her on March 21, 1908, so he could rob her of approximately one hundred dollars. *Right:* Louisa Blake would have done anything for her beloved only son, Grover, except give him money to stoke his drinking and gambling habits.

Grover brushed past her, and she followed him into the five-by-eight-foot pantry, where she kept jars of canned food, cleaning supplies, and the family toolbox.

"Grover," she said, "I asked you a question. Where were you?"

Paying his mother no attention, Grover opened the tool chest and extracted the claw hammer.

Puzzled, Louisa asked, "What are you going to do with that?"

"This?" he said, displaying the hammer. "I'm going to drive a tack in my shoe." Louisa shrugged and turned away from him, taking a step toward the kitchen.

That's when Grover threw the first blow, driving the hammer into the top of his mother's head. Dazed and confused, she turned to him and instinctively thrust her arms in front of her to fend off the attack, but her effort was futile. He battered her again. With terror blazing in her eyes, she opened her mouth to scream. Despite the whirlwind of questions spinning in her mind, she could only wheeze a single word: "Why?"

Her son sloughed off the unanswerable as Louisa surrendered to the incessant crushing blows, six in all—one over her right eye, three to the right side of her head, one behind her right ear, and one at the base of her brain. At least three of the strikes imprinted her flesh, leaving wounds the length and breadth of the hammerhead; the other three penetrated her skull. The final blow knocked her unconscious, and she dropped to the floor facedown in a heap.

Grover straddled his mother's body and hastily ripped open the throat of her dress. Fumbling for the satin pouch that always hung on a chain around her neck, he tore it loose. He figured the pouch contained at least Change to $100 in gold coins. He rose and then remembered his mother's gold watch and rings. He knelt back down and took them too.

After the Awful Deed

Clutching the stolen valuables, Grover took a moment to absorb the havoc that he alone had wrought. Blood spatters streaked the pantry walls and floor; his mother lay about two feet into the kitchen, blood pooling around her pulverized head. He stepped gingerly out of the room, tracking bloody shoe prints across the kitchen floor and into the dining room, where he pinched another forty dollars from his mother's purse. Upstairs, he stripped off his bloody clothes and stashed them under his mattress. After a quick bath, he dressed in his new brown suit and topped off the ensemble with a matching derby.

Outside, he took the hidden key from its nail on the front porch and locked the front door. He returned the key to the nail and hurried off to the Wallace Saloon, where his pal Orzo Reynolds would be waiting for him.

Orzo had already consumed several rounds by the time Grover entered the saloon, around two o'clock. Handing his buddy forty-five dollars and one of his mother's rings, Grover was champing at the bit to carry on with the plan he and Orzo had cooked up in the wee hours of that very morning in the Ike Robbins Saloon, the last stop of their all-night drinking binge.

Grover would later tell the Anderson police that Orzo convinced him they could make some money playing cards at a gambling house he knew of in Fort Wayne, then a bustling city of some sixty-three thousand, located about seventy miles north of Anderson. "Reynolds wanted twenty-five dollars," Grover stated. "He said if my mother would not give it to me, we could go down there and take it away from her."

Grover and Orzo knocked back a few more drinks at Wallace's before starting out for the first stop on their journey—Chesterfield, a mere six-mile jaunt. Drunk or sober, they could walk it in less than two hours, plenty of time to catch the next traction car to Yorktown.

Discovery

William Blake arrived home from his Wabash business excursion around six o'clock that Saturday evening, surprised that the front door was locked and the blinds drawn. Stepping inside the front door, he called out, "Louisa?" and proceeded to the kitchen. As soon as he laid eyes on the terrible, bloody scene, William rushed to his wife, who lay motionless on the floor, and attempted to revive her. Lapsing into hysterics, he ran out the back door and to his next-door neighbors, crying for help. They, in turn, notified the police.

Anderson police responded immediately and launched an investigation. They first questioned neighbors, who were unanimous in their observation that Grover was the only person seen entering and leaving the Blake house all day. Neighbors' statements, coupled with the younger Blake's absence, raised many questions. And the discovery of Grover's bloody suit hidden under his mattress prompted a manhunt that would soon extend statewide.

While circumstantial evidence did not bode well for Grover, many relatives and friends were slow to accept him as Louisa Blake's cold-blooded killer. Grover's grandfather, Andrew J. Blake, however, was not one of them.

"It is awful," the elderly Blake proclaimed, "just awful. We only hope and pray that when they bring Grover back, he'll be dead. I never want to see him again. Just think of it, a boy murdering his own mother, beating her brains out with a hammer."

Andrew Blake insisted that his grandson had gone "crazy." Insanity was the only explanation that made sense to him.

"Grover always was good to his mother," he said. "He kissed her every night before he went to bed and always told her, 'Sweet dreams, Mother.'"

The officers received their first clue to Grover's whereabouts from a young boy who had noticed Grover around noon strolling into Park Place, a neighborhood east of downtown and across the White River. When police searched Park Place, they found witnesses who had seen Grover with an unidentified man walking the road toward Chesterfield. The

Anderson police alerted Chesterfield authorities, who, in turn, learned that at four o'clock, Grover and another man had purchased tickets to Yorktown over the traction line.

The Suspects' Journey and Capture

Grover and Orzo boarded the late-afternoon traction car for Yorktown, a small community about thirteen miles northeast of Anderson. In Yorktown, they boarded the seven o'clock limited for Muncie. After arriving at that destination, the two traveled on to Westchester; and from there, they took the Grand Rapids and Indiana train to Fort Wayne, arriving at 10:00 p.m. Somewhere along the way, the two formulated a new plan—to keep heading north, all the way into Michigan.

Blissfully unaware that a posse was on their tail, Grover and Orzo took their sweet time at each stop, visiting saloons and freely spending money. Despite their reckless behavior, they maintained a two-hour lead on the band of law enforcement officers—the Madison County deputy sheriff, the Anderson police chief, the night captain, and the turnkey—who were determined to nab the two men and bring them home.

The officers' search of Muncie taverns reaped hearsay that Grover and Orzo had boasted to bar patrons about their intended junket to Michigan. The Anderson officers, in turn, alerted all the cities in eastern Indiana with details and descriptions of the wanted men. Fort Wayne police went on the offense, searching saloons and "sporting houses"—an early twentieth-century euphemism for brothels. The diligent Fort Wayne officers hit pay dirt when they turned up someone who had spent several hours drinking with the Anderson men. The witness told them that Grover and Orzo planned to board the Lake Erie train for Michigan on Sunday morning.

It was the break Anderson law enforcement officers needed. Two of them—the night captain and the deputy sheriff—boarded the next train for Fort Wayne and joined the local police early Sunday morning. Shortly after the officers converged on the Lake Shore depot, the Madison County deputy sheriff noticed Grover and another man walking toward them. Both Anderson officers dropped out of sight, while the Fort Wayne officers approached the two suspects, who were oblivious to their imminent arrest. All at once, the Anderson officers jumped into the open and seized the fugitives, relieving each of a .32 caliber revolver before shackling them and escorting them to the local jail. Grover and Orzo, for all their self-proclaimed cleverness, had walked right into the open arms of the law.

The *Anderson Morning Herald* reported that Grover turned deathly white during the arrest and shortly thereafter made a complete confession, freely admitting that he had hit his mother with a hammer—once—but he blamed her death on Orzo.

"Just as I got to the top of the stairs," Grover said, "I heard my mother make a sound like a scream. Reynolds rushed in and hit my mother another blow with the hammer, and I heard no more sounds." Grover claimed he ran downstairs and found Reynolds standing over Louisa's body with the hammer. "I asked Orzo if he had hit her," Grover continued, "and he said, 'I hit her and guess it will hold her for a while.'"

"Not so," Orzo countered during his own statement to the police. "I wasn't even there. I had no idea Mrs. Blake had been murdered, but I did wonder why Blake was acting so peculiar after he came back with the money."

In his own confession, Orzo claimed he had been at the Wise Pool Room in downtown Anderson at the time of the killing and offered names of a half dozen men who could substantiate his alibi.

The Anderson officers brought their prisoners home late that Sunday night by way of Wabash, Marion, and Alexandria. When the car reached the north corner of the Anderson jail yard, some two hundred men were waiting. Uncertain of the crowd's temperament, police rushed Grover and Orzo into the jail. Although it was reported that no one in the crowd uttered a single threat, Grover was trembling and sweating until he reached relative safety inside the prison walls.

The Trial

The murder had the entire city bristling with shock, outrage, and a perverse curiosity. Louisa's funeral on Monday at the Blakes' Madison Street residence attracted as many as a thousand callers, most of whom were denied entry and congregated in the street and on neighboring yards during the service. When the police chief and sheriff escorted Grover into and out of the house, the crowd stood back and watched in quiet contempt. Since Saturday night, Grover's grief-stricken father, William, had taken refuge in his room and refused to speak with or even see his son. "I never want to look upon his face again," he said.

William did, however, want his son to look upon his mother's face and asked the police to escort Grover to his mother's coffin the morning of the funeral. "Let him see her," William was quoted as saying. "May it bring to him the awful deed he has done."

Once Louisa was buried in West Maplewood Cemetery, the focus turned to the trial and prosecution of her killer. By Friday, the coroner had presented the result of his inquest, and the following Monday, a grand jury met. At first, William refused to pay for a lawyer to represent his son, forcing Grover to retain the county's pauper attorney. But as time wore on, the stern father broke down and hired one of the finest attorneys in Anderson, who crafted a rather weak defense that would present Grover as a good boy who made a bad decision.

On Thursday, April 9, Grover made his only court appearance before a capacity crowd that stood on their seats and craned their necks for a glimpse of him as he ambled toward the judge's bench. As expected, when court convened, the defense attorney entered a plea of guilty on Grover's behalf, leaving the sentence—life in prison or death by hanging—to the judge's discretion.

During the testimony that followed, neighbors, friends, and members of the Blake family spoke glowingly of Grover, noting Louisa's unbridled love for her son.

"My little brother was always sweet and loving to his mother," an emotional Mrs. Herman Biest, Grover's half sister, told the court. "No mother could ask for a more devoted son. He helped her around the house and would do anything for her. And every night, on his way to bed, he would kiss her forehead and tell her . . ." Biest paused to compose herself and dry her eyes. "He would tell her, 'Sweet dreams, Mother.'"

Biest's testimony prompted tears throughout the courtroom, and the sentiment apparently was not lost on the judge. When handing out the penalty, the judge cited Grover's youth and his previously clean criminal record as reasons for sparing him from the gallows. The judge then sentenced Grover Blake to live the rest of his life behind bars in the Indiana State Prison at Michigan City. Grover reportedly received the sentence without a blink and later remarked to Sheriff Smelser: "The judge treated me mighty nice."

Early Tuesday, April 14, Grover and Smelser boarded a traction car traveling east through Alexandria, Elwood, Hobbs, and Tipton. In Tipton, the two men caught the northbound Lake Erie and Western train for Michigan City. The *Elwood Free Press* ran a brief opinion piece on Thursday, April 16, about Grover's demeanor and appearance that morning. The piece stated:

> Blake slept well last night, ate a hearty breakfast, and left the jail in apparently as good spirits as though starting on a pleasure trip. . . . He rode in the smoking compartment from Anderson to Alexandria with Sheriff Smelser and conversed as glibly as if starting on a fishing trip. Strong men and women who were on the car shed tears at the bravado act of the young man, and many believed that deep down in the boy's heart that he was sorely tried, but was holding up in the company of those who knew him and would break down when the prison walls stared him in the face.
>
> Blake surprised those who saw him on the car this morning, he appearing not over eighteen or nineteen years of age, and his countenance open and frank, leading one to believe he would be the last boy on earth to commit such an atrocious crime. He smoked a cigarette on the way over, which had to be lighted by the sheriff and was not in the least abashed that he was heavily ironed and guarded. It was a character study that was deeply interesting to those who were fortunate enough to be on the car with the arch criminal of the age.

Newspapers chided Grover for his continued cool demeanor and apparent indifference. However, on Sunday, April 12, the *Muncie Sunday Star* reported that on the previous day, a "local paper" in Anderson had printed a letter penned by Grover in which he urged young men to beware of drink and bad company, pointing to himself as an example. Referring to his own fate, he also wrote, "There is but one chance left for me, and that is to give my heart to God, for He says, 'He that cometh unto me I will in no wise cast out,' and He will be true to His word." Some applauded Grover's letter as raw honesty, but others saw it as a selfish, last-ditch gimmick for sympathy.

It is interesting to note that Louisa had been meticulous in her effort to keep her son clean and sober. Had her efforts panned out, Grover likely would not have felt compelled to drink himself into a stupor. Months before her murder, she had put all the Anderson saloonkeepers on notice that under no circumstance were they to serve liquor to her boy. They all ignored her warnings and continued providing Grover all the alcoholic drinks he asked for. Ironically, had they honored Louisa Blake's heartfelt request, she might have avoided getting her brains beaten to a pulp at the hand of her drunken son.

Epilogue

The evidence against Orzo Reynolds was insufficient to warrant a trial. So on August 3, 1908, the same judge who sentenced Grover Blake to prison for life dismissed the affidavit against Reynolds and set him free.

William Blake asked the Indiana Parole Board to pardon his son in 1909, 1913, 1914, and 1918. Each request was denied. In early February 1920, William received a telegram from the Indiana State Prison asking what should be done with Grover's remains. William rushed to Michigan City, where, to his great relief, he found his son alive. Grover had contracted the flu, however, but he was improving. Prison officials apologized to William for the mix-up, and William returned to Anderson on February 6. A few days later, William received a second telegram from the prison advising him that his son had died after all.

The once carefree, handsome young man, whose life had been filled with so much promise, was laid to rest February 12, 1920, in Anderson's West Maplewood Cemetery. Buried beside him was the woman who had always been there for him and loved him so dearly, his proud mother, Louisa. Eighteen years later, when William joined them, the entire Blake family was once again, and forever, reunited.

PART II
WIFE KILLERS

4

DAN SNIDER AND THE STRYCHNINE SOLUTION

TIPTON, 1876

Tipton County folk were greatly saddened in late August 1876 when they heard the news that eight-year-old Mollie King had died of hydrophobia. Just a few days before, her little dog had suffered fits and died. So when Mollie took sick, physicians assumed the animal had infected her with rabies. Dying had been an agonizing ordeal for the girl, causing suffering so horrible that she had begged her doctors for relief.

Mollie's mother, Hannah King Snider, fell ill a few days later, complaining of the same symptoms her daughter had experienced, quickly developing muscle spasms, convulsions, fever, and vomiting. Like Mollie, Hannah also pleaded with her doctors for relief; however, she was more specific. "Please," she wailed, "*kill* me; give me something that'll take me out of this world."

Hannah did leave this world before a new day dawned, but many who knew her didn't believe she or her daughter had died of hydrophobia. They suspected Hannah and Mollie had been poisoned by Dan Snider, Hannah's opportunistic young husband of less than six months.

The whispers spread, seeping into every corner of the community, forcing Tipton County sheriff Robert Roberson and coroner Andrew Swope to acknowledge the possibility. On October 20, the coroner ordered that Mollie's and Hannah's bodies be exhumed and their stomachs sent to Henry Jameson, professor of chemistry at Indiana Medical College in Indianapolis, for analysis. Jameson returned his findings just five days later, attesting that both deaths were caused by strychnine poisoning. "My estimate on the quantity taken into the stomach would be from two to four grains," Jameson wrote, "which would be sufficient to produce death in any instance."

The next day, Tipton County judge Clark Pollard issued a warrant for Snider's arrest.

A Match Made in Hell

Daniel C. Snider was born in 1851 in Howard County near Russiaville. In 1873, he enlisted in the US Army. Marvin Pershing, editor and publisher of the *Tipton Advocate*, reported in the June 21, 1895, edition that Snider had served under General George Custer. However, Pershing was quick to note that Snider had not fought in the terrible Little Bighorn battle. Rather, Snider had arrived on the scene several hours afterward and was glad he had missed the wagon train. Serving two years as an infantryman in the Wyoming territory, Snider had sustained gunshot wounds to his left ankle and legs and lost three fingers on his left hand to frostbite. He was discharged on November 6, 1875, at the age of twenty-four. From there, he journeyed to Tipton, where he joined his brother, John, just in time to meet his future bride at John's New Year's Eve party.

Hannah King was a short, plump, olive-skinned thirty-eight-year-old widow who wore a perpetual scowl to complement a sorrowful demeanor. Her dead husband, David, a casualty of the Civil War, was a son of Tipton founder Samuel King. David had left Hannah a large spread of wooded, virgin land, which is probably what made her so attractive to Snider.

It was unclear what Hannah found so appealing about Snider, but it probably wasn't his boyish good looks. More likely, she was in the market for a provider and someone to tend to her property. Snider filled the bill. Although his five-foot-six frame carried too much weight, his stocky, muscular build made him appear strong and able-bodied. Nevertheless, he shunned hard labor and, consequently, was always broke, as Hannah's nineteen-year-old son, Cassius, noted in his November 16, 1876, deposition. "My mother said when she married him, he didn't have any money," Cassius stated.

Daniel C. Snider was convicted of poisoning his stepdaughter and wife in 1876 in Tipton County.

Meeting Hannah was the opportunity Snider had been waiting for, and he wasted no time in winning her over. The two formed an immediate friendship, which quickly developed into a courtship. On March 9, 1876, the couple married.

That summer, Hannah and Mollie accompanied Snider to Shelby County, southeast of Indianapolis, where they settled in for several weeks visiting with Snider's mother and father. On their return to Tipton, Mollie's dog became violently sick, and, within hours, it was dead. Everyone assumed the child's beloved pet had been a victim of rabies. Thus, when Mollie and Hannah came down with similar symptoms, their doctors mistakenly diagnosed their illnesses as hydrophobia.

Dr. J. M. Grove disagreed with the diagnosis. In his deposition for the grand jury on November 16, he stated, "I didn't have an opportunity to examine Mollie King, but I have seen two or three cases of hydrophobia and had no hesitation in saying that it was *not* hydrophobia. When I saw her, she drank water, which she could not have done had it been hydrophobia."

Another Tipton doctor, H. G. Evans, told the grand jury what he had seen when he visited Mollie at the height of her sickness:

She was drafted with mustard all over her spine, chest, bowels, wrists, ankles, palms, feet, knees, and elbows. She was shivering as though an electric shock was passing through her. Dr. Vickrey advised we get a tub of cold water and pour bucketsful on her head, which we did. We then put an ice cap on her head, but I am not sure our treatment was of any benefit. She gradually got weaker and died, I think in a coma. She had her first convulsion about three o'clock in the afternoon and died the next morning about five.

Evans testified that he had asked Mrs. Snider if there was any chance that the dog had bitten Mollie. "Her answer was, if there was, they did not know of it," he said.

Evans's wife, Georgia, had been at the Snider home the day Mollie died. She testified that Hannah complained of feeling ill. "Mrs. Snider thought she would die," Georgia Evans said, "same as Mollie, inside of a week."

Mollie had been dead ten days when Hannah took sick. Hannah's doctor, M. V. B. Vickrey, told the grand jury that Dan Snider sent for him. "When I arrived, I found Mrs. Snider laboring under a low-grade fever, what I would call typhomalarial. I prescribed a purgative pill and left some tonic powders."

By morning, however, Hannah's illness had grown alarmingly worse.

"I found a very serious change in her disease between the time I was there the night before," Vickrey said. "She was having convulsions and asked me to give her something to kill her. I thought it was on account of the pain she suffered. I had no suspicion she had been poisoned."

And finally, Hannah's neighbor, Amanda Bowlin, described the devastating final moments of Hannah's life. "We held her, Mr. Snider and I, while she had a spasm," Amanda said. "She asked the doctors if they would give her something to kill her, to take her out of this world. She repeated this two or three times."

A County Divided

"Dan didn't seem uneasy before he was arrested," Snider's brother, John, told the grand jury on November 16, when he gave his deposition. "Afterward, the sheriff said he didn't think Dan was the man he wanted."

Opinion about Snider's guilt was divided among the county's residents. Snider seemed like an agreeable man, not the type to commit a double homicide. And yet, more than anyone, he had the opportunity, motive, and means to do it. He was a young man who had taken on the responsibility of caring for a dour, depressed widow thirteen years his senior as well as her two children. Amid the many witness depositions recorded in preparation of his trial, several, including Cassius King's, mentioned that Hannah was so displeased with Snider that she planned to leave him.

"She told me they were not getting along right," Cassius told the grand jury. "Before she died, she said she intended to leave as soon as she got well enough."

Hannah's sister, Mary Ann Mount, corroborated Cassius's disclosure and revealed Hannah's claim that her husband had no use for her offspring. "Dan Snider wanted her to put the children out," Mary Ann stated. "He told her he couldn't live with them."

According to Mary Ann, not only did Hannah vigorously reject the suggestion of putting her children out, she told him to leave. "Hannah always said she would put her children out for no man," Mary Ann said with contempt.

Countering Cassius's and Mary Ann's claims, John Snider insisted his brother's marriage was just fine. "He never complained," John testified. "They got along very well." Obviously, John wanted to help his brother and presented him as a happy, involved husband and provider. Further, to evoke sympathy for his brother, John cast Hannah as emotionally unbalanced, even suicidal.

"She told me once," John said, "that after Dan and her were married, she had taken arsenic poison to kill herself. She said she had taken too much, and it vomited her, which is why it did not kill her.

"Mrs. Snider said that if she ever got in the family way again," John continued, "she would take poison. So, after she died, when Dr. Vickrey told me the rumor that she had been poisoned, I told him she might have done it herself."

Asked to comment on John Snider's claim that Hannah once attempted suicide, Mary Ann Mount responded brusquely: "I never heard of her trying to poison herself."

In case there was still a shred of Hannah's sterling reputation left for John to destroy, he concocted a story bolstered with gossip that she had murdered her two deceased children some ten years before. "Mrs. Jerre Farley and Mrs. Allen Giles sent word that they would swear Mrs. Snider told them she poisoned one of her children with strychnine," John said.

"Mrs. Snider told one of these women that she had smothered the other in a basket of rags. Jim Reed's wife told my wife, and Cliff Bowlin's wife told me."

Regarding John Snider's suggestion that Hannah had killed two of her children, Vickrey said, "It was my opinion that the children who died some years ago died with cerebro special meningitis."

Cassius King may have been the only witness to give voice to the unspoken suspicion that Dan Snider was a ruthless killer who originally had set his sights on the entire King family. Cassius told the grand jury that on the morning his mother and sister left with Snider for Shelby County, he had found a cup of coffee poured out for him. "I tasted it," he said, "and it was so bitter I did not drink it. I found the brewed coffee and poured some into another cup, and it tasted all right. Because of that, I suspicioned right after sister died that she had been poisoned."

The grand jury returned a verdict of murder in the first degree. The Snider murder case would be tried during the next session of the Tipton Circuit Court.

Guilty, Guilty, and . . . Guilty

The trial got under way in early February with Judge Pollard presiding. Representing the state were J. Fred Vaile, Nathan R. Overman, R. B. Beauchamp, and George H. Gifford, while John Green, Dan Waugh, and Joshua Jones argued for the defense. The courtroom battle was bitter and hard fought. The prosecution claimed Snider had killed to gain his wife's wealth, and the defense countered that Hannah was so despondent that she poisoned her daughter and then herself.

The twelve men of the jury were unconvinced by the defense's line of reasoning, and after deliberating all night, they convicted Dan Snider of first-degree murder, punishable by life in prison. However, the defense team appealed to the Indiana Supreme Court. After Snider served nearly a year in the penitentiary, the higher court reversed the lower court's decision and granted him a new trial. Snider was brought to Indianapolis in June 1878 and was retried. Officiating was Judge John B. Elam, who was elected prosecuting attorney of Marion County the next year and later practiced law with President Benjamin Harrison. After another fierce courtroom battle, the jury again convicted Snider. But this time, the jury found him guilty of the lesser charge of manslaughter, which prescribed punishment of two to twenty-one years in prison.

Obviously encouraged by the lighter sentence he had won for his client, lead defense counsel Dan Waugh appealed again to the Indiana Supreme Court. As before, the case was reversed, and Snider was brought back to Tipton to await his third trial.

In September 1881, the case was heard in Muncie, where it was presided over by Judge Leander J. Monks. Vaile and Cyrus Mellette argued for the state, and for the defense, Dan Waugh was assisted by Ralph Gregory of Muncie. Three is not always a charm, as Snider learned when the Muncie jury returned its verdict. After deliberating twenty-four hours, the jury found Snider guilty of second-degree murder and sentenced him to life in the Indiana State Prison in Michigan City.

According to *Tipton Advocate* editor and publisher Marvin Pershing, "This announcement struck most of our citizens like a thunderbolt from a cloudless sky." Pershing claimed that anyone who had heard the evidence overwhelmingly believed Snider would be acquitted. "Even men, who always have thought that Snider was guilty," Pershing added.

After that, Waugh abandoned his efforts to secure another trial for Snider and concentrated instead on securing a pardon. Through it all, Snider's number one advocate was his brother. John Snider poured all his resources—money, time, and energy—into efforts to gain his brother's pardon. Remarkably, more than eight hundred Tipton County citizens signed a petition demanding Dan Snider's freedom, as did every judge, every attorney for the defense, and even those for the state. In November 1893, after Snider had served seventeen years behind bars, then Indiana governor Claude Matthews caved to the pressure and pardoned him. According to Pershing, when Snider was released, the governor offered him some good advice.

"He warned him never to return to Tipton and risk stirring up old animosities," Pershing wrote. "Snider had every encouragement to lead an honest and upright life."

Unfortunately, Snider didn't take the governor's advice, and in June 1895, he made headlines again when he was arrested in Grant County for stealing a horse and buggy. The offense sent Tipton reeling. "Nearly all those who believed him innocent and stuck with him through the ordeal are now dumbfounded," Pershing wrote, "and when spoken to on the subject, they shake their heads as much as to say, 'He deceived us; perhaps he *was* guilty.' His friends are thoroughly disgusted."

Disgusted, indeed. Apparently, murder could be overlooked, but stealing a horse and buggy was an unforgivable sin.

"In fact," Pershing editorialized, "it is the general feeling that he should be sent to the penitentiary to the fullest limit that the law will allow. In fact, he should be kept there the remainder of his natural life."

Pershing wasn't one to mince words. Referring to Snider as "a common horse thief," Pershing gleefully reported that the Grant County judge had sentenced Snider to two more years in the Michigan City penitentiary. "Now, Dan," Pershing goaded, "tell us the truth. Did you or did you not murder your wife and little Mollie?"

Epilogue

Dan Snider walked out of prison for the final time on March 17, 1897, and married Emma Jane Stroup shortly after. He settled down and established himself as an upholsterer and carpenter. The Sniders moved to Tipton in 1910 and made their home on West Madison Street until 1920, when Emma met an unsavory demise.

On March 23, 1920, she was "burned to a crisp," according to the *Tipton Daily Tribune*. As she did every morning, Emma had risen before dawn to prepare breakfast. She thought she was pouring coal oil into the stove, as was her longtime practice. However, that morning, she inexplicably had picked up the can of gasoline. Her bloodcurdling shrieks drew her husband, who tried to tear the flaming clothing from her body and beat out the flames with his bare hands. Unfortunately, his attempts to save her failed, and, as the paper reported, Emma died within a matter of hours.

Snider's notorious track record with wives caused some in the community to speculate about what prompted Emma to pick up the wrong can that morning, but nothing ever came of it.

Snider, too, met a rather nasty end in Russiaville nine years later, on June 5, 1929, as he shuffled across a railroad track in front of an oncoming freight train. Then age seventy-eight and a resident of the Howard County village, Snider was on his way to the local fishing pond. He obviously saw the locomotive but apparently figured he had time to cross the track safely. Death came to him instantly and was far kinder than when it claimed his wives and little Mollie. The *Tipton Daily Tribune* noted that Snider's only visible sign of injury was a small scratch on his left hand.

Hannah's only living offspring—her son, Cassius King—spent his entire life in Tipton, where he raised a family, operated a successful trucking business, and enjoyed the community's respect. He died there in 1940 at the age of eighty-two.

Cassius was still a boy when he lost his mother and sister. What had it been like for him to live for years in such close proximity to the man convicted of murdering them? Perhaps the answer can be gleaned from Cassius's obituary. "His mother remarried after the death of [his father] David King," the death notice stated, "and her second husband, Dan Snider, was convicted of poisoning her and a daughter. The poisoned food prepared for them was also meant for Cassius, but he escaped."

Indeed, Cassius King escaped. Afterward, despite the horror of his mother's and sister's murders as well as his own near-death experience, he channeled his energy into living a life that reinforced the King family's legacy. His final message, however, revealed that he never forgot his brush with evil and wanted no one else to forget it either.

THE CASE OF THE DROWSY UXORICIDE

ARCADIA, 1911

Harry and Nellie Hiatt—he twenty-seven and she twenty-one—had been married four volatile years before Nellie packed her bags, loaded up their two small sons, and moved to her parents' farm near Cicero. Three months later, on Monday, June 5, 1911, with the mercury creeping north of one hundred degrees, Hiatt reached his boiling point and set out to fetch his family. When Nellie refused to come home, he chased her through the barnyard and shot her—twice in the back and once in the heart. His anger spent, he gaped with smug satisfaction at the dead woman sprawled on the ground at his feet, her blood flowing from the wounds his bullets had inflicted. Suddenly, the fog that had shrouded his conscience lifted, exposing raw remorse, and with blinding clarity, he bellowed, "My God! My God! What have I done?" Overcome by indefensible guilt, he fled across the road and into the woods, pointed his .32 caliber revolver at his temple, and pulled the trigger.

Surrender without a Fuss

Fortunately for Hiatt, he missed. The bullet had only grazed his thick forehead, inflicting a minor flesh wound. While he staggered about the woods, stunned and confused, news of his despicable crime was spreading through Jackson Township. Word quickly reached Cicero, provoking the victim's friends and neighbors to threaten a lynch mob to finish what Hiatt's poor aim had failed to accomplish. The mob might have followed through had City Marshall Fisher and Justice Meehan not reached Hiatt first.

The Cicero officers approached Hiatt with caution, demanding that he throw away his gun and surrender. Hiatt offered no resistance. He did as he was told and raised his arms.

"What is it that I've done?" he asked with a nervous stutter, his swollen brown eyes watering, the right side of his face streaked in blood. "Did I do something wrong?"

The officers led Hiatt to their rig and drove him directly to city hall. There, Hiatt's wound was dressed, while Fisher telephoned the Hamilton County sheriff's office in Noblesville. When Sheriff J. L. York learned that vigilantes were talking up a lynching, he lost no time securing an automobile so he and Deputy Charles Wheeler could get to Hiatt and transfer him the six miles to the county jail before trouble broke out. En route to Noblesville, Hiatt appeared restless and skittish. When the officers pressed him for an explanation about the shooting, he told them he and Nellie had been separated since March, but as for her murder, he maintained that he didn't remember a thing.

Nellie's mother, Amy May Voss, in contrast, remembered every detail. "I saw Harry coming up the road," Mrs. Voss told Sheriff York in her statement. "When I alerted my daughter, she ran out the back door and headed for the field where her father was plowing."

"She feared her husband?" the sheriff asked.

Mrs. Voss bobbed her head and shuddered. "Harry drove up to the house, climbed out, and barged in," she said, continuing her narrative. "He had a gun, and he was frantic."

Hiatt darted from room to room, looking for his wife. He didn't find her, but he did find his sons—three-year-old Estel and twenty-month-old Voss. They had followed their mother onto the back porch. Hiatt picked the boys up and kissed their cheeks.

"That's when he saw Nellie running across the barnyard," Mrs. Voss said. "He set the boys down and bolted after her."

Hiatt fired off two shots as he ran. Both bullets struck his wife's back. In an amazing show of resolve, Nellie kept going but, in her injured state, was quickly overtaken by her out-of-control husband. Grabbing her arm, Hiatt dragged her some twenty-five feet into the cowshed behind the barn, where he shot her again, this time in her left breast. The round pierced her heart. Mortally wounded, Nellie fell to the ground.

Mrs. Voss rushed out the back door after Hiatt. She had hoped to stop him before he hurt her daughter, but by the time she reached him, he had already fired three shots and was crossing the road, running for a cluster of trees about a half mile north of the farm.

Nellie Hiatt was buried three days later in Cicero Cemetery, following a lovely funeral at the Vosses' home. An unusually large number of people attended to pay their respects.

Meanwhile, Hiatt sat in his Noblesville jail cell, recuperating from his attempted suicide and insisting that he remembered nothing of the incident that killed his wife.

Indicted and Frightened

Hiatt stewed in the Hamilton County jail ten days while the grand jury investigated and deliberated his case. On June 16, he was indicted for murder in the first degree, also known in those days as *uxoricide*, the term for a husband's killing of his wife. Hiatt held fast to his claim that he had no memory of the killing, leading the state to believe he was setting the stage for a plea of insanity.

Hiatt's days and weeks behind bars with nothing to do but think dragged on. By mid-September, he was scared and desperate. He was facing the death penalty, and he wanted out.

Out is exactly what he got during the wee hours of September 22, thanks to an unknown accomplice with a skeleton key. When his empty jail cell was discovered six hours later, police were baffled. The only entrance to the jail was a large iron door that opened from the sheriff's office, which was accessible only from his private residence. The door had been securely locked when Sheriff York retired the night before, and it was locked the next morning when the turnkey took the prisoners their breakfast. How had Hiatt gotten free?

Police learned the answer from another prisoner, Allen Lewis, who told officers that he had been awakened at 1:00 a.m. by an animated Hiatt. The jail door was open, and Hiatt invited Lewis to escape with him. Lewis declined. Punishment for Lewis's crime, bootlegging, was relatively moderate; thus, he had no reason to run.

Had an intruder with a key slipped into the jail by way of the house during the night? Had one of the sheriff's family members opened the door? Had Hiatt managed to steal the key from the guard? While the mystery begged to be answered, the more pressing concern was, Where was Hiatt hiding? Officers figured that with a six-hour head start, Hiatt would have jumped the Chicago-bound freighter as it rumbled through Noblesville at 2:00 a.m.

A statewide manhunt had barely begun when little more than twenty-four hours later, the escaped prisoner returned to the jail in the custody of his father and brother, George and Roll Hiatt. They had found Hiatt the previous afternoon near Cicero as he wandered along the road to the family home, making no effort to hide and speaking with everyone he knew. After a brief visit with his family, they convinced him to return to jail, and he acquiesced.

"I only wanted to see my parents," Hiatt told the sheriff.

The Trial Begins

Hiatt appeared before Judge Meade Vestal on Saturday, October 7, for his arraignment and entered his plea: not guilty on the grounds of temporary insanity. His rationale was predictable and flimsy. How could he be guilty, he reasoned, when he couldn't recall a single incident connecting him to the crime? Or so he claimed.

Conversely, when the trial began on Monday, October 16, Hamilton County prosecutor R. R. Foland argued that Hiatt was guilty of murder beyond a reasonable doubt and should be hung. It had been almost twenty-five years since a Hamilton County prosecutor had argued for the death penalty. The prosecution's stunning recommendation forced the defense team, headed by W. R. Fertig, to fine-tune its strategy. Rather than claiming that Hiatt was merely insane, Fertig insisted his client's insanity was hereditary.

Bolstering the argument, Fertig stated that Hiatt's father was considered insane as a young man. Furthermore, he stated, Hiatt's mother was mentally unbalanced, and her mother and sister were both insane.

Hiatt displayed little interest in the proceedings, as if proving his dull mental acuity. While the courtroom was spellbound by witnesses' testimony, he frequently snoozed.

On the first day of the trial, the state's principal witness and the only eyewitness to the shooting—Nellie Hiatt's mother—delivered a heartrending account of the day her daughter was mercilessly gunned down. Mrs. Voss shed tears throughout the painful testimony, causing her to stop several times to regain her composure.

The other key witness for the state was Nellie's father, Albert Voss. At the time his daughter was fatally shot, Mr. Voss had been plowing the field down the road. Hearing the gunshots, he had scrambled off the tractor and sprinted to his daughter's crumpled body in the barnyard. He had no doubt about who killed her. "Every night for a month before my daughter's murder," Mr. Voss told the court, "a prowler had been creeping around the house and peeping through the windows."

"Did you see who it was?" Prosecutor Foland asked.

"I didn't see him," Mr. Voss grumbled, his voice trembling. "I didn't have to. I seen his foot tracks, and they were *his*." Mr. Voss pointed at the defendant.

"You're certain of that?" Foland asked.

"I measured 'em," Mr. Voss replied. "Next time I seen him, I told him he was welcome in our home any time, but I wouldn't put up with him sneakin' around the house, especially after dark."

"Did he stop?" asked the prosecutor.

Mr. Voss cocked his jaw and nodded. "Yes, he did. And he promised he'd never again threaten to harm my daughter."

Another witness, one of Hiatt's buddies, advised the court that on the Saturday before the shooting, Hiatt brought a concealed gun to the Cicero movie house where Nellie played piano.

Two young women who had been friends of Nellie's next took the stand and revealed that Hiatt often covertly followed his wife. On at least one occasion, he had a knife in his hand, they said. After the couple's separation, Nellie confided to her friends that she was afraid he would kill her.

In its effort to prove Hiatt's guilt beyond a reasonable doubt, the prosecution required two days to lay out its case. The defense took the same amount of time. Hoping to convince the jury that Hiatt was insane, and therefore innocent, his attorney presented a medical expert to testify that the defendant's skull was abnormally thick, a conclusion he based on the failure of Hiatt's bullet to penetrate his skull in his unsuccessful suicide attempt. A thick skull, the witness noted, was a condition that typically signals insanity. The defense cemented that assertion by next calling Hiatt's parents to the witness stand. They swore insanity

Harry Hiatt was convicted of shooting and killing his wife, Nellie, in her parents' barnyard on June 5, 1911. *Photo courtesy Indiana State Archives.*

was prevalent in both of their families for at least three generations. Following the defense's presentation, the prosecution requested three days to rebut. The case finally was handed to the jury at noon on Wednesday, October 25.

And the Verdict Is . . .

Twenty-four hours later, the jury had not returned its decision. In fact, the jury deliberated for fifty-five hours, which was unprecedented in Hamilton County. And when Judge Vestal revealed the jury's long-awaited decision, the courtroom's anticipation was doused with disappointment. The jury was deadlocked.

From the beginning, ten jurors believed Hiatt was guilty of first-degree murder and deserved life in prison, while the remaining two were convinced he was insane and should be acquitted. Those two jurors told the press they were willing to agree to a manslaughter verdict, but the other ten refused to yield.

The frustrated judge declared a mistrial and discharged the jury. The case would be retried at the start of the next session in January.

Hiatt was undoubtedly frustrated too. He had waited more than three months to learn whether death, life in prison, or freedom awaited him. Now he would have to wait two more months and sit through another trial. While a deputy escorted Hiatt back to his jail cell, a newspaper reporter caught up with him and asked how he felt about the verdict. A downtrodden Hiatt replied, "I'd rather go to the penitentiary than fool around this way."

Retried and Droopy-Eyed

When Hiatt's new trial convened on Tuesday, January 9, 1912, he maintained his plea of insanity. The next four days were consumed by the selection of twelve jurors from a pool of 101 men, the majority of whom said they placed no faith in such a plea as a murder defense. Further, Hiatt did nothing to ingratiate himself to the jury panel—ignoring what was going on around him, slumping over the defense table, resting his chin on his fists, and nodding off.

R. R. Foland made the opening statement for the prosecution the afternoon of Friday, January 12. He again called for the death penalty. The next day, Amy May Voss testified, as she had at the first trial, relating details of her daughter's slaying. It was an ordeal for her, and she broke down several times and cried.

A stream of witnesses, such as a Cicero schoolteacher who boarded at the Voss home, took the stand to describe instances when Hiatt had harassed and threatened his wife. In addition, to establish that the murder was premeditated, Nellie's brother, Floyd Voss, testified that the day before his sister's death, he saw Hiatt loading a revolver. When Floyd asked his brother-in-law about it, his response was, "You'll know in the morning."

The state rested its case at noon on Tuesday, January 16. Through it all, Hiatt dozed, and his attorney let him.

The defense's mission was to erode the prosecution's case. Fertig hoped to achieve that by convincing the jury that Hiatt was indisputably, irretrievably, emotionally insane—or that the notion was at least reasonably feasible.

The first witness for the defense was Hiatt's seventy-nine-year-old grandfather, Eliphalet Hiatt, who lamented that his wife's sister had been "incurably insane," two of his grandson's aunts were "mentally weak," and that his own son, George, father of the accused, was dimwitted.

When Hiatt's father took the stand, he told the court that his son had fallen into a vat of boiling water three years earlier at an Elwood glass factory. The scalding, the father claimed, contributed to his son's lunacy.

The president of the Frankfort, Indiana, school board then stepped up to reveal that the Frankfort superintendent, who had been Hiatt's first cousin, had been insane for months before he committed suicide the previous summer.

Next, each in a string of physicians was given a lengthy hypothetical quiz about Hiatt's sanity. In addition, they all agreed that Hiatt's allegedly thick skull was a telltale sign of insanity.

Following the doctors, ten Cicero-area residents who remembered Hiatt as a child took the stand. They did their best to substantiate the insanity claim by sharing anecdotes about a boy who suffered epileptic fits in church, stole money without shame, and failed to recognize his closest friends.

And finally, a farmer who saw Hiatt shortly after the June shooting attested to Hiatt's unsound mind, based on the glassy appearance of his eyes.

Still, the evidence became more peculiar. On the eleventh day of the trial, Hiatt's mother was called to testify on her son's behalf. After tracing the mental instability of her family tree, she confessed that her son had been "a nervous babe, crying and screaming almost constantly for a year." And, she added, the fact that he had been kicked in the head by a horse at a young age probably hadn't helped.

Alas, while the courtroom may have been enthralled by the defense witnesses' testimony, Hiatt could not stay awake.

The defense finally rested at noon on Tuesday, January 23. The prosecution took over, questioning two Noblesville doctors—A. R. Tucker and E. E. Wishard—for three days about Hiatt's sanity. Both doctors believed Hiatt was perfectly sane when he killed his wife, and both were certain the murder was premeditated. When their testimony ended, Hiatt's fate was a matter for the jury.

Fifteen hours later, at 9:34 a.m. on Saturday, January 27, the trial's sixteenth day, the jury returned its verdict. The panel had quickly brushed aside Hiatt's insanity plea and decided within two hours that he was guilty of murder in the first degree. They devoted the remaining thirteen hours to deciding his appropriate punishment. Thirty ballots later, the panel settled on life in prison.

When the jury foreman passed the verdict to Judge Vestal, Hiatt slouched in a chair behind his attorneys, his head propped on his right hand and his face turned to the wall. As the judge read the jury's decision to the crowded courtroom, Hiatt might as well have been a mannequin. He didn't flinch. He didn't blink. He never looked up.

First Day of the Rest of His Life

On Tuesday, February 13, 1912, a small crowd of curiosity seekers assembled outside the Hamilton County jail, eager for a last look at Hiatt. Well rested, spit shined, and dressed up in his suit, he was handcuffed to Sheriff York when he stepped outside and surprised the congregation with a public statement. It was his first in the more than eight months since he had murdered his wife.

"I guess I made a mistake," he said, his head bowed, his eyes averted from the onlookers' faces. "I wanted to shoot the man that come between me and Nellie, *not* her. But that day, when I went to the house, all I wanted was to talk to her, and what'd she do? She up and run away. It made me mad, and I sort of lost control and . . ."

"And you shot her," nudged a Noblesville newspaper reporter who was among the crowd.

Hiatt spun his head in the reporter's direction and grunted, "Uh-huh." He told the reporter he was sorry he hadn't taken the witness stand on his own behalf, so he could have revealed that the separation from his wife and her murder were the fault of the man who wrecked his home.

The sheriff grasped Hiatt's arm and whisked him through the crowd to the depot a few blocks up the street. There they met a deputy and boarded a train bound for Michigan City.

On their arrival, they were transported by automobile to Hiatt's final destination, the Indiana State Prison, where he began his life sentence.

Epilogue

Hiatt beat the odds. Adjusting well to prison life, he earned the reputation of a model prisoner, establishing himself as a trustee and valued library employee. The state granted him numerous temporary paroles from 1922 through 1936, allowing him the privilege of traveling unaccompanied to Hamilton County to visit his family.

Despite his exemplary behavior, the parole board denied his applications for clemency in 1933, 1936, 1939, and 1941. Finally, on October 8, 1943, Indiana governor Henry Schricker granted Hiatt his parole. At long last, Harry Hiatt was a free man.

He also was a reformed man who loved his family. He returned to Arcadia to be near the two sons whose mother he had stolen from them. Hiatt lived a quiet life in that community until his death on December 22, 1959, just nine days before his seventy-fifth birthday. He never remarried.

6

DEATH ON MAISH ROAD

FRANKFORT, 1932

Clinton County sheriff Dan Power drove his cruiser briskly along State Road 39, heading north out of Frankfort. His backseat passengers were twenty-two-year-old convicted wife killer Richard Gladden, securely handcuffed and closely guarded by deputized Frankfort merchant Clyde Louck sitting beside him. Frankfort police officer Clifford Gray was riding shotgun. Their destination that warm morning in April 1932 was the Indiana State Prison in Michigan City.

For the first ninety-three miles of the journey, Gladden appeared devil-may-care about the life sentence waiting for him, masking his fear and dread behind a facade of indifference. But after passing through the tiny LaPorte County town of Wanatah, where he read the "19 Miles to Michigan City" road sign, he grew somber. A few minutes later, as the sheriff's car rolled within eyeshot of the prison walls, Gladden remarked uneasily, "So this is where we're going."

"This is it," the sheriff affirmed. "This is where you'll spend the rest of your life."

Gladden huffed a little laugh and shook his head. "Naw," he said, "I'll be eligible for parole in six months, and I bet I don't serve two years."

Three months earlier, Gladden would have bet he'd never be accused of murder—let alone charged, convicted, and sentenced to life in prison. But that was before his twenty-one-year-old bride, Dolores, died in the front seat of his car.

Left: Richard D. Gladden was twenty-two when he was convicted of murdering his wife, Dolores, by carbon monoxide poisoning the night of February 1, 1932. *Right:* Richard Gladden's wife, Dolores, who died of carbon monoxide poisoning after she and Richard allegedly fell asleep in their car, parked just beyond the Frankfort city limits. *Photos courtesy the* Frankfort Times, *Frankfort Indiana.*

Dolores Gladden, DOA

Shortly before midnight on February 1, 1932, John Young, whose house overlooked State Road 28 on Frankfort's east side, was awakened by incessant banging on his front door. Disgruntled by the disturbance, Young greeted Gladden, who excitedly stammered, "My wife has been gassed, and I need an ambulance. Call eighty-eight!"

Young figured Gladden was drunk but made the call anyway, dialing eighty-eight—the number for Goodwin Funeral Home, which also operated the local ambulance. Young informed Gladden that he'd made the call and watched him stagger across the state road toward its intersection with Maish Road.

When ambulance driver William Goodwin responded to the call a few minutes later, he saw Gladden standing in the road waving a flashlight. Goodwin stopped, threw open the passenger door, and told Gladden, who appeared weak and upset, to climb in.

"What's the matter?" Goodwin said. "A wreck?"

"No," Gladden replied, "gassed—carbon monoxide!"

Gladden directed Goodwin to turn north onto Maish Road and proceed to his car, a Whippet coupe, parked about a half mile up the road, just south of the railroad tracks.

"What time is it?" Gladden asked.

"About midnight," Goodwin said.

"My God," Gladden gasped. "I've been out here since eight thirty."

Gladden explained that he and his wife had pulled over to talk, and because it was below freezing, he had left the car running to keep warm. He wasn't sure when they had dozed off, but when he awoke around ten thirty, he couldn't rouse his wife. His first thought was to get her to the hospital, but the motor had stopped and wouldn't restart. He had no alternative but to take off on foot to find help.

Easing the ambulance alongside Gladden's car, Goodwin spotted Dolores in the front seat, her drooping head pressed against the passenger-side window. Goodwin acted quickly to move the unresponsive woman into the ambulance and rush her to the Clinton County Hospital.

There, a nurse assessed Dolores's vitals and summoned Dr. W. L. Hammersley. The doctor reached the hospital within minutes and immediately went to work on the unconscious woman, trying to resuscitate her. But it was useless. Dolores was dead. After that, several events quickly went into play that would forever alter the course of Richard Gladden's life.

Hammersley would later report to the *Frankfort Morning Times* that he had noticed two bruises on each side of Dolores's neck. Although he said they were "hardly discernible," he was nonetheless compelled to notify Clinton County coroner Frank Strange and prosecutor Millard Morrison without delay. At their recommendation, Gladden was taken into police custody on the spot, and Strange performed an autopsy at Weidner and Kent Funeral Home. Morrison characterized Dolores Gladden's death as "surrounded by mysterious circumstances" and called for a grand jury the next day, although the autopsy report would not reach Frankfort authorities until the end of the week.

Interment and Internment

Gladden had met his soon-to-be bride, Dolores Renfrow, in January 1930 in Kansas City, Missouri, where he attended Sweeney Automobile and

Members of Frankfort's police department posed in 1935 for this photograph. Among them are then mayor Dan Power (*seated, fourth from left*), who was Clinton County's sheriff in 1932. Power drove Richard Gladden to the Indiana State Prison, where Gladden was to serve a life sentence. *Photo courtesy of the Frankfort, Indiana, Police Department.*

Aviation School. The couple married three weeks later and briefly made their home with Dolores's mother and stepfather. Soon after, Gladden's school went out of business, leaving him to look for work while Dolores clerked at Woolworth's. Within a month, he landed a job at a local cafeteria, and he and Dolores moved into a rooming house. The couple relocated to Frankfort in January 1931, but over the next year, Dolores returned to Kansas City several times to visit her mother, Dorothy Titsworth.

A grief-stricken Titsworth rushed to Frankfort after learning of her daughter's death. Arriving on Wednesday, February 3, she spoke with Gladden in his jail cell that afternoon. The two met again the next morning at Weidner and Kent to bid an emotional goodbye to Dolores. Mortuary owner Oswell Weidner would later testify that Titsworth asked her son-in-law several times if he had killed Dolores, and each time he swore, "I never touched her."

Two days later, Titsworth took her daughter home for interment at Soldier Cemetery in Jackson County, Kansas.

Gladden retained local defense attorney Frank S. Pryor. No charges had yet been filed, so Pryor immediately petitioned for his client's release. However, on Saturday, February 6, the grand jury indicted Gladden for first-degree murder. Pryor and Gladden appeared before Clinton circuit court judge Brenton A. Devol on February 8 to request a bail hearing. The *Frankfort Morning Times* was there and reported that Gladden looked "far different from the debonair young man who was a familiar figure on the streets of the city during the past few months. He had not shaved for several days and the strain of his incarceration was clearly evident."

When Pryor returned to Devol's court on February 20, he proclaimed his client's innocence and argued for his release on bond pending trial because, he said, "the evidence is not evident nor the presumption strong." The prosecuting attorney challenged the bond, and the hearing dragged on several days, producing nineteen witnesses for the state. Pryor motioned for dismissal on February 26, after his two expert witnesses—doctors from Indianapolis—refused to testify without remuneration. While the motion quashed Gladden's chance for bail, the hearing provided him a preview of the state's strategy: overwhelm the jury with a barrage of theories and see what sticks.

The trial was set for Monday, April 11.

The Trial Begins

On the first day of Gladden's long-awaited trial, he appeared gaunt and pale. Because the majority of prospective jurors, all twelve of them men, had formed strong opinions about Gladden's guilt, jury selection took the entire day and a good portion of the next.

Day one, although long and mind-numbing, ended with a dramatic flourish when Dorothy Titsworth suddenly sashayed into the courtroom and collapsed onto the chair next to Prosecutor Morrison.

Gladden was taken aback by Titsworth's unexpected presence. The last time he had spoken with his former mother-in-law was the day he said goodbye to his wife at the funeral home. Had Titsworth returned as a witness? If she had, was she there for his defense or his prosecution? Gladden had to know.

He rose from his seat at the defense table and, before the deputy could stop him, leaped in Titsworth's direction.

Recoiling, Titsworth thrust her hands before her and shrieked, "Get away! Get away!" As if that weren't enough to turn the courtroom into a tizzy, Titsworth screamed, "Dolores came to me from 'spirit land' and told me *you killed her!*"

Although the *Frankfort Morning Times* chose not to report Titsworth's odd outburst until after the trial had ended, interest in the case rippled through the community once Tuesday's paper hit the doorsteps. By the next day, courtroom seating was so scarce that spectators were hiring stand-ins to save seats for them. The going rate was twenty-five cents per hour.

Prosecution vs. Defense

Laying out his case during opening statements, the prosecutor cast several gossamer-thin, unsubstantiated scenarios that, he said, would prove Gladden's guilt beyond a reasonable doubt. Morrison insisted that any one of them—strangulation, drugging, motor tampering, a rubber hose, disharmony in the marriage, and life insurance—was more than enough to convict Richard Gladden of murder in the first degree. Should Morrison win a conviction, the jury would decide whether Gladden's punishment would be death or life in prison.

Pryor responded with promises. In the coming days, he said, the defense would offer irrefutable, rock-hard evidence to dismantle the state's circumstantial allegations.

Allegation 1: Gladden Was Cheating on His Wife

For shock value, Morrison laid out the one theory guaranteed to offend the jury's sense of morality and stir emotions. Morrison called Gladden a "feckless adulterer." He claimed Gladden had been hatching a "nefarious scheme" for months to "exterminate" his wife. The motive, Morrison asserted, was money and another woman.

Pryor laughed at Morrison's assertions and countered with a lecture on circumstantial evidence. "A grand jury indictment must not be confused with evidence of guilt," he stressed. "Richard Gladden is an *innocent* man. He loved his wife dearly. Finding her unconscious in his car, he did everything humanly possible to revive her. When his efforts failed, he rushed to obtain medical assistance."

Pryor also assured the jury that the Gladdens had been highly religious and took their marriage vows seriously. "In fact," he said, "the Sunday night preceding the fatal Monday night, the young man and his wife attended church, as they frequently did. Such habits are not those of one with adultery—or murder—in his heart."

Allegation 2: Gladden Plotted a Life Insurance Payoff

On Wednesday morning, April 13, Morrison called three witnesses affiliated with three different insurance companies. Their testimony revealed that Gladden was the beneficiary on three life insurance policies with a face value totaling $11,000.

While the policies may have seemed suspicious to the prosecutor, Pryor called them the sensible precautions of a responsible married couple. His cross-examination showed that the policies had been taken out with Dolores's knowledge and consent. Besides that, she was the beneficiary of a $5,000 policy taken out on her husband.

Allegation 3: Gladden Tampered with the Heater

Morrison relentlessly quizzed Gladden's younger brother, Robert, owner of the Whippet coupe in which Dolores had died. Questions focused on repairs made as recently as January 31 to the car's heater. Robert told the court that the gas line, as well as the heater, frequently malfunctioned and that his passengers complained about headaches, which he also had experienced. The prosecutor scoffed at Robert's answers, suggesting that the car had been tampered with.

Pryor questioned a local mechanic, who testified that the car's manifold heater was faulty. He said its grease- and soot-covered outlet tube could have caused carbon monoxide to leak into the car's interior.

Allegation 4: Gladden Piped Carbon Monoxide into the Car

Morrison displayed a piece of rubber hose found in the car's trunk. He asserted that Gladden had used the hose to convey poisonous gas fumes from the exhaust pipe to the car's interior.

In response, Pryor's mechanic testified that the hose was too short.

Allegation 5: Gladden Drugged Dolores

Morrison said Gladden had drugged his wife with luminal, a commonly used sedative. Pryor called on R. H. Harger, associate professor of toxicology at the Indiana University School of Medicine. Harger said tests showed conclusively that only two foreign substances were present in Dolores Gladden's organs—carbon monoxide and a trace of acetylsalicylic acid, also known as aspirin.

Allegation 6: Gladden Strangled Dolores

Bruises on Dolores's neck led Morrison to conclude that Gladden had strangled his wife.

However, Frankfort doctor A. G. Chittick testified that strangulation had not contributed to Dolores Gladden's death. "We did not think so as the marks were not seemingly deep," Chittick said. "The finding of air in the lungs also would disprove that deduction."

Allegation 7: Gladden Was Heartless

Morrison tried to cast the defendant as a coldhearted killer by focusing on his impassive demeanor. First, he questioned a Frankfort patrolman, who testified that Gladden hadn't shed a single tear the night his wife died. Next, the ambulance driver told the jury, "Gladden displayed no outward signs of emotion."

To counter the attack on his client's emotional conduct, Pryor spoke of Gladden's reaction to seeing his wife's corpse laid out in the "slumber room" at Weidner and Kent. "He knelt beside her body at the funeral parlor and cried bitterly," Pryor said.

Allegation 8: Gladden Was Drunk

John Young, whom Gladden called on for help the night of Dolores's death, said Gladden had acted "queer" and was probably drunk.

In response, Pryor asked Dr. Ivan Carlyle, former Clinton County coroner, to list the effects of carbon monoxide poisoning. Carlyle testified that prior to death, victims experience extreme weakness, general lassitude, headaches, and dizziness—any one of which might be mistaken for drunkenness.

Allegation 9: Gladden Was a Convicted Felon

The prosecutor revealed that in 1929, Gladden pleaded guilty in a Missouri-based US federal court for pilfering the US mail. As punishment, he was sentenced to one year and one day at the federal reformatory at Chillicothe, Ohio.

Pryor confirmed the allegation was factual, but it was a non sequitur. The sentence had been suspended, and Gladden was placed on probation for three years. To his client's credit, Pryor said, because of good conduct, probation had been reduced to two years, and Gladden was sent home.

Allegation 10: Gladden Was a Loser

Morrison presented Gladden as a ne'er-do-well who shunned work and sponged off his family. The prosecutor pointed out that both of Gladden's grandmothers had been "indulgent benefactors" for most of his life. But recently, both women had had their fill of his laziness and had cut him off.

When it was Pryor's turn, he painted his client as a victim of lifelong setbacks, dating back to age three, when his mother died. After that, his father relinquished all parental responsibilities and left his son's rearing to his grandmothers. Thus, he said, Gladden never had the benefit of a two-parent family or a strong male role model.

Gladden Testifies

Gladden took the stand on Thursday, April 21—day nine of the proceedings. Pryor's line of questioning was surprisingly brief, beginning with, "I will ask that if, on February 1, 1932, you murdered one Dolores Gladden."

"I did *not*," Gladden responded brusquely.

"I will ask," continued Pryor, "if you loved your wife."

At this point, Gladden drew a handkerchief from his pocket and dabbed at his eyes. (The *Frankfort Morning Times* reported that no tears were visible.) "I did," he said.

"I will ask," said Pryor, "if you bought any tablets at the drugstore on the night of February 1."

"Yes," answered Gladden, "luminal tablets."

"That's all," Pryor said and returned to his seat.

However, before the judge could adjourn for the day, Pryor turned to Gladden and asked one final question: "Did you cry at the police station that night?"

"No, I didn't," Gladden replied.

"Why not?" Pryor probed.

"Death is something that has had much effect on me," Gladden said. "But with Dolores, I just couldn't realize it. . . . I knew she was gone, but I couldn't realize it."

Verdict

In the prosecution's dramatic closing argument on Tuesday, April 26—day twelve—Morrison insisted Gladden had drugged, strangled, and gassed his wife for insurance money. Advancing to within a few feet of Gladden, he pointed an accusing finger and shouted, "You've got blood on your hands, Mr. Gladden, and you know it." With that, Morrison sat down, and the state's prosecution of Richard Gladden ended.

Pryor's closing argument followed. He was emphatic that without one shred of hard evidence, all Morrison's claims were circumstantial.

The case went to the jury at 10:40 a.m. Wednesday, April 27. Nine hours later, the courthouse bell rang, signaling that the panel had reached a decision.

Deathlike silence fell upon the courtroom as the clerk read the verdict: "We the jury find the defendant, Richard H. Gladden, guilty of murder in the first degree; and we the jury recommend life imprisonment."

All eyes shifted to Gladden. Slumped in the chair, he displayed nothing—not surprise, not sadness, not anger.

The next morning, Gladden stood before Judge Devol for formal sentencing. Devol asked him if he had anything to say before judgment was pronounced.

Gladden peered straight into the judge's eyes and answered clearly, "Though the jury has found me guilty, I'm *not* guilty."

Later that day, Gladden moved into his new digs in Michigan City, and Pryor filed a motion for a new trial. Devol overruled it.

The Gladden trial had been one of the longest in Frankfort's history. It also was the first in Indiana that tried and convicted a defendant for murder by carbon monoxide.

Shown is the northeast view of the Indiana State Prison in the 1930s. The prison, located in Michigan City, was home to Richard Gladden from 1932 through 1966, when he was pardoned by Indiana governor Roger Branigin. The prison also became home to several other convicted killers featured in this book, some of whom died there. *Photo courtesy Bass Photo Co. Collection, Indiana Historical Society.*

Epilogue

Gladden maintained his innocence for the rest of his life. At the outset of his prison term, he was confident his sentence would be reduced, just as his sentence for mail tampering had been.

He never changed his story about the night Dolores died—that her death was an accident and that he was no murderer. Initially, he was certain regaining freedom would be a matter of convincing the right person that he had been framed.

The following February, the *Kokomo Tribune* reported that Gladden had met with a Kokomo attorney about seeking a new trial. Gladden claimed that he'd been "railroaded" and had evidence to prove it. But nothing came of it, and there were no other reports about a new trial.

Gladden might have won parole had he changed his attitude. The March 1954 edition of *Mechanix Illustrated* magazine carried a story that mentioned his case, and Gladden responded a few months later with a letter to the editor. In it, Gladden wrote: "It might interest you to know that I am still doing life in prison because I will not ask for a parole. A parole is the tempering of justice with mercy, and I have always contended that there has been no justice in my case. A pardon or discharge is all I'll take."

Several years passed before another word about Richard Gladden was printed. Then, on January 16, 1962, a number of Indiana newspapers carried a story reporting that his request to have his sentence commuted had been denied. The brief story was largely forgettable, except for a curious quote from the former Clinton County prosecutor Millard Morrison: "Had [Gladden] not been convicted, a very great effort would have been made to have hung him on the courthouse lawn."

A file at the Clinton County Historical Society contains a handful of clips about Gladden, along with a photocopy of a handwritten note to him from former Indiana governor Roger Branigin dated November 23, 1965. It reads:

Dear Mr. Gladden

Thank you for the letter. Your case will be reviewed at once.

Sincerely,

Roger D. Branigin

Branigin and Brenton Devol, the judge for Gladden's case, had been partners in a Lafayette-based law firm for many years before Devol died in 1950. Had Gladden known? Was that association the reason Branigin moved so quickly on Gladden's request?

Gladden next made news on February 11, 1966. The *Frankfort Morning Times* headline read, "'Lifer' Gladden Nears Parole." After spending thirty-four years behind bars, he had a change of heart about tempering justice with mercy. Gladden walked out of prison a free man the following October.

Never able to reassemble the pieces of his shattered life, Richard Gladden quietly lived his remaining years in Tippecanoe County. He died on December 30, 2007, at age ninety-seven. He was interred in Lafayette's Rest Haven Memorial Park, but at his request, a tombstone in Soldier Cemetery of Jackson County, Kansas, bears his name. It is engraved next to that of the grave's occupant, Dolores Gladden.

It is impossible to miss the irony in his small, long-overdue act of defiance. Richard Gladden finally had the last say.

7

CHIRKA AND RASICO

INDIANA HARBOR AND TERRE HAUTE, 1913–14

> The fact that a few doses of capital punishment for murder in Indiana would not be a bad thing as evidenced by the fact that during the past week, five murderers were taken to the Michigan City prison to serve life sentences. Hardly a paper can be picked up nowadays that does not tell of some murder in Indiana. An epidemic seems to be sweeping the state, and something a little harsher than kind words is needed to stop it.
>
> *Alexandria Times-Tribune*
> February 5, 1912

The year was 1913. Almost daily, newspaper headlines throughout Indiana shouted stories of murder. Yet, to the chagrin of die-hard capital punishment advocates, convicted killers were being spared the gallows. Although the state had hanged thirteen of them since 1897, none had paid the supreme price since 1907. In the intervening years—thanks to a lively abolitionist movement led by the Women's Christian Temperance Union, educators, and clergy—the stiffest penalty given to perpetrators of even the most heinous murders was life behind bars.

Countering the steady drip of the pacifists' hard-line contention, state legislator Rowland H. Jackson of Ripley County introduced a bill in January 1913 calling for an electric chair to replace hanging at the state

John Chirka, *top*, was convicted of shooting and killing his wife, Mary, in their kitchen on May 15, 1913. And Harry Rasico, *bottom*, was convicted of shooting and killing his wife and toddler son on September 13, 1913. Both men, who had never met, were executed shortly past midnight on February 20, 1914, at the Indiana State Prison. Chirka and Rasico were the first men executed by Indiana's newly installed electric chair. *Photos courtesy Indiana State Archives.*

prison in Michigan City. Indiana should "keep up with other states in the manner of disposing of murderers," he said, asserting that the superiority of the chair over other means of capital punishment had already been demonstrated.

Not all the senators agreed. "It is murder just the same, whether we hang or electrocute murderers," said Senator Traylor of Jasper, who vowed to vote nay for the bill.

Senator Grube of Plymouth also promised to vote against the bill, not simply because he opposed the death penalty but because he resented being part of a system that promoted hanging.

Jackson again insisted that electrocution was the most humane method for delivering capital punishments, arguing that it produced instantaneous death.

Although the Jackson bill passed both houses by a huge margin, with so few hangings in the state, an electric chair hardly seemed warranted. That's likely the reason the legislators decided not to install the death chair or to appropriate the funds until Indiana's next convicted killer was sentenced to die.

John Chirka

Some three months later, on the morning of May 15, Mary Chirka sat at her kitchen table in Indiana Harbor, a small community in Lake County, enjoying breakfast with two of her tenants, Mr. Popa and Mrs. Comes, when her forty-year-old husband, John, charged in through the back door. He was in a drunken stupor, as he often was, demanding his wife give him fifteen cents and a ticket to their twelve-year-old daughter's school program the next evening.

Mary was accustomed to her husband's lack of civility and knew better than to egg him on. Without uttering a word, she rose from her seat at the table, picked the coins from her pocketbook, and followed her husband into the bedroom. There, in the privacy of their room, John whirled around, aimed a .38 Smith and Wesson revolver at his wife, and fired two shots point blank. The first hit Mary's right side; the second lodged in her left breast.

Her mind swirled in confusion. How could she have not seen this coming? John was far from easy to get along with, but life with him had at least been predictable—chaos, threats, beatings, police intervention, arrests, and, of course, the reconciliations. She had always asked him to come back, and he always had. But the bond that united them wasn't love. It was a symbiotic need. She needed him to take care of her and their four children. He needed her to cook and clean and make him feel like a man.

Shocked and bleeding profusely from her wounds, Mary backed away from her husband. As she staggered into the kitchen, a third shot rang out, striking her in the back and killing her instantly.

Chirka shifted his attention from his bloody wife lying on the floor to the shocked man and woman sitting at his table. His anger surged. "I'll kill you, too," he shouted at them.

Mr. Popa lunged at Chirka and seized him by the throat. While the two men struggled for control of the gun, Mrs. Comes escaped to the safety of the next-door neighbor's house, where she telephoned the police. They arrived quickly, and Chirka surrendered without resistance.

"The man was too drunk to explain his act," said Indiana Harbor police sergeant Billy Hughes. "It's doubtful he fully realized what he had done."

After Chirka sobered up, he shrugged off his vile act and revealed not an ounce of remorse. In fact, the *Lake County Times* of Munster reported that while Chirka was questioned by East Chicago police sergeant Mike Gorman, he bragged about killing his wife. "She had it coming," Chirka said. "I ought to have killed her years ago."

Such talk did nothing to help save his hide two weeks later, when Chirka's case was considered by the grand jury. Nor did his apathy help him four months later, when he was tried for murder in the Lake Circuit Court. Although the *Lake County Times* reported on September 16 that the trial in Judge W. C. McMahon's courtroom would last several days, the jury reached its decision in just two.

Standing before his audience—court attachés, attorneys, newspaper reporters, a handful of friends, and his brother—Chirka portrayed stoic indifference as the court clerk read the verdict. "We, the jury," the clerk said, "find the defendant guilty and fix the penalty at death."

Chirka looked over his shoulder and gazed at his brother. A long moment passed between them, and Chirka's cavalier demeanor darkened. Terminal reality seemed to set in.

On September 22, Judge McMahon set January 9, 1914, as the date for Chirka's execution. He was going to be electrocuted.

Harry Rasico

Nine days before Chirka learned his fate, thirty-five-year-old Harry Rasico journeyed to Terre Haute and murdered his wife and son. Waiving his right to an attorney, Rasico pleaded guilty the next day, and on September 20, the state prescribed its punishment. Rasico was the first convicted killer in Indiana sentenced to death by electrocution.

Harry Rasico and Bertha Benton met and married in 1906. They made their home in Vincennes, and at the time of the tragedy, they were the parents of five children ranging in age from six to sixteen months. Although Bertha was a few months into yet another pregnancy, the Rasicos hadn't been happy for a long time. A beautiful, vibrant woman of thirty-two, Bertha found life with Harry, a career chicken picker, a difficult proposition. She often needed a break from her life with him and traveled to Terre Haute to spend time with her family.

A few days before her death, Bertha and her youngest child, eighteen-month-old Walter, had journeyed the sixty miles from Vincennes to Terre Haute to visit her brother, Luther Benton. Bertha had promised to return to Vincennes on Friday, but after she failed to show up, Harry set out for Terre Haute, telling his oldest son, Paul, "The next time you see your mother and father, they will be in wooden boxes."

Understanding his father's promise, Paul immediately wired a telegram to his mother, warning of his father's threat and impending arrival. Bertha ignored the warning. She was used to Harry's temper and no longer feared him.

Rasico reached Luther Benton's Lafayette Avenue home in Terre Haute early Saturday evening and expected Bertha to go downtown with him for a few drinks. She told him no. Luther had offered to babysit Walter so that Bertha, her sister-in-law, and a girlfriend could enjoy a girls' night out. She would talk with her husband later, she said, and walked out the door.

Rasico was furious. His wife had demeaned him in front of her family, and there would be hell to pay. He would make sure of it.

He stormed off for town and ducked into the first saloon he saw. There was nothing like a good, stiff drink for strengthening a man's self-esteem. Unfortunately, a regular saloon patron, who didn't like Rasico's looks, picked a fight.

Rasico was no match for his aggressor, and he took a number of wallops before he was thrown to the floor like a rag doll and relieved of his money. Humiliated and hopping mad, Rasico stumbled out of the tavern and into a pawnshop, where he traded his coat for a revolver and a few bullets. With his new acquisition tucked in his pocket, he made his way back to Luther's house, where he hunkered down with his toddler son, Walter, and waited for Bertha.

She finally returned around ten o'clock, and Rasico followed her into the bedroom, demanding to know where she had been.

"We went shopping at the five and dime," she answered, fawning over little Walter asleep on the bed. "I bought some presents for the children, and then we went to a moving picture to—" Her gaze was drawn to the silver object at the foot of the bed, and she couldn't finish her sentence. She gasped. It was a gun.

Rasico made a dive for the weapon, and Bertha ran screaming toward the front door. Rasico took aim at his target and fired. The bullet struck Bertha's right thigh. She bolted outside and fell to her knees. Rasico sauntered over to her and pointed his gun at her head. Shaking and sobbing uncontrollably, she rolled her tear-filled eyes upward and took in her husband's sneering bravado. She was powerless. She had only one chance of saving herself and the life of her unborn child. She raised her arms heavenward and begged for her life.

"Please, Harry, don't kill me," she whispered. "Think of the children."

Rasico smirked, as if savoring the terror he had wrought. Satisfied, he squeezed the trigger, discharging a bullet into Bertha's brain. Her dead body crumpled to the sidewalk.

Terre Haute police officer Larry O'Donnell was patrolling the neighborhood when he heard the first shot, and he ran in the direction of the commotion. After O'Donnell heard the second shot, he spotted a woman sprawled in a front yard. He rushed inside the house as the third shot rang out and found Rasico in the bedroom, peering down at the tiny boy with blood gushing from the hole in his chest. Before O'Donnell could intervene, Rasico pressed the tip of the gun's barrel into his temple and pulled the trigger. To his chagrin, the cartridge was a dud and did not fire.

O'Donnell arrested Rasico without incident and summoned medical help for the baby. Little Walter passed away en route to the hospital.

At the jail, Rasico spoke freely about what he had done but showed no sign of remorse. "My only regret is that I did not succeed in killing myself," he said. "I tried, but the cartridges I saved for myself wouldn't go off. I won't pay a nickel for a lawyer. I'll plead guilty and go to the electric chair."

Justice moved swiftly. The grand jury convened the following Tuesday, September 16. Within twenty minutes, it returned two indictments charging Rasico with first-degree murder. He was arraigned within ten minutes, and he pleaded guilty to both charges, telling Vigo Circuit Court judge Charles M. Fortune that killing his wife was the sole purpose of his journey from Vincennes to Terre Haute that Friday night.

"I warned her," he said. "I told her not to come here, but she wouldn't listen. She said she'd be back Thursday, and when she wasn't, I came here. I had been planning to kill her for months, and I'm glad it's done."

Although the judge hoped to pass sentencing within a few days, he appointed two medical doctors, T. C. Stunkard and M. A. Boon, to evaluate Rasico's mental condition as a preemptive measure to a possible insanity defense. In the meantime, because Rasico vowed to commit suicide if the opportunity should arise, he required round-the-clock monitoring.

The doctors declared Rasico sane within two days, thus removing the only barrier to his destiny. Rasico learned his fate on Saturday, September 20, when he returned to Judge Fortune's courtroom and stood before him.

The judge instructed the state to immediately transport the prisoner to the Indiana State Prison. "And there," the judge said, looking directly into Rasico's eyes, "before sunrise January 16, 1914, the warden will apply an electric current of sufficient intensity to produce death to your body, and that current will continue until you are dead."

Rasico didn't even flinch. He was escorted back to his jail cell, where he resumed his game of solitaire.

Governor Ralston's Dilemma

With two Hoosier wife killers sentenced to die by electrocution on his watch, Governor Samuel Ralston faced a serious problem: How would the state pay for the chair's purchase, installation, and maintenance? The previous legislature had passed the bill that abolished hanging and substituted it with electrocution, but it had neglected to appropriate the estimated $3,000 necessary to implement it.

Ralston, who personally opposed the death penalty, had hoped to serve his term without the stain of an execution. Instead, he found himself with not one but two executions to deal with as his second year in office was just beginning. Furthermore, the executions had already created a dilemma for him. According to the attorney general, payment for the chair could be drawn from the governor's contingency fund, and doing so would signify his support of capital punishment. Conversely, should he refuse to draw from his contingency fund, the public might conflate it as a refusal to uphold the law.

The decision marked a significant juncture in Ralston's young administration. Two weeks after Chirka's and Rasico's executions were ordered, Ralston announced his decision. Payments for purchasing and installing a state-of-the-art electric chair at the Indiana State Prison in Michigan City would come from the governor's contingency fund.

While prison officials set to work constructing an electrocution chamber, capital punishment abolitionists protested, and petitions calling for commutations for Chirka and Rasico were circulated.

Behind one of the petitions was East Chicago attorney John Meade, who had represented Chirka during his murder trial. He was certain Chirka was insane and said neither he nor the prosecuting attorney expected the case to result in a death penalty.

It was Meade's contention that, despite Chirka's reputation for disorderly conduct, he was a hard worker who took good care of his family, sometimes working twenty-four hours at a stretch. The Chirkas had buried three children, Meade pointed out and emphasized that Mrs. Chirka had driven her husband from their home, forcing him to sleep in a shed for months. Consequently, according to Meade, in the weeks leading up to the shooting, Chirka had become a nervous and physical wreck.

"There was no denial he killed his wife," Meade argued, "but in all justice, the sentence should have been life in the asylum for the criminally insane."

Among the groups appealing to the governor's humanitarian side was an assembly of clergymen who represented various churches in cities throughout Indiana. Like Meade, they implored Ralston to reduce the condemned men's sentences to life imprisonment on the grounds of insanity.

Arguably, the most heartrending plea for Chirka's life came from his daughter, Mary, who wrote a letter to Governor Ralston begging him to spare her father for the most compelling of reasons—love. The letter, dated January 7, 1914, read:

Dear Governor,

Today is our Christmas, and today and tomorrow, my brother, Felix, who is 4, will be here. My sister, Edith, is 12 years old. I am 8. Tomorrow we go to Michigan City to say goodbye to my papa, John Chirka. Please, Mister Governor, do not let him die.

Your friend, Mary Chirka

Just one day after Mary mailed her letter to the governor, acting on the recommendation of prison officials that both executions should occur on the same day, Ralston granted Chirka and Rasico reprieves until February 20. When little Mary learned of her father's reprieve, she reportedly wept for joy and told reporters, "The governor is a good man, and I will write to thank him for saving Papa's life for this time."

Mary's elevated opinion of the governor wouldn't last long, however. On February 12, Ralston issued a statement that he would not interfere with the death sentences of Chirka and Rasico. He assured the public that the executions would be carried out as planned on February 20.

Five days later, Mary and her brother, Felix, dropped in to visit with Governor Ralston at his Indianapolis office. When the children entered, Mary took hold of Ralston's hand and kissed it. "Won't you please save my papa?" she said.

Embarrassed, the governor retracted his hand and crisply told her, "I can do nothing more, and I shall not interfere further in your father's case. Regardless of my personal sympathies, I must perform my duty."

And with that, the children were ushered out of the office.

Chirka and Rasico's End

When February 20 arrived, the official word from the warden, Edward J. Fogarty, read, "Both men met death bravely. They walked to the death chair without a tremor. Religion sustained them in their last hours."

Witnesses to the executions other than prison officials were not allowed, which didn't set particularly well with members of the press. Editorials about the state-administered deaths complained that the executions, as well as the preparations, had been conducted so quietly that were it not for the gaggle of reporters holed up in the makeshift pressroom at the prison that night, no one would have even suspected something unusual was afoot.

According to newspaper accounts, on the afternoon of February 19, Chirka's three children spent fifteen tear-filled minutes with their father.

The scene could have squeezed anguish from a stone, one area newspaper reported. As for Rasico, his four children did not journey to Michigan City to say goodbye. They had called on him once in September at the Terre Haute jail, but he turned away and refused to talk.

At the stroke of midnight on February 20, Rasico, accompanied by a prison guard and a pastor, walked out of his cell and headed down the cold, cheerless corridor toward his death. Two physicians, two guards, the warden, and two unidentified, unseen "electrocutioners" were waiting to see him off.

The papers reported that Rasico had projected a calm demeanor as he was strapped into the chair and an electrical conductor was attached to his head and another to his leg. At 12:07 a.m., Warden Fogarty signaled the executioners to drop the switch, delivering twenty-three hundred volts of electricity through Rasico's body. The physicians pronounced him dead at 12:15, and his body was removed.

Ten minutes later, at exactly 12:25 a.m., the ordeal was repeated as Chirka took his first step of a short trip that would end with his last breath. According to the newspapers, Chirka was strapped into the chair at 12:30. When the electrical currents coursed through his body five minutes later, he stiffened and strained against the straps. When he stopped moving, the executioners pulled the switch again. That time, his body remained still. Chirka's official time of death was 12:58 a.m.

In the hours and days following the executions, Governor Ralston made it clear that, while he personally did not favor the death penalty, he couldn't fulfill his office properly if he stood in the way of Indiana law. Justice had prevailed, he said, despite the petitions delivered to him bearing the signatures of seventeen thousand Indiana citizens calling for the state to spare the lives of the two condemned men.

Immediately following the February 20, 1914, executions, the *Lake County Times* ran an impassioned, anti-death penalty letter to the editor on its front page. In part, the letter read:

> *In cases of no other forms of crime do we [impose death], and surely a rational people, with a well-organized government, ought not to act thus in the highest and most sacred realm of all—human life. . . . We are sorry for our great state of Indiana. Heaven hasten the day when the deliberate taking of any human life, in a civilized state shall be no more.*
>
> A Reader, Crown Point, Indiana

In the hundred-plus years since Chirka and Rasico tested the functionality of the state's first electric chair, sixty Hoosier killers were put to death, either in the same chair or new-and-improved versions of it. The last such death occurred in 1994. Since then, seventeen executions in Indiana have been administered by lethal injection, the last occurring in 2009.

The debate regarding the humanity of state-administered deaths and whether they serve as a deterrent to murder continues today.

Ralston's Rationale

On February 12, 1914, Governor Ralston sent a letter to Indiana State Prison warden Edward J. Fogarty. In it, the governor explained in detail why he felt it was his duty to let the courts' sentencing stand, despite the fact that the governor profoundly abhorred state-sanctioned murders.

The February 13 edition of the *Indianapolis Star* ran a front-page story about the governor's lengthy communication, along with a sidebar containing an abbreviated version of its highlights. That sidebar follows:

Points Made by Governor Ralston in Refusing Clemency to Chirka and Rasico

Whether or not the death penalty should be inflicted in these cases was for the courts and not for me to determine.

In deciding these cases of life or death, I cannot ignore the rights of society nor forget the two wives slain by the hands of the men who have taken a pledge before heaven to love, cherish and defend them.

I propose to do what I can to make wife killing an exceedingly dangerous thing under my administration. I cannot close my eyes to the fact that the killing of wives is becoming more and more frequent in the commonwealth whose laws I have sworn to have executed.

While I am governor of Indiana, the man who is sentenced to death for the killing of his wife will have to make an extremely strong showing to move me to the exercise of executive clemency on his behalf.

PART III
TO ERR CAN BE MURDER

8

MANHUNT FOR THE
IN-LAW OUTLAWS

ORLEANS, 1906

Scared, hungry, and nearly exhausted, John Roby and Oliver Haycock had been on the run for hours, trudging through forty-one miles of the cold, rain-soaked wilds of Orange and Crawford Counties in Southern Indiana. At first, they figured to make it to the Ohio River, where they would cross over to the safety of Kentucky. But as night gave way to daylight, each step toward freedom triggered more regret and tugged at their conscience. They had never been outlaws before, and what happened back at their house in rural Syria had not been their intent.

The evening before—Saturday, March 31, 1906—Roby, a tall and handsome twenty-four-year-old farmhand, who, as noted by the *Indianapolis Star*, "if properly attired, would be a man of attractive appearance without the characteristics of a ruffian," and Haycock, his agreeable but not overly bright twenty-year-old brother-in-law, had been seated around the kitchen table with Roby's wife, Alice, and their baby. One minute, they were enjoying a quiet supper together, and the next, they were embroiled in a shoot-out with two men they had never seen before. They supposed the strangers were part of the "mob" their neighbors had promised to send to even the score in their ongoing feud. If Roby and Haycock's assumption had borne out, what followed could have been deemed self-defense. But they had been wrong. Dead wrong.

The next day, Sunday, as the sun approached its midpoint overhead, Roby spotted a search party some distance away, and he led Haycock deeper into the woods. Slogging on, they reached the outskirts of Pilot Knob at dusk. Their stamina spent, they collapsed under a tree and snacked on walnuts while they considered their options. They hadn't asked for trouble, and they didn't want to spend the rest of their lives as fugitives. They saw only one way out. They would turn themselves in and take their chances. Satisfied with their decision, they hiked the fifteen miles north to Rego, where Roby's mother and father lived. The next morning, after a few hours' sleep and a hearty breakfast, they set out for Orleans to turn themselves in. They hadn't gone far when they saw the men rushing toward them. They had but one choice. They put up their hands.

Officers Down

Orange County sheriff Louis Maris learned the terrible news Saturday evening that his deputy, Harry Smith, had been killed in a shoot-out while serving an arrest warrant at a farmhouse six miles south of Orleans, and Constable Robert McCabe was wounded so severely that he might not live.

The story going around claimed the shooters were a couple of ne'er-do-well farm boys—John Roby and Oliver Haycock. Earlier that day, they had gotten into a tussle with their neighbors, John Elrod and Charles Phillips. According to witnesses, a verbal confrontation escalated to fisticuffs, and after Roby had bloodied Phillips's face, Haycock shot Elrod in the arm. As soon as word reached the sheriff's office, Smith and McCabe rode out to the Roby farm to have a chat with the troublemakers and bring them in.

Arriving at suppertime, Smith snuck around behind the house and entered through the back door, while McCabe opened the front door and walked in. Area newspapers reported that the officers' intrusion was met with a lethal "fusillade" of gunfire. Roby shot Smith twice—once in the back, where the bullet lodged in his spine, and once in the heart. Seeing what happened, McCabe ran outside and fled for shelter, but his escape was slowed down when Haycock shot him in the back. While Smith lay dead on the kitchen floor, McCabe managed to crawl to the safety of a nearby home, although the prognosis for his recovery was grim.

Sheriff Maris was brokenhearted over the death of his young deputy. He wasted no time rounding up a posse, reportedly two hundred men strong, to undertake what would become one of Indiana's most intense manhunts. They headed south, and at ten o'clock that night, he and a dozen men on horseback drew their guns and surrounded the Roby place. Maris dismounted and charged into the house. Except for Harry Smith's body, he found no one there. Neighbors reported that the "desperadoes" had stolen Smith's money and revolver and run off on foot. Most believed the men were headed for Kentucky, where they had family and friends.

Roby's wife, not wanting to interfere with her husband and brother's flight for freedom, had taken her child and sought shelter at a neighbor's.

The sheriff notified surrounding communities to remain watchful for the murderous fugitives and send word if they were discovered. In Paoli, an angry mob stormed the main street. If Smith's killers were captured alive, chances were good they would be hanged.

Twenty-four hours had passed since the murder, and the posse had scoured Orange and Crawford Counties. Riding hard through the wild forest of Southern Indiana, the men and horses were exhausted by nightfall. Most of the posse bunked at a farm near Pilot Knob, while a few of the men rode on to the mouth of Blue River to keep an eye on the banks of the Ohio. In the darkness, the fugitives easily could have hitched a ride on a skiff and crossed the river into Kentucky, where the chances of capturing them would be greatly diminished.

Captured and Escorted to Safety

By Monday morning, April 2, Smith's body had been transported to his father's home in Orleans for viewing. Hundreds of residents turned out to pay their respects, while on the streets throughout the city, the cold-blooded murder was the only topic of conversation.

At the same time, a number of posses were scouring the territory between Paoli and the Ohio River. Many were on foot, others were riding fast-running horses, and still more were driving wagons and buggies powered by galloping steeds. In Paoli, emotions were ready to explode over the murder of the county's beloved deputy, and Sheriff Maris wasn't certain he could control a determined lynch mob if such a threat should materialize.

Luckily for Roby and Haycock, they were captured that day by a lawman skilled at keeping them alive. On a hunch, former Orange County sheriff Edward R. Lashbrook led his posse to the home of Roby's mother near Rego and had a talk with her. He described the mood of the Paoli townspeople, particularly their eagerness for a hanging, and suggested she speak with her son and his brother-in-law about turning themselves in. Lashbrook promised to do everything he could to keep the two men safe, but if they didn't go with him, they were as good as dead.

According to the *Indianapolis News*, Roby and Haycock stepped outside the house and raised their hands high, offering no resistance as they walked toward the sheriff's posse. Within seconds, they were surrounded and searched, and Roby was relieved of the pistol hidden in his pocket.

As Lashbrook promised, he kept the men safe. Rather than escorting them ten miles north to the jail in Paoli, Lashbrook directed the men to climb into one of the carriages—Roby in front, seated between Lashbrook and one of the county officers; Haycock in the back between two guards, one of them clenching a pistol with an eight-inch barrel at the ready. From there, the carriage, along with several of the posse's horsemen and wagons, launched their forty-mile race to Jeffersonville in an effort to outpace the potential vigilantes.

According to the *Indianapolis News*, authorities in the four counties along the route—Orange, Crawford, Harrison, and Floyd—were alerted, and security was tightened. To avert potential violence by mobs, misinformation was leaked that the prisoners would be escorted to Salem and put on the Monon train for their destination. When the expected course of action failed to materialize, word began to spread that the killers actually were traversing the pike from Rego to New Albany. Curiosity seekers waited along the thirty-two mile stretch of road, straining for a glimpse of the killers as the caravan whisked by lickety-split. The convoy moved as quickly as possible to dissuade troublemakers, stopping only once, for dinner in Greenville, where a crowd turned out to taunt the prisoners. As the *Indianapolis News* reported, one of the onlookers shouted to Roby, "You don't look heavy enough to break your own neck."

If the comment ruffled Roby, he didn't show it. As the newspaper noted, he grinned affably and said, "Oh, I guess I am heavy enough for that," causing Haycock to burst into laughter.

Throughout the rugged eight-hour journey, the pair kicked back as if they were on a pleasure trip. "When [Roby and Haycock] ate their supper," the *Indianapolis News* reported, "they devoured the food with the gusto of wood choppers."

The next stop was New Albany, where Lashbrook and his prisoners boarded a train bound for the Indiana Prison South at Jeffersonville. Arriving at 10:30 p.m., Roby and Haycock were immediately locked in separate cells in solitary confinement and were not allowed to converse with each other or to anyone except prison officials.

Acted in Self-Defense

During an exclusive interview with Roby, the *Indianapolis News* reported that he, as well as Haycock, talked freely about their crime and insisted they had acted in self-defense.

Roby said he had visited John Phillips's corncrib midmorning Saturday to fetch a few ears to feed his horse but was stopped by his son, Charlie, and his buddy, John Elrod. They ordered Roby to put the corn back. When Roby refused, Phillips picked up a club and twice struck Roby's head. As Roby fought back, bloodying Phillips's face, Haycock, who was working nearby, grabbed his revolver and ran across the barnyard to help. That's when Elrod pulled his gun and fired several shots at Haycock. He missed, and Haycock fired back, one shot hitting Elrod's arm. Phillips and Elrod ran away, but not before warning Roby and Haycock that they would return with a mob.

Roby told the *Indianapolis News* reporter:

> We were sitting down at the supper table, when I heard a noise and thought the mob was coming. One man was at the south door, and a big man [Smith] came in the north door. He did not say anything, and I did not know who he was. . . . He walked into the sitting room, and Oliver followed him. And so did I. Just as I reached the door between the kitchen and the sitting room, Smith fired at me. He kept his gun drawn, and when he grabbed Oliver, I shot [Smith]. I guess I shot twice and hit him both times. I was so excited, I didn't know what I was doing.

Roby claimed he thought the intruders had been sent by Phillips and Elrod as vengeance for their earlier run-in. Insisting he shot Smith to save Haycock's life, Roby swore he didn't know the intruder was a deputy until later. Haycock admitted to firing at McCabe, but only to protect his sister and her baby, which she held in her arms. Both men contended the officers broke into the house and fired first.

"I do not know how we will get out of this," Roby said. "I never had anything like this on me before."

The next day's *Indianapolis Star* reported that both Roby and Haycock were confident that if they were to receive a fair trial, the mitigating circumstances of the shooting would vindicate them.

By the end of the week, area papers reported that the Orange County Grand Jury was expected to investigate the incident that left Deputy Harry Smith dead and Constable Robert McCabe seriously wounded. Sheriff Maris said the sentiment against Roby and Haycock remained unfavorable in Paoli, and he planned to ask Governor James Frank Hanly to send the militia when the cases were called for trial.

To Plea or Not to Plea

The Orange County Grand Jury convened on Monday, April 9, to consider the case against Roby and Haycock and was in session all week. On Friday, the jury indicted both men with charges of first-degree murder. The following Monday, April 16, during the predawn hours, Sheriff Maris and two deputies escorted the two brothers-in-law from Jefferson to Paoli for their arraignment in the Orange County Circuit Court. The sheriff knew the county's emotions over Smith's murder were still explosive; thus, he did not share the news of Roby and Haycock's arrival out of concern for their safety.

Later that morning, Roby and Haycock were brought into the courtroom to face Judge Asa Elliott for their arraignment. When the judge asked whether they had consulted with legal counsel, the men answered they had not. The judge then appointed local attorney William Throop to defend them and called for a ten-minute recess to allow Roby and Haycock to confer with Throop.

When court reconvened, Roby and Haycock entered pleas of not guilty, and the judge set their trial for May 1. The proceeding had been rather routine. Shortly after, however, while Roby and Haycock awaited their trip back to Jeffersonville for safekeeping, they had a change of heart. The reason for their reversal has been lost to time, but it prompted their return to the courtroom to stand for the second time that day before Judge Elliott.

The reprise was as unusual as it was confounding. Both men withdrew their plea of not guilty, pleaded guilty, and braced for their punishment. In the next heartbeat, Judge Elliott sentenced them to spend the balance of their lives behind bars at the Indiana State Prison in Michigan City.

The next morning after breakfast, Roby and Haycock were handcuffed together and placed on a train for the long ride north to Michigan City. Accompanying them was Sheriff Maris, who reported his dismay that the prisoners had prevented him from sleeping for three nights straight. He was looking forward to being done with them.

Epilogue

Roby and Haycock's story never deviated from their belief that the intruders, Harry Smith and Robert McCabe, had been sent by their neighbors in retaliation for the scuffle earlier that day.

Over the next twenty-two years, Roby and Haycock appeared before the parole board numerous times. The first time, March 27, 1911, the *Indianapolis News* reported that a petition submitted for their release contained nearly a thousand signatures. Their legal counsel at the hearing argued that the men had not received a fair chance to defend themselves in court and had been induced to plead guilty, even though circumstances of the case would not have supported it. The counsel maintained that the excitement following Smith's death prompted authorities to advise the men to make the plea.

Had it not been for the *Indianapolis News*'s coverage of the parole board hearing, Roby and Haycock might have been released at that time. But the publicity had brought the hearing to the attention of friends of Smith, and two weeks later, they filed their own petition in protest. Thus, the paroles were denied. If the proceedings had been conducted in secret, the *Muncie Morning Star* asserted, there would have been no opportunity for those protesting to take a stand.

Haycock ultimately convinced the board that it was Roby who fired the shot that killed Smith, and Governor Samuel Ralston signed Haycock's parole on November 15, 1915. A year and a half later, after Haycock violated his parole, it was revoked by Governor James Goodrich. Haycock was never seen again.

When Roby appeared before the state board of pardons in June 1917, Mrs. C. C. Warrington, an attorney from Fort Wayne, turned the tables

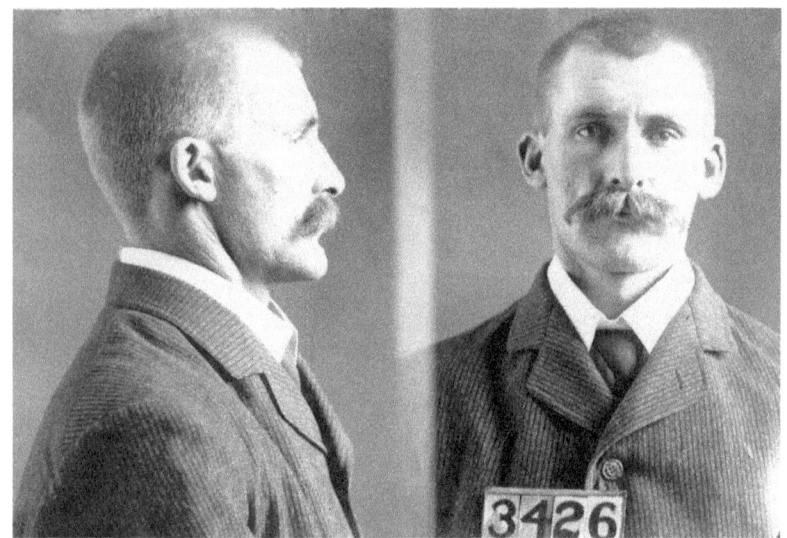

Brothers-in-law John Roby, *top*, and Oliver Haycock, *bottom*, were given life sentences at the Indiana State Prison for shooting and killing an Orange County sheriff's deputy on March 31, 1906. Both men were paroled—Haycock in 1915 and Roby in 1922. *Photos courtesy Indiana State Archives.*

by insisting that Haycock, not Roby, was indeed the shooter whose bullet took the life of Harry Smith. It was a nice try, but ultimately unsuccessful.

Roby finally won his parole on July 11, 1922, and he returned to Paoli with his wife. When the *Indianapolis Star* reported his release, the story explained that Roby had struggled for eleven years with the parole board to earn the pardon. "Papers in the case allege Roby and his brother-in-law, Oliver Haycock, were 'railroaded' to prison 19 years ago," the newspaper wrote, "when they were induced to enter pleas of guilty to the murder of Harry Smith, [deputy] sheriff of Orange County. Haycock was released several years ago."

In the final chapter of the Roby-Haycock saga, Haycock vanished, his whereabouts unknown since 1917. And Roby, at the age of forty-six, in his sixth year of freedom, on June 8, 1928, quietly passed away.

How different these young men's lives might have turned out if only Roby and Haycock hadn't fought with their hotheaded neighbors that Saturday morning, or if Smith and McCabe had politely knocked at Roby's front door instead of barging in.

9

THE BLACK SHEEP OF GOLDSMITH

GOLDSMITH, FRANKFORT, AND LEBANON, 1929

When night fell on Frankfort that wet, dreary Saturday in mid-October 1929, Clyde Jones and a couple of his buddies were huddled at the end of the bar in Rogers' Poolroom, a popular hangout on North Main Street. Jones gave a furtive glance at the three men who stepped inside, each clad in a dark suit, a light-gray overcoat, and a brown slouch hat. Jones knew one of the men, Orville Green, a Frankfort police officer. He didn't know the others, but he would learn soon enough that they were Frankfort police captain George Zook, a stocky, quick-tempered fifty-two-year-old, and Patrolman Amos Hamilton, a tall, congenial string bean of thirty-four. Green stayed by the door as the other two men approached Jones.

Jones's mild interest in the Mutt and Jeff look-alikes turned to intense unease when they walked right up to him, defiantly penetrating his personal space. His alarm bells sounded when the older man stepped forward and, without introduction, ordered him to come with them to the police station for questioning.

Jones choked back the cocktail of fear, suspicion, and panic surging in his belly. Stalling to settle his jitters, he flashed his two new pals an agreeable sneer as he stroked his black, pencil-thin mustache with his left pinky.

"All right," he said, surreptitiously inserting his right hand into his jacket pocket, where his .45 caliber automatic lay in wait. Like a spoonful of Bromo-Seltzer, the pistol never failed to settle his heartburn. He had become an expert marksman during his army years and could drive a nail with a bullet at forty paces.

The stocky man moved a half step sideways, waggled a thumb toward the front entrance, and barked at Jones, "Skedaddle."

Jones assumed a cavalier attitude, gave a nod, and started for the door. The man followed, and the tall guy fell in behind him.

Sinewy but sturdy, at five-foot-ten and 175 pounds, Jones typically would have given pause to adversaries. But a recent ankle fracture had left him with a temporary, inconvenient limp. So that night, he clenched a cane in his left hand and shuffled through the pool hall scanning patrons' faces in hopes of recognizing a sympathetic ally. He found none. Approaching the front door, Jones locked eyes with Patrolman Green, whom he had met two years before while he was a brief guest at the Frankfort jail, and extended his right hand.

"Hello, Orville," Jones said.

Green's everyday street clothes confused him. Was Green still a cop? Was he acquainted with the two men escorting him out? Were they cops, too, or were they gangsters sent by his old nemesis, Otto Davis, to take him for a ride?

"Hello, Jonesy," Green said, grasping Jones's hand and giving it a shake.

The short exchange between the two was the epitome of civility, despite Jones's apprehension about his situation. Racking his brain, he concocted a slapdash plan in less than a heartbeat and slid his right hand back into his pocket. He grasped his trusty weapon and resumed his walk through the front door. The instant his foot hit the Main Street sidewalk, he bolted for the alley, sparking a chaotic blaze of gunshots.

Eyewitnesses' stories differed, but two facts were indisputable: Officer Amos Hamilton took a bullet in the face, dropping dead on the spot, and Clyde Jones got away.

Bad Boy

The Joneses of the town of Goldsmith were regarded throughout Tipton County as one of its finest, most upstanding families—except for their

Clyde Jones of Goldsmith, Indiana, was convicted of shooting and killing Frankfort police officer Amos Hamilton on October 12, 1929. Jones served nearly sixteen years in the Indiana State Prison before he was paroled by Indiana governor Henry Schricker in 1945. *Photo courtesy the* Frankfort Times, *Frankfort Indiana.*

son, Clyde, born in 1905. Clyde's consistently irreverent behavior won him the reputation as the Jones family's bad boy. No one wanted him to succeed more than his parents, Richard and Amelia, did, but despite their help and encouragement, he could never quite get his life together. During a troubled childhood as the reputed town bully, Jones frequently got into fights. After he carved up a bunch of his opponents with a pocketknife, leaving some of them looking like mincemeat, he gave in to his father's wishes in 1921 and joined the US Army. For the next three years, he served in Panama as an infantryman. After Jones's discharge in 1924, he moved to New York City, where he was employed as an electrician for New York Edison. But in 1927, back home again in Indiana, he was arrested in Frankfort for auto banditry. He had fallen in with bad company that resulted in a low life of bootlegging, armed robbery, and selling stolen auto parts. Rumors claimed he was connected to Chicago gangland.

Jones spent six months in the state penal farm at Putnamville for the trouble in Frankfort. When he got out, he moved to Chicago, bought a garage, and started anew. He was only twenty-five and had plenty of life ahead to redeem his early transgressions. But Jonesy, as his friends called him, couldn't shake the urge to steal something every now and then.

Frankfort police officer Amos Hamilton was shot and killed by Clyde Jones during a shootout in a Frankfort alley. Hamilton is Frankfort's only police officer killed in the line of duty. *Photo courtesy Frankfort Police Department.*

The Getaway

Jones was scrambling west down the alley when a bullet ripped into his right side about four inches above his hip, tore through his kidneys, and lodged in his left side. Fire turned in his gut like a red-hot poker, but he ran for his life. At Columbia Street, he staggered across the parking lot south of the heating plant and pressed on through the driveway of the Matrix Elevator. Reaching the building, he was unable to take another step and collapsed in its shadow. His belly hurt like hell. Sprawled on the hard ground, he clutched his pistol for dear life. How many rounds remained? How many had he fired? He fished a handful of lead-nose bullets from his pants pocket and began feeding them into the magazine. After the fourth, it was full again.

Darkness beckoned, but giving in was a weakness Jones rejected. He forced himself upright onto his feet and stumbled along the dark backstreets until he reached an alley leading north to Morrison Street. From there, he doubled back and hobbled to the intersection of Morrison and Main. His machine, a Columbia touring car, was parked curbside on the northeast corner, exactly where he'd left it. He pitched his cane, climbed in behind the wheel, and pressed the starter. The car rumbled to life, and he pulled away, driving north on Main Street. At the filling station on the corner of Barner, he turned west. He made a right at Rossville Avenue and drove a couple of blocks to 1108, where he pulled into the driveway and eased the car to the rear of the house.

His strength draining, Jones crawled out of the car and started for the back door before he stumbled and fell. "Cuddy," he called out. "Cuddy." After a long moment, his friend, forty-three-year-old Charles Cudahy, came out.

"I'm in a jam," Jones groaned, showing Cudahy the wound in his side. Cudahy flinched at the sight and lifted Jones to his feet. "What happened?"

Jones moaned and shook his head. "Not sure. They said they were cops, but they could've been Davis's boys."

Cudahy helped Jones inside to the spare bedroom and stashed his .45 under the bed.

Capture and Arrest

Frankfort police were frantic. They issued an all-points bulletin to law enforcement agencies throughout the Midwest. They phoned Tipton County sheriff Jesse Devault and Tipton's chief of police, Jesse Coleman, urging them to drive to Goldsmith and watch the Jones house. They asked radio stations in Indianapolis and Chicago to broadcast news of the shooting and to tell listeners to be on the lookout for the fugitive killer. And all through the night, they questioned everyone they could find who might have been acquainted with Jones.

One of the acquaintances provided a list of addresses in and around Frankfort and Goldsmith, as well as Chicago, where Jones might be hiding. Among the locations was Cudahy's Rossville Avenue home.

Shortly past dawn on Sunday, Captain Zook summoned both the day and night forces. He announced that an anonymous tipster had told him where Jones was hiding and that any attempt to capture Jones would be met with lethal resistance. Zook, law enforcement officers, and a few dozen friends of Amos Hamilton drove to Cudahy's. The heavily armed police, wearing bulletproof vests and carrying tear gas bombs, surrounded the premises and guarded the doors and windows. Zook ordered them to shoot to kill anyone who resisted.

Frankfort police captain Charles Schultz pounded on the front door. "Police," he yelled. "Open up!"

When no one answered, he drew his gun, clutched a tear gas bomb, kicked open the door, and burst inside. Pausing in the living room, he peered down the long, dark hallway to the back of the house. That's where he spotted Cudahy, standing at the far end, saucer-eyed and rigid, looking like a Thrasher's Department Store mannequin.

Schultz shouted, "Where's Jones?"

Cudahy came to life, diving into the nearest room and slamming the door.

Fearing Cudahy might have an arsenal at his disposal, Schultz hesitated. As he weighed his options, the air crackled with danger. All at once, behind him, the telephone rang, shattering the stillness. One, two, three, four times it rang. Schultz called out again: "Cudahy!" No response. The lull made him even more uneasy. He sensed Cudahy gaining the advantage. The situation called for a preemptive measure. He tossed the tear gas bomb to the end of the hall and backed out the front door. Patrolman Marvin Disinger, stationed at the rear of the house, opened a window and hurled a second canister of tear gas inside.

Noxious fumes quickly claimed the house. Penetrating every crack and crevice, tear gas leached into the rooms where Jones and Cudahy hid. It was more than Cudahy could take, and he ran outdoors, gasping for air, his eyes burning, his hands raised above his head. Officers readied for the subject of their attack to follow, but after a reasonable amount of time with no sign of Jones, they grew impatient.

Schultz broke the window of the bedroom in which Jones was sequestered and climbed through. He found Jones curled up on the mattress, mortally wounded, bleeding, and trembling under a pile of covers. Disinger joined Schultz, and they dragged Jones out of bed. Without giving him a chance to grab a coat or even slip on his shoes, they forced their weak, barefoot prisoner through the broken glass to the open window and pushed him out. From there, they prodded him to the waiting police car and shoved him into the backseat.

"Hello, Jonesy," said the officer behind the wheel. It was Orville Green. "Fancy meeting you again."

Schultz climbed in beside his barely conscious prisoner and slammed the door. He gave a nod, and Green floored the accelerator. The car streaked down Rossville Avenue like a meteor. Jones was in bad shape, probably near death, but Green steered the speeding car over the bumpiest of Frankfort's brick-paved streets and squealed around corners, deliberately tossing Jones back and forth, up and down. Schultz and Green smirked with satisfaction.

With no regard for Jones's deteriorating condition, the officers transported Jones straight to the jail, where he was arrested by Zook and locked up. Cudahy, who arrived separately, also was arrested as an accessory after the fact for aiding and assisting.

Shock, Anger, Shame

Frankfort was in shock. Amos Hamilton had been a beloved family man, father of two young children, a churchgoer, and a war veteran to boot. The morning after his death, as news spread through the city that the shooter had been captured, thousands of people swarmed the jail, demonstrating outrage, demanding justice. Fearing the worst, police officers calmed the mob with assurances that Jones would soon die from his bullet wounds. In response, cheers erupted, and the mob dissipated triumphantly.

While Frankfort reeled, Tipton took the news more or less with a shrug. The *Tipton Daily Tribune* reported the shooting and Jones's capture, but not without reminding readers that Clyde Jones had long engaged in a life of crime. The report called him the Jones family's "black sheep."

The grand jury convened on Monday morning, October 14, while Jones, burning with fever and eating morphine to quell his unbearable pain, lay in his jail cell awaiting death. Four days later, the grand jury returned an indictment, charging Jones with first-degree murder. Because of his weakened condition, Jones would not be arraigned until November 27.

When that day arrived, a much-improved Jones entered Judge Brenton Devol's Clinton County courtroom leaning on Sheriff Fred Need and chief of police John Haffner for support. Facing the judge, Jones entered his plea: not guilty. Next, his pauper attorney, Paul Laymon, stated his intent to file for a change of venue. Two days later, the judge granted the change and moved the trial to Boone County. Before another week had passed, Jones would climb into the back seat of Clinton County prosecutor Gilbert Adams's sedan for the sixteen-mile trip along State Road 39 to the Boone County jail.

The trial was slated for January 20, 1930. The countdown to Jones's fate—freedom, life behind bars, or death in the electric chair—was on.

The Trial Begins

Jury selection took the entire day of Monday, January 20. The next day, at 9:45 a.m., Boone County circuit court judge John W. Hornaday rapped his gavel, calling order in the packed courtroom and setting Clyde Jones's murder trial in motion. Hornaday could not know the coming days would bring an explosive tinderbox of confusion; contradicting, mangled stories; unsubstantiated theories; and foggy recollections. Testimony would weave together a web that would be nearly impossible to unravel.

Jones's family—his father and mother, three brothers, and two sisters—were seated in the front row, lending support to their son and brother. The Reverend C. E. Dunlap, pastor of the Jones's Goldsmith church, took a seat at the defense table next to the defendant. According to the *Frankfort Morning Times*, Jones was faultlessly dressed and all smiles, appearing cheerful and intently focused on every detail. But other news outlets had a less affable take, reporting that Jones appeared nervous, continually fidgeting and rubbing his palms with his handkerchief.

In their opening statements, attorneys for both sides carefully laid out their cards. The stories they told about the night of October 12 couldn't have been more different. They were, in fact, diametric opposites.

The state claimed it was an open-and-shut case: Jones killed Hamilton with premeditated malice. But the defense cried foul. "If a bullet from Jones's gun killed Hamilton," argued Defense Attorney Laymon, "it was fired in self-defense. . . . The two men marching Clyde Jones out of the poolroom were strangers to him. He didn't know they were policemen. He thought they were hoodlums, acting on behalf of a man named Otto Davis, taking him for a ride."

Laymon dug deeper in his effort to plant a fertile seed of doubt, pointing out that if his client had meant to kill a police officer, he wouldn't have waited for a Saturday night, when half the town was on the streets. Jones had been in Frankfort for weeks before the shooting, Laymon said, noting that if his client had wanted to kill a police officer, he'd already had plenty of opportunities.

Laymon paused. The room grew uncomfortably still as he looked from juror to juror, momentarily locking eyes with each man. It almost seemed as if he were reading their minds. Resuming his oratory, he spoke sharply. "I don't think this jury will ever know why the officers went to the poolroom in plain clothes or why they didn't take Jones's gun away from

Frankfort police chief Troy Bacon is shown in 2018, displaying the weapon used by Clyde Jones to fire the bullet that killed Officer Amos Hamilton on October 12, 1929.

him," he said. "Throughout this trial, the defense asks only that you jurors uphold your promise to keep your minds open until all the evidence is in."

Over the next four days, the temperature outside was below zero, but the air in the courtroom sizzled. The state had called nearly two dozen witnesses to the stand. They ranged from police officers to a former Frankfort mayor to ex-convicts, a Methodist minister, and pedestrians who had been strolling past the poolroom as the shots rang out that fateful Saturday night. Eyewitnesses to the shooting gave testimony about who fired first, the number of shots fired, and the locations of Jones, Zook, and Green when Hamilton dropped.

Responding to the concerns posed by the defense, Police Chief John Haffner testified that on the Monday or Tuesday before the shoot-out, he had given orders to Zook to apprehend Jones without a warrant on suspicion of a felony. He said the city didn't furnish uniforms for the police and that the men frequently worked in their civilian clothes. And what Jones mistakenly believed at the time of the arrest was irrelevant, he said. In the end, what mattered most was the ballistics. The bullet that killed Hamilton appeared to match the steel-jacketed balls in Jones's gun.

Pros and Blows

On Friday, January 24, the prosecution called Mildred Davis, wife of Lafayette tavern proprietor Otto Davis, to the stand. Mrs. Davis would be the trial's only female witness. Small and pretty, the twenty-year-old woman swept through the courtroom like a breath of spring air and took the seat on the witness stand. The *Frankfort Morning Times* reported that although Mrs. Davis looked like a fresh-scrubbed high school pupil, she articulated her answers with confidence.

"Yes, I've been with Clyde Jones," she told the defense attorney on cross-examination. "We've been together lots of times."

Laymon flinched. "Together?" he said, his eyebrows converging to a V. "Together in what way?"

Mrs. Davis's face flushed. She shook her head and waved off the implication. "It wasn't like *that*," she insisted. "We never did anything wrong."

"What about your husband?" Laymon asked. "He must have believed something inappropriate was going on between you and Jones."

"Yes, he did," she said in a hushed tone. "Otto threatened to kill him."

Laymon folded his arms and considered what his witness had said. If he could convince the jury that Jones actually did fear Otto Davis, there might still be a chance for acquittal.

"Thank you, Mrs. Davis," he said. "You're excused. No more questions." Mildred Davis stepped down from the witness box. As she returned to her seat, Laymon looked to the judge and said, "Your honor, the defense calls Otto Davis."

A beat passed before Davis rose from his seat in the gallery and strutted to the witness stand. His eyes blazed with anger. Seizing the opportunity to bolster his client's claim of self-defense, Laymon fired off a series of questions at Davis: What was the motivating incident that made you turn on Jones? How did you threaten him? What was the outcome?

Davis said Jones spent a lot of time at his home and was always welcome. Everything was okay for months, he said, until Jones started to forget he was a guest. Their friendship suffered after the morning in July when Jones and Mildred went out to pick up some groceries and didn't come home until late afternoon.

"It made me so mad," Davis said, "that by the time they got home, I was in bad shape. I went upstairs and got a shotgun and told Jones to get the hell out of there."

"Did he?" Laymon asked.

"No."

As if that episode wasn't enough to test a man's patience, Davis had blown his stack a few weeks later, when he found his wife with Jones at the Clinton County Fair. Davis told the court that Mildred left him after that, and they had been separated ever since. But there was more. Davis admitted that on the night of the shooting, he was the one who tipped off Zook that Jones was at the poolroom.

For a while, the defense's case seemed to be on solid ground, but the prosecution did its best to dismantle it with a series of witnesses. First, the *Frankfort Morning Times* reporter testified that Jones had told him he carried a gun out of fear of Davis, but Jones also admitted he might have known George Zook was a police officer. Zook substantiated the possibility when he testified that Jones's assertion of not recognizing him and Hamilton as police officers was pure bunk. They had met two years before, he said, when Jones was in the Frankfort jail for auto banditry.

The final blow to the defense came when the prosecution called Basil Castle, who had been incarcerated at the state penal farm with Jones in 1927. Castle said he had overheard a group of Frankfort inmates talking about the raw deals they had gotten from the police in Frankfort. Jones had remarked, "If I ever have a chance to get even with Zook and [former Clinton County sheriff Elza] Webster, I'll do it."

Expectations had been high that Jones would take the witness stand to tell his side of the story, but ultimately he didn't. Perhaps his defense team decided not to risk presenting his testimony for the prosecution to rip to shreds. Such a decision was reasonable and typically would be compensated for with a powerful summation.

However, after the Clinton County prosecutor gave his closing argument on Monday, January 27, defense attorney Paul Laymon was expected to take his turn. Instead, he took a pass. "The court may instruct the jury to what the law is," he told the judge, setting off a cascade of gasps rippling through the courtroom.

As the *Frankfort Morning Times* reported, "The spectators were clearly disappointed."

It was a most perplexing strategy.

Verdict

The judge turned the case over to the jury shortly before noon. The courtroom was at maximum capacity, and several hundred more bystanders lined the hallways to await the verdict. The wait wore on into the night, but the crowd stayed put.

The jury reached its verdict after breakfast the next morning, nearly twenty-four hours later, on the twelfth ballot. The eleven previous votes had ended eleven to one, the one holding out for manslaughter.

After the jury filed into the courtroom, the foreman handed the sealed verdict to the court bailiff. The bailiff passed the verdict to Judge Hornaday, who opened it and gave it a read. Stone-faced, he handed it back to the bailiff to read aloud.

"We, the jury," the bailiff said, "find the defendant, Clyde Jones, guilty of murder in the first degree."

Jones reportedly showed little emotion. As the *Lafayette Journal and Courier* reported, "He received the verdict without the flutter of an eyelash," although he was clearly surprised. Customarily, the longer a jury deliberates, the better the outcome is for the defendant. Jones had hoped a compromise for manslaughter might be possible. Would his penalty be death in the electric chair or life in prison? He would have to wait four more days to find out.

Mrs. Hamilton, widow of the slain patrolman, had been in attendance at the trial almost daily but was not present when the verdict was read. She was informed of the outcome by Mrs. Orville Green. "It doesn't make any difference what they do to him," Mrs. Hamilton told the *Frankfort Morning Times*. "It would never make up for my loss."

On Saturday, February 1, Jones returned to the Boone County courtroom to learn his fate. Accompanying him were his attorneys. Not one member of his family was there. When Judge Hornaday handed down the sentence—life in prison—Jones sighed with relief. His life had been spared.

"It might have been worse," he said to his attorney.

But he told the *Frankfort Morning Times*, "I don't think I got a fair trial. Actually," he added, "I'm surprised they found me guilty."

Before leaving the courtroom, Jones thanked the jurors and members of his defense team. When Laymon bid him goodbye, Jones replied, "Oh no, not goodbye. It's just so long."

The following Monday, February 3, the Boone County sheriff drove Jones to the prison in Michigan City to begin the first day of the rest of his life.

Epilogue

On February 7, 1930, four days after Jones entered prison, Charles Cudahy was found guilty of involuntary manslaughter, but his sentence was suspended three weeks later.

Jones's father, Richard Jones, was killed on April 29 that year, when he inexplicably walked into the path of a Tipton Ice Cream Company truck on State Road 31.

Otto Davis, who would forever be known as "the man who started the trouble at Frankfort that resulted in the murder of Amos Hamilton," became a fugitive, dodging warrants that charged him with forgery and fraud.

In a shocking twist to the Jones case, on August 15, Captain George Zook went home, turned on the gas, and committed suicide. The public was told he was despondent over losing his job with the Frankfort police, but not everyone believed the story. During Jones's trial, the defense attorney introduced suspicion of Zook's complicity in Amos Hamilton's death, even suggesting it had been Zook's bullet that killed his fellow officer. Thus, some wondered whether Zook's motivation for suicide might have been guilt rather than unemployment.

Over the next fifteen years, Jones—known as Prisoner No. 13625—asked for a new trial four times. The last request, made in June 1943, received widespread press coverage because of its unique angle: Jones had been studying law and would serve as his own attorney in the Boone Circuit Court. He had prepared a seventy-five-page appeal in longhand and spoke two hours making his plea to the judge. He claimed he had been convicted on George Zook's perjured testimony. Jones swore he had not fired the bullet that killed Amos Hamilton. Rather, he said, the lethal shot had been fired by Zook, who, according to Jones, held a vendetta against Hamilton. Although the court expressed admiration for Jones's moxie in his masterful preparation and plea, the judge denied his request.

However, on March 12, 1945, Jones's fondest dream finally came true. Citing Jones's "exceptionally good adjustment," Indiana governor Ralph F. Gates granted him parole—and his freedom. Two weeks later, Jones walked out of prison and never looked back. He returned to Tipton for a year, and from there, he moved to Fresno, California, to be near his brother Fred and start fresh.

Clyde Jones's obituary in the November 2, 2000, *Tipton County Tribune* indicated he had indeed adjusted, living to age ninety-five. He had been a father, a painting contractor, a numismatist, active with senior citizen programs, and involved with the Fresno County Sportsman's Club. He even founded the Four-Wheeler Club, perhaps out of nostalgia for his days as a mechanic.

Who knows why Clyde Jones ran away that night at the Frankfort poolroom? Who knows why—or if—he fired the shot that killed Amos Hamilton? What is known is that over time, Jones changed for the better. He proved his worth, earned a second chance at life, and made the most of it. Sadly, the same breaks evaded Amos Hamilton. Who can say why life happens as it does?

PART IV
LOVED TO DEATH

10

HE WAS HER MAN, BUT HE DONE HER WRONG

FRANKFORT, 1950

Leland "Lee" Holliday occupied a corner booth in a smoke-filled Frankfort tavern while the final game of Indiana's 1950 high school basketball tournament flickered across the TV screen behind the bar in glorious black and white. Holliday, a thirty-nine-year-old mechanic, loved Hoosier basketball. However, the game that interested him most that cold Saturday, March 18, was the one heating up between him and the attractive brunette nestled beside him. He and Mabel McGilton, a visitor from Missouri, had met by chance a couple of hours before, and things were progressing quickly.

Meanwhile, Holliday's longtime girlfriend, twenty-nine-year-old telephone operator Frankie Miller, was waiting for him at his second-floor apartment at 254 South Columbia Street. She had been there since 8:00 p.m., when her shift ended at Indiana Bell. It was now almost nine. Where was Holliday? Frankie didn't know, but she had an inkling.

Her mind shifted into overdrive and conjured all sorts of scenarios. She grew antsy. Holliday didn't have a phone, so she hiked across the street to the boardinghouse, where she rented a sleeping room. The house had a phone, and she was welcome to use it. She picked up the receiver and dialed the number for the Marine Room, the bar where Holliday was

Frankie Miller, *center*, is shown in the Clinton County courthouse on her way to the courtroom, where she was tried for shooting and killing her lover, Leland Holliday, in the spring of 1950. To Frankie's right is her sister, Dickie James. To her left, behind her, is Clinton County sheriff Maynard Lewis. The man in the back is unidentified. *Photo courtesy Clinton County Historical Society, Frankfort, Indiana.*

a regular. When the waitress answered, Frankie said, "Is Lee Holliday there?"

"Yes, he is," the waitress said.

"Is he drunk?" Frankie asked.

"Doesn't seem to be. Do you want to talk to him?"

"Nuh-uh," Frankie said, "but . . ." She hesitated before asking the question that was tearing her apart. "Is he alone?"

The waitress's reply confirmed what Frankie already knew: the man she loved was a lousy cheat who wasn't worthy of a woman like her. Anger coursed through her veins and burned like sulfuric acid in her soul. She thanked the waitress, returned the telephone receiver to its cradle, and traipsed back across the street. Entering Holliday's dark apartment, she bypassed the light switch and sank into the couch. And seethed.

Shortly past ten o'clock, Frankie stood at the window watching Holliday on the street below walking toward the apartment. With him was a woman she didn't know. Frankie held her breath, hoping the obvious was anything but. But when Holliday opened his car's passenger door and the woman climbed in, Frankie's emotions exploded, propelling her down the stairs, out the front door, and into the street.

Lunging at Holliday, Frankie slapped at him and demanded, "What's the meaning of this?"

He pushed Frankie away and called her "crazy."

Incensed by Holliday's insulting response, Frankie glared at the woman in the front seat. "If I were you, I'd get out," she said through gritted teeth.

McGilton shook her head and smiled smugly. "Sure, I'll get out," she said, "when Leland tells me to."

Frankie yanked the back door open, scrambled inside, and yelled, "Get out!"

McGilton didn't budge. "You're not being very ladylike, are you?" she said in a patronizing tone that snipped Frankie's last thread of dignity in half.

Frankie had invested twelve years of her life in Holliday. They loved each other. He was going to marry her. He was her man, and she wasn't about to let this whore steal him away. "Do you have any idea how long Lee and I have dated?" she snarled.

The woman shrugged and said she didn't care.

Leland Holliday was shot and killed instantly in his apartment during a lovers' quarrel with his girlfriend, Frankie Miller, on Sunday morning, March 19, 1950. *Photo courtesy Clinton County Historical Society, Frankfort, Indiana.*

Frankie glared at Holliday. "I thought I was the only woman you cared to screw," she said with disgust. She paused. It was his cue to reassure her, to apologize, to ask for forgiveness, to throw that bitch out. But he said nothing. Another beat passed, and Frankie lashed out, "I suppose you'll screw her before the night's over." With that, she slid out of the car and hissed over her shoulder, "You'll be sorry."

She stomped back upstairs to the apartment. She was furious and wanted to ruin everything Holliday had ever owned. When she heard the car drive away, she set to work, pouring Coke and beer over Holliday's furniture and his clothes. But that wasn't nearly enough to squelch her rage. She wanted him to pay. She wanted him to pay big-time.

"I made up my mind then to kill him," Frankie would later tell the police, "regardless of whether he came home today or two weeks from today.... I got his shotgun out of the kitchen closet and loaded it myself."

She gathered all the love letters she had written to Holliday and scattered them over the kitchen floor. Pleased with the mess she had created, she stretched out on the couch and fell asleep.

At approximately 1:30 a.m., Holliday strolled through the front door, waking Frankie. Hanging up his coat, he greeted her in a cordial tone and strolled into the kitchen. He switched on the light and stopped. Turning to her, he said, "You kind of tore things up, didn't you?"

Clenching Holliday's Montgomery Ward Western sixteen-gauge shotgun, Frankie stepped to the kitchen doorway. He took a look at her and dismissively turned his back.

"Lee," Frankie said, pointing the gun at him, "I'm going to kill you."

For a brief moment, time seemed to freeze, and in what felt like slow motion to Frankie, Holliday began to pivot back toward her. Satisfied that she finally had his attention, she fired. The bullet entered through the back of his neck, ripped through his jugular, and exited through his throat. Holliday's body hit the floor.

With her plan consummated, Frankie leaned over Holliday and avowed, "I love you." But he couldn't hear her. He was dead.

Frankie flipped the spent shell out of the gun and reloaded. She planned to kill herself, but instead, she placed the gun on the couch and ran out of the apartment. She ran six blocks, all the way to the west side of the courthouse square, and entered the Main Street police station. Approaching the officer on duty, Desk Sergeant Gilbert Clidence, she calmly said, "Gib, I've just killed Lee."

Her pronouncement was stunning, considering Indiana's penalty for first-degree murder was life in prison or death in the electric chair. But perhaps Frankie already knew that an all-male jury could be had. All it would take was a little tit for tat.

Love and Other Dangerous Emotions

Frankie Miller and Leland Holliday's love story began in 1938. Frankie Harrell was just seventeen—and a virgin, she claimed—when she moved from her mother's home in Kokomo to Clinton County and started working on the Lee Baker farm, located between Jefferson and Mulberry. Holliday, then twenty-seven, showed up one day and liked what he saw. He and Frankie began to date almost immediately and as often as possible, typically at least three times a week. The relationship appeared to flourish, despite one tiny flaw: Frankie's new boyfriend was a married man. There is no way of knowing when Frankie found out about Mrs. Holliday or when Mrs. Holliday learned about Frankie. However, Mr. Holliday had to have known that gossip about his reckless infidelity would eventually reach his wife. It did, of course, and when the Hollidays divorced in 1949, Frankie was the driving force.

Sometime between 1945 and 1947, the Harrell-Holliday relationship hit an irreconcilable bump, and Frankie moved back to her hometown of Tamms, Illinois, where she had been born Deborah Harrell on August 9, 1920. She had lived in Tamms until she was fifteen, spending at least five years in an orphanage with her twin brother, Alfred. Not long after returning to Tamms, she met and married Harland Miller, and the two settled in nearby Cairo.

Within months, however, the luster on her new life began to dull, and soon the marriage was on the fast track to divorce court, emboldening Frankie to reconnect with Holliday in February 1948. Although the Millers tried to reconcile their differences, Frankie ultimately was unable to resist Holliday's magnetic pull. By April, Harlan Miller had thrown in the towel, and Frankie was back in Kokomo, living with her father. In early 1949, she moved to Frankfort to live with Holliday. For appearances' sake, she maintained a room at the boardinghouse across the street, although she and Holliday planned to marry as soon as their divorces became final.

Confession, Confinement, and Charges

Following Frankie's stunning pronouncement to the Frankfort police desk sergeant that she had killed her fiancé, four officers rushed to Holliday's apartment. What they found there made them ill.

Holliday's lifeless body was sprawled facedown on his kitchen floor. Several pints of his blood had flowed from the bullet hole in his throat and pooled all around him. Scattered about the room were dozens of blood-soaked love letters written to him in happier times by the woman who shot him dead.

Back at police headquarters, lead investigator Lieutenant Glen Nickols and Officer Harry Gladden secured a formal confession from Frankie and turned her over to Clinton County sheriff Maynard Lewis. Because the Clinton County jail was not well suited for women, Lewis transferred Frankie to the neighboring Boone County jail, which provided separate accommodations for male and female inmates.

Clinton County prosecutor Tom Robison called for a grand jury to hear witnesses' testimony about the murder and to determine the appropriate charge. When the grand jury convened the following Friday, March 24, Frankie declined to testify, taking the advice of her attorneys John Downing, Hollis Davison, and chief counsel Frank S. Pryor, who represented her when she divorced Harland Miller the previous year. Before the end of the day, the six-man jury had indicted Frankie with a charge of first-degree murder.

Frankie showed up for her arraignment on the afternoon of Tuesday, April 4, attired in a smart green suit. She appeared nothing like the reports published by many out-of-town newspapers that described her with sexually suggestive adjectives, such as "torrid blonde," "shapely," and "buxom divorcée." With Pryor at her side, she strode confidently into the crowded courtroom. Not until the clerk read the indictment did she shed a tear.

As Judge Fred Campbell asked for her plea, she replied in an almost inaudible tone, "Not guilty."

Frankie Goes to Court

The courtroom was packed for opening statements at 9:00 a.m. on Wednesday, May 24, 1950. Prosecutor Robison spoke first, revealing that the state had waived its right to seek the death penalty but would ask for life imprisonment. He vowed to prove beyond a reasonable doubt that Frankie Miller had killed her lover in cold blood with malice and premeditation.

For the defense, Hollis Davison offered a glimpse into the team's strategy to present Frankie Miller not as her lover's killer but as his victim. Concluding, Davison planted the seed of doubt. "When you hear what happened that night," he said, "you will realize that it was *not* murder because there was no premeditation. The events of the night were the result of the love she had for Holliday."

The prosecution called its first witnesses, Frankfort police sergeant Gilbert Clidence and officers Harry Gladden and Charles Woodward. Most damning to the defense, perhaps, was testimony from Woodward, who quoted Frankie as saying, "I killed him, and I'm glad of it." Similar testimony was given the next day, when Lieutenant Nickols stated that the night of the shooting, Frankie had told him, "I killed Lee. I'm glad I killed him. Had I not have did it then, I would have did it later. I have given him everything I have, and now I feel empty."

In an effort to discredit the witnesses' testimony, Pryor conducted an impassioned, lengthy cross-examination, pressing each witness for the minutest detail. He picked apart their interpretations of each word Frankie uttered, every detail of her behavior and demeanor the night of the shooting, and every encounter with her since. Leaning in close to their faces, he grilled the witnesses hotly and made them sweat.

Pryor was a natural thespian. However, his theatrical performance tended to morph into overt hyperbole that fueled onlookers' emotions. That day, Pryor's cross-examinations repeatedly incited the courtroom galley to erupt in rowdy chatter and laughter, prompting reprimands from the judge, who finally threatened to clear the courtroom if spectators couldn't contain their outbursts.

On the trial's fourth day, Thursday, May 25, Mabel McGilton, the woman Holliday met the night of his murder, took the stand and drove the courtroom's tension to its breaking point, further challenging the spectators' poise. McGilton, who was described by the *Frankfort Morning Times* as a "not unattractive brunette," spoke of meeting Leland Holliday at the Frankfort bar, his encounter with Frankie outside his apartment, Frankie's "You'll be sorry" threat, and Holliday's final three hours of life. McGilton's testimony reportedly caused Frankie to weep "convulsively" and McGilton to stop several times to regain her composure.

After the defense passed on cross-examination, the prosecutor stoked the fervor by calling to the stand William Goodwin, the Frankfort undertaker who transported Holliday's body from the bloody kitchen to the funeral home. Frankie had not stopped crying since McGilton started her testimony, and when Goodwin identified Holliday's clothing and shoes, Frankie grew nauseated. The judge called a five-minute recess to allow her an opportunity to regain her composure and to inhale fresh air at the open window.

The day's proceedings ended with the state's surprise piece of evidence—Frankie's missing purse, the one she had carried the night she left Holliday's apartment for the last time. From inside it, Robison pulled out a note Frankie had written to Holliday. It read, "Lee, darling, I love you. I need some money. Not much. 50¢." Across it, in a different handwriting, were the words, "I love you, too." The purse also contained the fishing

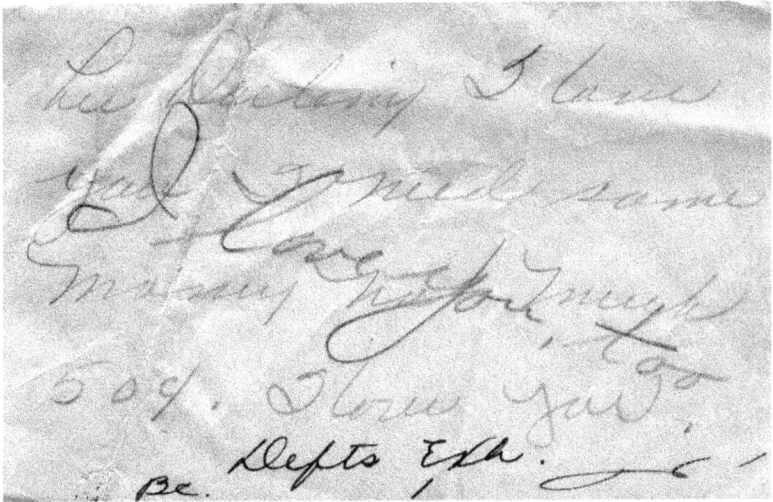

During the Frankie Miller trial, the state submitted this note found in the purse she carried the night of the shooting. The note reads: "Lee, darling, I love you. I need some money. Not much. 50¢. I love you." Across it, in a different handwriting, were the words, "I love you, too." *Photo courtesy Clinton County Clerk's Office, Frankfort, Indiana.*

license Frankie and Holliday had acquired during a trip to Michigan in July 1949. It listed them as husband and wife.

The prosecution opened day five of the trial—Friday, May 26—with Joe Robertson, the cab driver who transported Frankie and one of her girlfriends, Clarice Smith, throughout Frankfort during the early-morning hours of March 4, 1950, while they looked for Holliday. The driver testified that Frankie had said, "I'll kill that son of a bitch if it's the last thing I ever do." They never did find him.

After Robertson's testimony, the state rested its case.

The defense called its first witness, Rush Robison, sheriff of Boone County, who characterized Frankie as disconnected from reality for the first three days she was locked up in his jail. She "stared into space and seemed oblivious of her surroundings," he said. He also swore that her neck and left arm were bruised, and one of her breasts looked red. To prevent chafing, he said, she had stuffed toilet tissue around the breast.

Frankie's twin brother and her father introduced a new element of the Miller-Holliday relationship for consideration—that Holliday had abused Frankie. Frankie's friend Clarice not only disputed the cab driver's claim

Frankfort defense attorney Frank Pryor, who represented Frankie Miller, as well as Richard Gladden nearly twenty years before, was involved in numerous high-profile cases, union issues, and politics. Here, Pryor (*standing*), is shown with then Indiana state representative (and future US senator) Birch Bayh (*left*) and Indiana governor Harold Handley (*second from left*) at dinner, ca. 1958. (The man at right could not be identified.) *Photo courtesy Clinton County Historical Society, Frankfort, Indiana.*

that Frankie had threatened to kill Holliday but also confirmed the Boone County sheriff's assertion about the burns on Frankie's breast and said Holliday had burned it with a cigarette.

With that, amid a surge of spectators' chatter, the trial was adjourned for the week. When court resumed on Tuesday, May 30, the long Memorial Day weekend had done nothing to temper the sensational atmosphere in Judge Campbell's courtroom.

Day six started with a string of witnesses dishing up an earful of shocking testimony about Miller and Holliday. First was the doctor who found burns on Frankie's breast when he examined her. Then Frankie's former boss at the Woolworth lunch counter testified that during the time Frankie had worked for him in late 1948 and early 1949, Holliday constantly pestered her, making her nervous and driving her to tears. Ultimately, her boss said, Frankie quit the job to get away from Holliday. Discounting previous testimony that painted Frankie as cavalier about killing Holliday, Frankie's sister, Dickie James, told the court that Frankie was so distraught over Holliday's death that she declined to speak with visitors at the jail. In an effort to cement the feelings the defendant shared with the victim, the defense spent the balance of the day reciting excerpts from a collection of Frankie and Holliday's love letters.

Pryor ended Tuesday's proceedings with a provocative promise about the next day: Frankie's fate would go to the jury, but not before the twelve-man panel heard her story. In her own words. From her own lips.

Defense Drops Bombshell

The moment the spectators and reporters had been waiting for finally arrived on the morning of Wednesday, May 31, when a demure Frankie Miller, dressed in a neatly tailored suit, stepped onto the witness stand. The scene evoked all the noir of a Raymond Chandler novel as the defense's line of questioning painted Frankie as the victim of Holliday's emotional and physical abuse. Her well-rehearsed direct testimony lasted more than two hours. The prosecution's cross-examination lasted almost as long.

The *Frankfort Morning Times* reported that Frankie overshadowed everything that had occurred in the courtroom the day before. "Her story of the twelve years she knew Leland Holliday was impressive," the paper reported, "partly because of her demeanor of patience and partly because of an air that was refinement even in the face of questions that called for humiliating confession."

Other papers weren't as delicate in their reports of Frankie's performance. Some of them used even less sensitivity in reporting the defense team's explosive piece of evidence—the cigarette burn scars on Frankie's breast.

The *Dixon (IL) Evening Telegraph* tossed aside any pretense of journalism when it ran the story under a headline reading, "Frankie Bares Her Story to Jury." It wrote, "Frankie Miller, 29-year-old divorcée on trial in

Frankfort, Ind., for the murder of Leland Holliday, bared her breast to an all male jury behind closed doors to show where he allegedly branded her with a lighted cigarette to 'remind me that I belonged to him.'"

Frankie's bare breast likely pulled more sway with the jury than a week's worth of testimony, exactly as the defense team intended. Curiously, any mention of the breast-baring incident was absent from the *Frankfort Morning Times*. The stunt—the stuff of TV courtroom dramas—was almost certainly the invention of courtroom maestro Frank Pryor.

The prosecution did its best to rip apart the defense's sensational portrait of Frankie as the victim, suggesting that the burns on her breast were self-inflicted. "There was no evidence of them until two days after Holliday was slain," the Clinton County prosecutor insisted.

It was an allegation worthy of consideration. Frankie's jail cell had been cloaked in privacy, and certain visitors—such as her attorney, Frank Pryor, and Boone County sheriff Rush Robison—were allowed unmonitored access. In addition, she had won the sympathy of the sheriff's wife, Nellie Robison, who even testified on Frankie's behalf. It was not at all clear when the cigarette burns were inflicted or by whom.

During the closing arguments, which took most of the next day, Thursday, June 1, Pryor implored the jury to show mercy, reasoning that, under the law and the evidence presented, Frankie had not murdered Leland Holliday. The Clinton County prosecutor rebutted Pryor's argument with sarcasm and calm analysis. "Homicide. Malice. Premeditation," he said. "That's *murder* in the first degree."

The prosecutor concluded shortly before 4:00 p.m., and Judge Campbell turned the case over to the jury.

"Has the Jury Reached a Verdict?"

Everyone expected deliberation to extend into the next day, but in just over three hours, the bailiff called everyone back to the courtroom for the verdict.

Seated at the defense table, Frankie appeared nervous, frequently closing her eyes and biting her lip. After the last juror had taken his seat, Judge Campbell asked whether the jury had reached a verdict. The foreman replied, "We have, your honor," and the verdict was read: "Guilty of manslaughter."

Shaking her head vigorously, Frankie buried her face in her hands and sobbed.

Although it wasn't the outcome she had hoped for, manslaughter carried far lighter punishment than the first-degree murder verdict the prosecutor sought to obtain.

Frankie endured a long weekend in her Boone County jail cell awaiting her formal sentencing. Returning to the Clinton County courtroom Monday morning, she learned her fate: she would spend two to twenty-one years in the Indiana Women's Prison in Indianapolis. Dry-eyed, her emotions spent, she only shook her head.

The Boone County sheriff transported Frankie to Indianapolis the following day, Tuesday, June 6, 1950. The *Kokomo Tribune* reported that on the way to jail, she commented, "I don't suppose I would have shot Lee if he hadn't brought that other woman there."

Epilogue

Frank Pryor's career took an upward turn the following August, when he was appointed director of the Indiana Republican State Labor Division. Nevertheless, he continued working on Frankie's behalf, accomplishing feats that less enterprising attorneys would have deemed impossible. Consequently, Frankie quietly walked out of prison a free woman on June 5, 1952. She had served exactly twenty-four months. Pryor had made good on his promise that if she behaved, he would spring her as early as possible.

Frankie's release largely eluded the scrutiny of the press. Not a single word about her parole appeared in the *Frankfort Morning Times*. Perhaps that was due to the untimely death on June 10, 1950, of Robert Starr, the *Frankfort Morning Times* reporter who had covered the Frankie Miller story from the start. Had Starr lived, he likely would have reported on Frankie's parole. And had he continued to follow her story, perhaps she could not have so easily slipped unnoticed into her new life in Kokomo. As it turned out, Frankie assumed her given name, Deborah, and faded into obscurity.

Court records and legal files can no longer be located, and few Frankfort old-timers remain who remember anything about the case. However, a bit of digging in public records can produce enough pieces of Frankie's life to confirm that after her release from prison, she never again viewed the world from inside a jail cell. In December 1952, the *Kokomo Tribune* reported that she had applied for a marriage license. That marriage didn't work out, and in 1956, she married again. That time, it was for life. In May 1993, the *Kokomo Tribune* reported her death at age seventy-two. A photo of an unassuming, grandmotherly woman accompanied the obituary.

Ironically, the woman who briefly dominated the headlines from coast to coast decades before passed quietly. In all likelihood, outside her family and close friends, no one—not even the obituary writer—knew the deceased was the notorious Frankie Miller, the woman scorned who "killed her man 'cause he done her wrong."

Frank Pryor Inserted High Drama into Every Case He Tried

Had Frankfort's legendary defense attorney Frank Pryor not chosen law as his profession, he might have given P. T. Barnum a run for his status as "Greatest Showman."

Pryor's obituary in the February 16, 1981, edition of the *Frankfort Times*, referred to him as Frankfort's most flamboyant defense attorney.

"He was a legend," said Carol Grafton, Pryor's partner in the 1970s. Grafton also called his former partner "a master at captivating a jury."

According to former Clinton County prosecutor Millard Morrison, who prosecuted the 1932 Richard Gladden case, spectators would pack the courtroom just to watch Pryor's electrifying performances.

Frankfort Times managing editor Ray Moscowitz referred to Pryor as "a flamboyant guy with expensive suits and alligator shoes." "But beneath that flamboyance," Moscowitz said, "was a tremendous legal mind that no one could underestimate." Pryor also cared deeply about people, Moscowitz added, particularly the underdogs.

"He could usually invoke and play up to the jury's sympathy," said Frankfort lawyer Tom Robison, who prosecuted the Frankie Miller case.

Grafton agreed. "He could take a jury in the palm of his hand," he said. "He was the greatest thing in the courtroom you've ever seen."

11

FAIRY'S GRIM TALE OF MURDER ON LaFOUNTAIN

KOKOMO, 1908

Fairy McClain-Miller was as bold as she was fetching. Headstrong and independent, the twenty-four-year-old's fiery disposition mirrored her abundant reddish-bronze curls. The avant-garde behavior she demonstrated shocked many in her straitlaced Kokomo community, but she didn't care. Fairy was a proud, modern woman. It was 1908, and she was full of life.

Her second divorce wasn't yet final, but that didn't stop several smitten Howard County bachelors from fawning over her. Jesse Worley "Pete" Osborn was one of them. Osborn, who some called "Blubber" for obvious reasons, was, by all accounts, a bloviating bore, nine years Fairy's senior, but his father was a highly respected Greentown farmer and former Howard County commissioner. Perhaps it was the Osborn family's high standing that compelled Fairy to tolerate Worley's advances, listen to his yammering, accept his gifts, and come to his room over the livery stable. Frequently.

Being seen with Fairy Miller on his arm offered advantages to Osborn too. She afforded him prestige, boosted his confidence, and lent proof that he was a desirable man. When he fell for her, he fell hard. However, the romance was doomed from the beginning because Osborn already answered to another lover—whiskey—and its hold on him was far more potent than any woman's.

Besides an addiction to alcohol, Osborn had a vitriolic temper. Booze and unbridled anger were a toxic combination that too often manifested in physical abuse directed at Fairy. By spring, Fairy had endured enough of it, and she severed her relationship with Osborn. Losing Fairy was more than Osborn could bear, and his desperation came to a head late Tuesday night, April 7, 1908.

Fairy was spending the night at her Aunt Mattie Nay's house on LaFountain Street. Fairy, her thirteen-year-old nephew, Noel, and her aunt had been asleep in the front bedroom for a couple of hours when they were abruptly awakened by rapping on the front door. Fairy got up and answered. Greeted by an intoxicated Osborn, she turned and went back to bed without saying a word. Osborn followed her into the bedroom.

Annoyed, Mattie asked him what he wanted.

"I want to talk with Fairy," Osborn replied.

"You're drunk," Mattie said. "I should call the police."

"I may be drunk," he said, "but I didn't come here to make rough house. I swear I won't cause any trouble."

At first, Mattie, Noel, and Fairy didn't perceive the intrusion as a danger. They knew Osborn well. Following the death of Mattie's husband, Osborn had boarded at her home for a time. After he moved out, he visited often. So when he entered the bedroom uninvited, no one felt particularly threatened.

Osborn staggered to Fairy's side of the bed and coaxed, "Get up, Queen, and come talk to me."

"No. I will *not* talk to you," Fairy snapped. She pulled the bedclothes tautly under her chin and said, "I have no use for you, Worley, and after the way you treated me, I'll *never* have anything to do with you."

Osborn grunted and asked her again, this time with exaggerated sweetness, to get out of bed so they could talk. When she refused to budge, Osborn took a new tack. He hovered over her, positioning his lips a few inches above hers. "If you won't talk," he said, "how about a kiss?"

Outraged, Fairy shoved him away and scooted herself upright in the bed. "Get away!" she shouted. "Get out of this house!"

"Come on, Fairy," he begged, "and give me a kiss."

Fairy again ordered him out of the house. Her rejection was more than Osborn's bloated pride could endure. He evidently felt that the only option he had left was to show her, as he had so many times before, who's the boss. Grabbing her wrist, he demanded, "Get up and fight."

"No," she hissed, "I'll not fight, but if you don't get out of here now, I swear, first thing in the morning, I'll tell your father what you've done."

Osborn went silent. His hands formed fists that clenched and unclenched, clenched and unclenched. "Fairy," he finally said as he reached into his coat pocket and withdrew a revolver, "you vex me so."

Fairy didn't even flinch. "I'm not afraid of you or your gun," she said. "You can't scare me, but I don't want you scaring auntie and Noel. So *go away!*"

Eyeing the gun, Mattie yanked her son from the bed and hurried him out of the room and out of the house. They had reached the front porch when they heard a shot, and they began to run down the steps. As their feet hit the ground, they heard another.

Manhunt Ensues

Mattie Nay was headed for her next-door neighbor's when she saw Osborn dash from the house and run away into the darkness. Osborn's next moves perplexed local law enforcement for two weeks.

Mattie roused her neighbor and called the police. When the officers arrived, they confirmed Fairy had taken two bullets, one squarely in her forehead and the other over her left eye. The coroner, W. H. Harrison, said Fairy likely died instantly from the first shot.

A manhunt was immediately launched. Police officers searched Osborn's rented room over the Vonderahe Livery Barn, where they found more than one hundred .38-caliber cartridges, the same size that killed Fairy. Police alerted rail personnel to keep watch on all outgoing trains. They also telephoned law enforcement in surrounding cities about the killing and asked them to keep a close lookout.

Howard County sheriff Joe Lindley was relentless in Osborn's pursuit. That very night, he rode his horse through the rain to Greentown to pay a call on Osborn's parents, Oliver and Sarah. The *Kokomo Daily Tribune* reported, "The old people were deeply shocked to learn of their son's rash act, but they threw no light on his whereabouts. They had not seen him for some little time."

The sheriff left Greentown around 3:00 a.m. and rode straight through to Kokomo. The paper noted that "the roads were heavy, and the horse was

Fairy McClain-Miller of Kokomo was shot and killed in her bed during a quarrel with Jesse Worley "Pete" Osborn on April 7, 1908.

fagged." It was nearly five o'clock when Lindley arrived back at his office. After a brief break, Lindley was back out making his rounds, visiting a number of Osborn's known haunts and looking for his hiding place.

On Wednesday, even though Osborn was still at large, a grand jury indicted him, and the Howard County commissioners offered a fifty-dollar reward for his capture. Lindley believed Osborn was still in town. Osborn's acquaintances agreed that he lacked the financial resources to travel. He rarely worked and was known throughout Kokomo as a "tin horn sport." He often asked friends to float him small loans and relied on his parents for handouts.

The *Kokomo Daily Tribune* reported that police had "sweated" several of Osborn's "boon companions," who had been drinking with Osborn the night of the shooting. No one admitted to knowing Osborn's whereabouts.

By Thursday, April 9, a countywide dragnet had been put in place, and all city and county law enforcement officers were assigned to the manhunt. The next day, the Kokomo newspaper reported that, despite law enforcement's vigilance, Sheriff Lindley and Constable Oscar Welty believed Osborn had escaped.

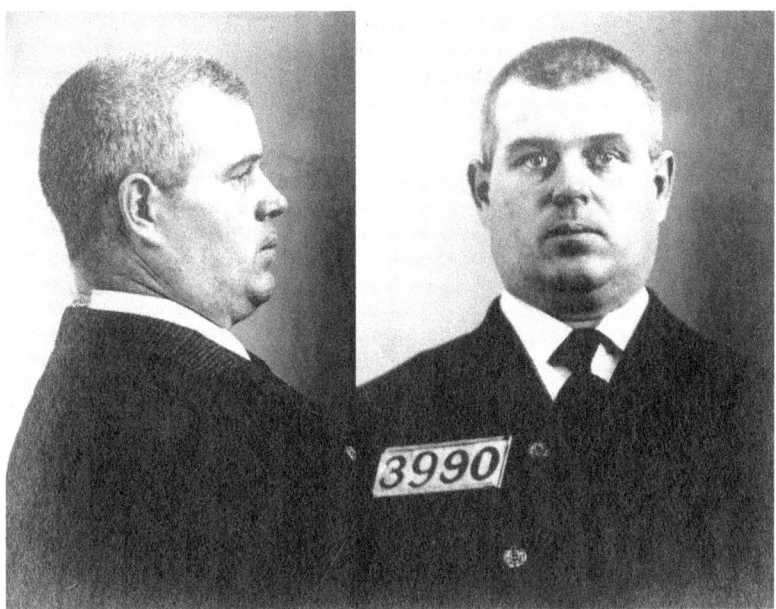

Jesse Worley "Pete" Osborn (sometimes referred to as "Blubber") shot and killed his main squeeze, Fairy McClain-Miller, in a fit of rage. *Photo courtesy Indiana State Archives.*

On Monday, April 13, the Howard County commissioners upped their reward in hopes of attracting the services of several freelance detectives. They also circulated a "Wanted for Murder" flyer throughout the entire country advertising a $500 reward.

Lindley followed every lead, working day and night, exhausting every possible scenario. After two weeks, it became evident that the fugitive had escaped Howard County and perhaps even the state. Lindley was certain, however, that Osborn eventually would make a blunder that would lead to his arrest.

The Great Escape

Osborn's house of cards crumbled on the night of Friday, April 17, after he was spotted lurking around the Logansport railroad yards. The Pennsylvania operator who recognized him notified a yardman. The yardman called in two patrolmen. They immediately nabbed Osborn and sent word to Howard County. Sheriff Lindley boarded the next train for Logansport, and by morning, he was back in Kokomo with his prisoner.

"It is all hazy," a humbled, subdued, and incarcerated Osborn told a *Kokomo Daily Tribune* reporter the next day. "I'll tell it as straight as I can."

After the shooting, Osborn fled straight east, following the railroad tracks to Greentown. The destination was his parents' farm. "It was about three o'clock when I got to the barn," Osborn said. "I crawled into the hay and hid. The hay was wet, and the wind got cold, and I thought I would freeze."

Although he hadn't had a bite to eat since Tuesday evening, he stayed put until dusk Wednesday rather than risk being seen sneaking into his mother's kitchen. Under the cover of darkness, Osborn entered the house, talked with his parents, stuffed himself on his mother's cooking, changed clothes, and formulated an escape plan. With his belly and pockets full, Osborn struck out on foot, heading northeast.

He reached Wabash late Thursday and caught a train north to Grand Rapids, where he stayed Friday night. He spent Saturday and Sunday aimlessly riding the rails from city to city. On Monday morning, the train he was riding chugged into a tiny, northern Michigan mill town called Trout Creek. It was there that he had a change of heart.

It was snowy and cold. He quickly realized that he was unqualified for a mill job, the only work available. If he wanted to eat, he would have to shoot his own game—deer, bear, or perhaps raccoon and squirrel. He would starve to death up here.

"All that took the sand out of me," he admitted to the reporter. "I decided to come right back home, and the quicker I could, the better it suited me." Osborn caught the next train south. He hoped to get to Greentown without incident to seek his parents' guidance. If they advised him to turn himself in, that's what he would do.

"I got into Logansport Thursday afternoon," he said. "I stayed at a little rooming house until last night and meant to take the Panhandle freight at eight or nine o'clock and ride to the water tank north of town, where I would get off and walk home while it was still dark. That was the first I had tried to ride a freight, but as you know, they got me."

Arrest

Osborn was a broken man, remorseful, full of shame, and scared. The *Kokomo Daily Tribune* reported that Osborn sat on a stool at the county jail—"his hair matted, his eyes heavy from loss of sleep, and his face haggard with the fatigue of the hunted man"—as he shored up the courage to confess his crime to an audience of city and county officials, including the sheriff, the coroner, and the prosecutor.

Attempting to put Osborn at ease, Sheriff Lindley said, "Pete, tell us the whole truth. It will be better for you to make a clean breast of this whole bad business."

Osborn nodded but remained silent, prompting Coroner Harrison to prod him. "Isn't it true that you had been drinking when you went to Mrs. Nay's home looking for Mrs. Miller," Harrison said, "and then you got into a quarrel with her and shot her?"

Osborn looked the coroner squarely in the eye for a long moment before answering. "That is about what happened," he said. "You may as well put it down that way."

"Do you know why you shot her?" the coroner asked.

"I loved her," Osborn said, "but when she said she would have nothing more to do with me and called me names, I became enraged. I lost control, and before I realized what I was doing, I drew my revolver and fired on her."

As he continued, Osborn spoke fondly of Fairy. He disclosed that they had been "extremely intimate" and were engaged for a while. However, he said, Fairy couldn't be faithful. He acknowledged that it angered him greatly when he saw her with other men, and he admitted that the previous year, he had lost control and hit her. After a few more physically abusive incidents, Fairy had gone to the police, resulting in his arrest on an assault and battery charge. She was set to testify against him in court but backed out at the last minute.

Osborn confessed that he'd been a drunk for years and had been on a three-day binge prior to the shooting. Even so, he assumed full responsibility—sort of—for killing the woman he loved. "Drink has killed the sweetest, innocent girl that ever drew breath," Osborn said. "I did not do it, though I did hold the revolver in my hand, but it was that damnable spirit of booze that committed the murder. Drink simply turned me into worse than a beast because I killed the one I loved above all."

When the interview concluded, Lindley led Osborn's father, who had been waiting in the jail office, through the corridors, past the cells, and up the iron stairway into the cheerless little room where Osborn waited.

The *Kokomo Daily Tribune* wrote, "With his massive chest heaving, his lips quivering, and his eyes filling with tears, Jesse Worley Osborn arose and grasped his father's hand. For a moment, he looked into the face of the brokenhearted man, who stood by him in every crisis of his life and was still standing by him."

Osborn went on to tell the reporter, "That old man is the finest gentleman who ever lived. This trouble of mine is nearly killing him, and I am afraid it will kill Mother. It doesn't make any difference what becomes of me, but it isn't right that they should suffer."

Perhaps that was the instant Osborn decided not to put his family through the disgrace and expense of a trial. What he had done was indefensible, he said, and he would take whatever punishment is decreed without complaint.

"Whiskey and an insane infatuation for a woman have brought me to this," Osborn said, "and I have got to take the consequences."

Hearing and Sentencing

Osborn appeared nervous at his Howard Circuit Court hearing for arraignment on Thursday, April 23, 1908. Accompanying him was Conrad Wolf, the attorney retained for Osborn by his parents. Once the indictment was in the court's hands, Wolf asked Judge J. F. Elliott to dismiss the first-degree charge with assurances that Osborn would forgo a trial and plead guilty to murder in the second degree on one condition—that witnesses Mattie and Noel Nay be allowed to testify.

Wolf said the Nays' testimony would show that Fairy McClain-Miller's killing was not premeditated. Second-degree murder was defined as murder without premeditation and did not carry a death penalty. If Wolf's strategy was successful, Osborn would be spared hanging and instead be subject to life in prison. The judge agreed to the condition and continued the hearing for a day to accommodate Wolf's request.

Osborn returned to court on Friday, April 24, and pleaded guilty to second-degree murder with the agreed-to stipulation. After the Nays testified, Judge Elliott dismissed the first-degree murder charge and accepted Osborn's plea. The sentence would be passed the next day.

"The penalty provided by the statute for the crime of second-degree murder is imprisonment for life," Elliott told Osborn on Saturday, April 25. "It is therefore the order of this court that you be committed to the Michigan City penitentiary for whatever period you may live."

When the judge concluded, Osborn dropped his head. His fate was sealed. He returned to his cell and submitted to one last interview by the *Kokomo Daily Tribune* reporter who had covered the case from day one.

"Have you any plans for your prison life?" asked the reporter.

"No definite plans," Osborn said, "except that I shall strive to be a model prisoner. I am going to begin my sentence with a determination to conform strictly to the prison rules."

"Do you think you will ever be set at liberty?"

"I shall do the right thing in prison," Osborn said, "and I believe the time will come when I will be set free."

"In the event your liberty should be restored," the reporter said, "would you renew your old habits?"

"I shall never taste whiskey again as long as I live," Osborn said. "If I could have my chance in life over again, I would know the things to shun, and first of all would be whiskey."

"Then you thoroughly regret all this bad business?" the reporter asked.

"Yes, I do," replied Osborn, his voice husky, his eyes moist. "I cannot tell you how deeply I regret it. I cannot excuse myself for it. I cannot blame anyone but myself."

The Long Goodbye

On Tuesday, April 28, the day before he was to be escorted to Michigan City, Osborn asked to speak with the *Tribune* reporter one more time. He wished to make a "statement of gratitude." It would be his swan song.

"First of all," Osborn began, "I want to thank Sheriff Lindley for his kindly treatment and for the good advice he gave me to make a clean breast of my crime. I thank Coroner Harrison for the consideration he showed me in his examination. . . . Prosecutor Cooper and Judge Elliott for the fairness with which I was treated. . . . And gratitude to the kinspeople and friends who brought me fruit and flowers. . . . The remembrance of such things will serve to cheer me in many a dark and lonely hour."

Osborn also composed a sermonette to warn the boys and young men of Kokomo about reaping what they sow, as if guidance from a convicted murderer carried a shred of credibility.

But perhaps it did. The next morning, Wednesday, April 29, a few hundred people gathered at the Lake Erie and Western depot, crowding the platform to see him off. As the train pulled from the station, Osborn shed tears and said to Lindley, "Well, Joe, this is my goodbye to Kokomo. I wonder whether I will ever see the old town again."

Epilogue

Osborn never saw the old town again. The State Board of Pardons considered his parole requests several times between 1913 and 1919. A December 5, 1919, *Kokomo Daily Tribune* article reported that he was a model prisoner and displayed repentance for his crime. However, the obstacle to his clemency consistently had been Fairy McClain-Miller's family. The board vigorously protested Osborn's release each time a new request came before it.

After his December 1919 pardon request was turned down, Osborn submitted no further requests. He died of acute appendicitis on July 25, 1920. He was forty-six. His family brought him home for the funeral at his brother Ed's home in Greentown and buried him in the Osborn plot.

With his death, the advice he imparted to the boys and young men of Howard County twelve years before had come full circle. Jesse Worley Osborn reaped exactly what he had sown.

PART V
DEADLY DECISIONS

12

MURDER ON ANDERSON AND MAIN

ELWOOD, 1903

Andrew Jackson "A. J." Baker and Etta Kaiser never admitted to an extramarital dalliance, but Etta's husband, Frederick, suspected as much. The notion had eaten at him since the days he worked for Baker's meat market, almost a decade before. Sober, Kaiser lacked the confidence to challenge Baker face-to-face about his suspicions. But drunk, he was a tiger. That is why at 6:00 p.m. on Thursday, September 3, 1903, at the busiest corner in downtown Elwood in front of at least a dozen witnesses, Kaiser confronted his wife's alleged lover. Unfortunately, the confrontation backfired, and twenty minutes later, Etta's marital status had deteriorated from adulteress to widow.

Shot in Plain Sight

By morning, the town was in an uproar about the scandalous incident, thanks to the *Daily Record*'s blow-by-blow details, laid out under a banner that screamed, "Elwood Disgraced by a Foul Murder," and an encapsulating, two-column headline that read, "Frederick Kaiser Shot and Killed by A. J. Baker." The newspaper noted that Kaiser's murder was the first

When A. J. Baker drew his gun and shot Frederick Kaiser on September 3, 1903, he did it at this busy Elwood intersection of Anderson and Main Streets. *Photo courtesy Elwood-Pipe Creek Historical Society, Elwood, Indiana.*

to "stain the fair name of Elwood" since the city's incorporation three decades before.

Although the *Daily Record* blasted Baker for the shooting, calling it "cold-blooded" and "unprovoked," eyewitness accounts were sketchy and varied.

Marion County resident John P. Angle told the newspaper that he had stopped Baker outside Saylor's Drug Store, at the intersection of Main and Anderson Streets, to inquire about the time of the next interurban rail service to Indianapolis. As they chatted, Kaiser, who was drunk, approached Baker, berating him and accusing him of sleeping with his wife. After a heated exchange, Kaiser leaped forward with his fists clenched and took two swings at Baker's head. The second punch connected just below Baker's right ear. Without hesitation, Baker whirled as he drew his .38 Smith and Wesson and fired point-bank into Kaiser's chest. Clutching his right breast, Kaiser staggered backward, slammed into the corner mailbox, and crumpled to the ground. His blood spreading around him, he gasped and writhed in pain.

Elwood police officer Charles C. Henze had been inside Saylor's Drug Store when the shot was fired. Rushing outside, he saw Kaiser standing less than six feet from Baker, his right arm extended, still pointing his weapon at Kaiser. Henze immediately threw himself at Baker and wrestled the firearm from his hand.

"I couldn't help it," Baker grumbled at Henze. "I had to do it. This man [Kaiser] has been hounding me for months. That man there [pointing to Angle] saw what he did to me." Baker nonetheless went quietly with Henze but smugly remarked that Kaiser "was done for."

Other bystanders gave statements, but none had witnessed the events that led to the shooting.

Smith's Ambulance service transported Kaiser the few blocks to Dr. Dick's office, where the doctor met Kaiser at the foot of the stairs, prepared to tend the wound. But when he realized the bullet had plowed through Kaiser's right breast and lodged in his back, the doctor offered no hope.

Kaiser died a few minutes later.

Baker stuck to his story that he had feared for his life when he shot Kaiser. However, the fact was, Kaiser was unarmed and drunk. He couldn't even walk a straight line. Furthermore, Baker, at sixty-two, was robust and tall compared to the forty-year-old Kaiser's diminutive stature, leading many in Elwood to believe Baker had overreacted and could have quelled the confrontation peacefully. The absence of marks on Baker further affirmed that his action had been unnecessary. As details of the killing spread through town, rumblings of a mob began to build. Nervous Elwood police tightened security in preparation for Baker's transfer to the Madison County jail in Anderson, some thirty miles away.

Background

Baker and his wife, May, had made their home in Elwood since the early 1890s. An expert butcher, Baker ran a market at 119 South Anderson Street, where he offered his customers a variety of fresh, salted, and smoked meat. He also established a successful business buying and selling livestock.

Before they settled in Elwood, the Bakers had resided in Muncie and later Marion, operating meat markets in both cities. It was in Marion, where Kaiser lived and worked for Baker, that the bad blood started to brew. During that association, Kaiser accused Baker of sleeping with his wife, and Baker complained of Kaiser tailing him. Even after both families moved to Elwood, the accusations and stalking continued and grew progressively worse. In fact, according to the *Daily Record*, there had been at least one similar, potentially tragic incident earlier that year involving a drunken, combative Kaiser and Baker's cocked revolver. The situation might have ended with a fatality had police not intervened.

At the time of Kaiser's death, his wife and children were visiting relatives out of town. Mrs. Kaiser later told the *Recorder* that when she'd last seen her husband, he had been abusive, quarrelsome, and drunk. "Fred has drank for years," she said.

"When in his cups," the *Indianapolis News* wrote in its September 4 coverage of the murder, "Kaiser frequently upbraided his wife, and often threatened to kill her."

Kaiser's supporters—either oblivious or indifferent to the reports of his abuse—banded together to raise funds for Baker's prosecution. As the *Daily Recorder* reported, they intended to ensure Baker wouldn't go "unwhipped of justice."

Baker shrugged off the surge of antipathy. He figured once the grand jury reviewed his case, he would be exonerated. But he figured wrong. When the grand jury convened a month later, under the direction of Madison County prosecutor Albert Vestal, Baker was indicted on a charge of first-degree murder.

Baker's attorneys set to work immediately, hoping to get him released on bail while he awaited trial. But the court of public opinion had already found him guilty of shooting down a "poor, defenseless fellow," and many who knew Baker worried he would jump bail if he were released. Their concern was cemented October 28, when the *Daily Record* reported a statement by Vestal. "Baker is worth in the neighborhood of $25,000," the prosecutor said, hiking Baker's bottom line in hopes of stoking fear, "and he would sacrifice his entire fortune to escape the county."

In a strange turn of events, Madison circuit court judge McClure overturned the grand jury's verdict on November 6 and unilaterally decided evidence was insufficient to hold Baker for either first- or second-degree murder. Accordingly, he reduced the first-degree charge to manslaughter and fixed bond at $10,000.

McClure's decisions sparked an unprecedented outpouring of reaction. Baker's friends sought signatures for the bond from the most influential men of the city. While Kaiser's pastor announced from the pulpit that he would not go on the bond, and the president of the Citizens Exchange Bank would not allow anyone connected with his bank to support the bond. Ultimately, the feeling against Baker was so strong that Judge McClure was censured.

The Trial

Baker, whom many considered a pompous, self-absorbed snob, initially showed little concern about the killing. It wasn't until he departed Elwood for the Madison County jail in Anderson that he finally displayed even a modicum of distress. However, even then, he refused to make any sort of statement, referring questions to his attorney, H. F. Willkie, father of the 1940 Republican presidential candidate Wendell Willkie.

Despite Baker's presumed wealth, he never was able to post bond. Thus, he had no choice but to remain in the Madison County jail to await his trial, which didn't start until Tuesday, January 19, 1904.

Vestal made his opening statement late that afternoon before a packed Madison County courtroom. He laid out the prosecution's case, dramatically claiming Baker twice robbed Kaiser—first, taking the love of his wife and, second, Kaiser's life. On the other side of the aisle, Baker's defense team argued that Kaiser had been the aggressor. Baker might have ended up dead, they claimed, had he not drawn his gun and fired.

On the second day of the trial, sensationalism reigned supreme. To the delight of spectators who crowded the courtroom, the defense attorney read a statement from Mrs. Kaiser, who had taken up residence in Pennsylvania and refused to return for the trial. According to her statement, her husband was "insanely jealous," especially when drunk. Although he usually carried a pistol, the day he was gunned down on Main Street, he was not armed. Mrs. Kaiser was adamant in her denials that she had ever engaged in "criminal relations" with Baker or that they had ever been alone—except for one time when she had run into him at an unnamed hotel and accepted his invitation to dinner. In short, her deposition denied all the charges made against her character and inadvertently exonerated Baker.

The prosecutor proceeded to shred Mrs. Kaiser's claims by calling Anderson resident W. A. Harlan to the stand. Harlan swore he had seen Baker and Mrs. Kaiser sitting together on the front porch of his neighbor's house "until dark, and then the two went into the house [and] locked the doors." Even more shocking, Harlan testified, the residents of the house were out of town. More shocking still, he'd seen Baker leaving the house the next morning—"out the back door." To further cast doubt on Mrs. Kaiser's deposition, a couple who ran a rooming house in the town of Orestes testified that "Baker and a woman resembling Mrs. Kaiser passed as many as a dozen nights at their place as husband and wife."

And just when Baker thought it couldn't get worse, Vestal called six of Kaiser's neighbors to the stand, including a twelve-year-old girl. Each testified that they had frequently seen Baker visit the Kaiser home when Mr. Kaiser was away. One witness swore she had occasionally observed Baker stay as long as two hours, which brought laughter throughout the courtroom.

It was damning testimony, indeed, causing serious damage to Mrs. Kaiser's reputation and quite possibly destroying the defense's case. Baker had an opportunity to set the record straight the next day from the witness stand, but his denials of wrongdoing were anticipated and broke no new ground.

The defense took its turn on day five of the trial and crafted a strong case that supported Baker's claim that he had acted in self-defense when he shot and killed Frederick Kaiser. A number of Elwood police officers took the stand, saying they had admonished Kaiser for his pursuit of Baker. Several Elwood citizens swore they had seen Kaiser accost Baker numerous times. And Mrs. Kaiser, in her deposition, said her husband told her he would kill Baker.

The final witness said he had recently seen Kaiser aggressively follow Baker down a stairway, growling, "Damn you! I'll fix you. You're a dirty coward."

By the time the defense finished calling its witnesses, much of the public sentiment had shifted to Baker's favor. Once it was clear why Baker feared Kaiser, the shooting didn't seem as rash as originally believed. However, almost no one condoned the overwhelming evidence that Baker and Etta Kaiser had been sleeping together.

Presentation of evidence and closing arguments on both sides were completed the evening of Wednesday, January 27, and the case was turned over to the jury. Everyone expected a verdict within twenty-four hours, but when the jury had not reached a verdict two days later, rumors of jury tampering emerged.

"The jurymen are maintaining a sphinx-like silence," the *Daily Record* reported January 29, "and have asked for the bailiff only two or three times, while no instructions have been requested from the judge."

The wait finally ended at 4:30 p.m. on Saturday, January 30. After deliberating seventy-two hours, the jury issued a statement. It wasn't what anyone had expected or hoped for.

The jury was hung.

While eleven members of the jury agreed Baker was guilty and voted for conviction, the twelfth man disagreed. The eleven like-minded jurors pleaded with the lone dissenter for hours, trying to convince him of Baker's guilt, but he would not budge. He held fast for acquittal, and the result was a mistrial.

The *Daily Record* reported that Baker received the news of the jury's indecision with "rather a glad face," relieved that the outcome wasn't worse.

The *Daily Record* suggested that the jury had been "fixed," but the prosecutor refused to act on that line of thinking. Instead, he prepared for the new trial, asserting that the state was in a position to make an even stronger case against Baker.

Awaiting a New Day in Court

Baker would remain in the Madison County jail until his new trial, thanks to another failed attempt to raise bond. Unable to run his businesses from his jail cell, Baker's financial woes mounted. Elwood businessman James Campbell filed suit against Baker in early June on an unpaid $400 note. Campbell alleged Baker owned property in Elwood and New Lancaster but had transferred it to his wife and brother to keep it from creditors. Thus, in addition to his first-degree murder charge, Baker was accused of fraud. When it rains it pours.

Two days later, the *Daily Record* ran a front-page story reporting that Baker's assets were nearly exhausted. His attorney fees thus far had amounted to $1,700, it stated, and his attorneys had filed suit to collect. Another of Baker's creditors filed suit the following day for payment of $200, and on August 18, his storage plant, valued at $1,545, went into receivership. If that weren't bad enough, the newspaper's story also noted that the strain of the ordeal had physically aged Baker by at least ten years.

On the first anniversary of the murder, the *Elwood Call-Leader* reported that, when Baker was arrested, his assets totaled "in the neighborhood" of $15,000. "Now," the newspaper wrote, "it would be hard for him to raise

$10." An unnamed source told the *Daily Record* that even if Baker were acquitted, he would leave jail a pauper.

Awaiting his new trial, Baker began to feel he would not get a fair trial in Madison County. After much finagling, his attorneys were able to get a change of venue to Hamilton County.

New Trial, New Outcome

While locked up, Baker was unable to make a living, and the bills accumulated. To keep up with them, he was forced to sell his property and other assets, leaving his wife little choice but to move back to Muncie to live with her mother.

Baker's second trial was to have gotten under way in Noblesville on June 14, 1904, but at the last minute, the proceeding was postponed to the fall term, a delay of five months. The defense told the court it needed the additional time to find the traveling man who had witnessed the shooting. The defense considered his testimony vital to their case.

The postponement was devastating to Baker. Even if he were acquitted, five more months without an income would ruin him.

When the new trial finally started on November 21, 1904, more than a hundred witnesses on both sides of the case—including Etta Kaiser, who said she could keep quiet no longer—had received subpoenas.

Two days later, the *Indianapolis News* reported that the star witness, John Angle, the traveler who had been talking with Baker at the time of the shooting, disappeared again, and Mrs. Kaiser changed her mind. She would not testify, nor would she provide a deposition.

The new trial, devoid of surprises, turned out to be a tired rehash of the first. The prosecution's case hinged on establishing an adulterous affair between the defendant and the victim's wife. But after the judge deemed testimony to that effect would be inadmissible, the state had no motive for murder and rested its case with little chance of winning.

Baker had convinced the prosecutor months earlier to drop the first-degree murder charge in exchange for a plea of guilty to the lesser charge of manslaughter. But when the defense took over and Baker testified, he refused to honor the agreement. Instead, he maintained his innocence, arguing that he was the victim of Kaiser's erratic stalking and abusive threats. Baker insisted Kaiser had struck him on the side of the head with some sort of makeshift weapon and then reached into his hip pocket. Baker swore he assumed Kaiser was going for a gun. "I didn't want to do it," Baker blustered from the witness stand, "but the man was a maniac. I was certain he meant to kill me, and I had no choice but to defend myself."

Some two dozen character witnesses followed Baker on the stand. After they all attested to his outstanding moral fiber, the case went to the jury shortly before dinner on Saturday, November 26. Twenty-two hours later, the jury sent word to the court that it had reached a verdict. The defense felt optimistic.

News of the jury's pending announcement spread throughout the city. By the time Baker was escorted into the courtroom, nearly one hundred curiosity seekers were packed in to greet him. Baker appeared calm despite the mounting tension. Judge Christian asked the jury for its verdict, and the jury foreman handed over a folded sheet of paper.

The judge unfolded the paper and studied it. After a long moment, he raised his eyes to the courtroom, inhaled a deep breath, and announced, "The jury finds the defendant not guilty and recommends acquittal." Speaking directly to the defendant, the judge said, "You are at liberty to go, Mr. Baker."

Baker didn't stir. Dazed, he just sat there. The judge had to tell him a second time, "Mr. Baker, you are free to go."

Baker had always held hope for acquittal, and once he fully comprehended that his nightmare was over, that he was again a free man, he broke down and wept. Several minutes passed before he regained his composure. As he exited the courtroom, his friends rallied around him, shaking his hand, patting his back, and calling out cheers of congratulations. While Baker's few staunch friends were overjoyed by the trial's outcome, the Elwood community was mostly outraged.

Epilogue

Baker told the *Muncie Morning Star* in a December 1, 1904, interview that the ordeal had left him bitter, and he should never have been held for the shooting. As for his plans going forward, he said he would remain in Muncie for the balance of the winter and return to Elwood in the spring and resume his business. "I am going back to face my accusers," he said, "and bring back the lie to their own doors. I will compel them by sheer force of character to hide the prejudice which they feel."

But he never did. Instead, he purchased a meat market in Indianapolis later the same month.

There was no love lost between Baker and Elwood, as the *Daily Record* stated in its January 21, 1905, edition. "A. J. Baker, the murderer of Fred Kaiser, has evidently had enough of Elwood. After being declared not guilty, although a dozen men saw him shoot down a defenseless man as a policeman would shoot a dog, he went to Indianapolis where he is conducting a grocery and meat store, and is not backward about letting Elwood people know that he is doing well."

As a parting gift to Elwood, Baker refused to pay his debts, including his attorney fees. Baker stewed in his anger another twenty-four years before he died April 21, 1929, of chronic cystitis. He was eighty-eight. He was buried in the Beech Grove Cemetery in Muncie. No stone marks his grave.

Baker's wife, May, who had stood by her man throughout the murder trial despite enduring the humiliation of her husband's alleged adulterous behavior, survived only five months without him. She died on September 11 that same year.

13

THE STRAWTOWN MURDERS

STRAWTOWN, 1907

Thirty-year-old James W. Hensley likely supposed a great many men would enjoy being pinned beneath a mound of excited women. However, at that moment, he wasn't one of them.

The McClintock women—Manilla, Cora, and Mary—were savages, walloping him from here till next Tuesday with their dainty fists and pointy-toed shoes. Provoking such spite was not what Hensley had set out to do that crisp autumn morning. He had wanted only to speak with Mary about making her his wife. If not for her overprotective father and brother butting in, Hensley would have been spooning with Mary and no one would have gotten killed. He had been careless to let himself be taken down by these lunatics and, worse, to let them wrench his gun from his hand. If they didn't use it now to fire a round into his brain, he feared he might die of humiliation.

The Intrusion

It was Thursday, October 3, 1907, and Hensley—an equine-faced, five-foot-seven, 127-pound foreman for the National Automobile Works of Indianapolis—had grown tired of waiting for eighteen-year-old Mary to defy her family and come to him. More than a year had passed since Mary's father, Walker McClintock—one of the meanest cusses Hensley ever had the misfortune to cross—had ambushed Mary and him at the train station in Indianapolis to sabotage their plans to elope. Mary's family thought that because his divorce from the current Mrs. Hensley wasn't yet final, he wouldn't be suitable husband material. The way Hensley saw it, his marital status had nothing to do with the way he felt about Mary. She was the love of his life, and he wouldn't wait another day to reclaim her.

The northbound traction car from Indianapolis arrived in Noblesville at 9:00 a.m., and Hensley stepped off. Renting a rig at Albert Fox's livery stable, he boasted that he was on his way to get his wife, referring, of course, to Mary.

Hensley pulled up in front of the McClintock farmhouse, about a mile northeast of Strawtown, shortly after noon and yelled for Mary's forty-two-year-old brother, Enoch, to come out.

A few seconds later, Enoch pushed open the screen door and strolled onto the porch. "Hensley?" he said, at first not believing his eyes. Enoch hadn't seen his old fishing buddy since the time he'd run off with his little sister. "What brings you here? You hankerin' to go fish?"

"Not this time," Hensley said. "I'm here for a bigger catch. Is Mary home?"

Enoch jammed his hands in his trouser pockets and sauntered down the front steps and into the yard. "Mary's here," he said.

"Will she see me?" Hensley said, hopeful.

"Not likely," Enoch told him. "She's feelin' poorly and took to her bed."

"Too poorly to see me?" Hensley persisted.

Enoch crossed the yard and walked up to the buggy. Hensley offered his hand, and Enoch shook it. "We figured we'd seen the last of you after that bad business last year," Enoch said. "I don't have to tell you how Pa feels about you."

"I reckon he'd like to kill me," Hensley said.

"I reckon," Enoch said as he climbed onto the seat beside Hensley. "Let's you and me go for a little ride."

The two men drove down the road a piece and were gone for a half hour. Although Hensley never revealed what they talked about, it's likely they partook of the half pint of whiskey he had brought along. When they returned, Hensley parked the rig next to the house and followed Enoch inside, despite Manilla McClintock's protests about having Hensley in her home.

Walker McClintock was a strong and fit seventy-one-year old. A man of few words, he would sooner use his fists to settle a beef than waste time conversing. When Hensley entered the house, Walker called his son aside and firmly advised him to get the scoundrel off the premises. Enoch promised that Hensley would be gone within the hour and convinced the elder McClintock to join his older daughter, Cora, in the upstairs sunroom for the interim.

Manilla begrudgingly served her son and Hensley a bite to eat. When they finished, Hensley rose from the kitchen table and unexpectedly strode into Mary's bedroom, shut the door, and locked it.

Blazing fury consumed Manilla. Turning to Enoch, she hissed, "Get your pa."

The Killings

Enoch, Walker, and Cora were descending the stairs when the first scream erupted from Mary's bedroom. The trio raced to her door. Finding it locked, they attempted to force it open, while Manilla dashed into the room next to Mary's and threw open the adjoining door.

"Watch out!" Mary screamed. "He's got a gun, and he threatened to kill me."

The rest of the family rushed in behind Manilla and froze. Hensley faced them from across the room, his .38 bulldog pointed straight at them.

Manilla gritted her teeth. "Jim," she said with forced restraint, "it's time to leave. I want you out of my house."

Hensley offered no response.

"Get out!" Manilla's anger surged. "Get out . . . *now*!"

Hensley sneered. "I'll leave, but not without Mary."

A terrified Mary caught her father's eye and mouthed, "No." Without hesitation, Walker bolted toward Hensley. He intended to choke the life out of the worthless varmint but halted abruptly when Hensley aimed his pistol at him and pulled the trigger. The hammer clicked but failed to discharge a bullet. Seizing the opportunity, Walker leaped forward and locked an arm around Hensley's throat.

As Walker choked off Hensley's air supply, Manilla and Cora shoved their unwelcome guest out of Mary's room and into the kitchen. Hensley swung his fists, unintentionally dropping his gun, but he could not muster a solid punch to dislodge the old man's grip.

Suddenly, Enoch appeared behind Hensley and slammed a stock of wood into his head. Dazed, Hensley turned. Clutching Enoch, Hensley managed to drag Enoch as well as Walker down.

Hensley eyed his pistol lying on the floor, inches from his fingertips. Sandwiched between the McClintock men, he thrust his arm forward and groped for the gun. Curling his finger around the trigger, he aimed blindly and fired. The bullet entered Walker's heart and exited the back of his head. Hensley pushed the lifeless body aside, struggled to his feet, and fired again. The second shot ripped through Enoch's neck, spewing blood like warm beer. Shocked, Enoch staggered from the house and into the barnyard, where he dropped to the ground. Within minutes, he had bled to death.

Accounts differ on what happened next.

According to the Tuesday, October 8, 1907, *Hamilton County Ledger*, after Hensley killed Walker and Enoch McClintock, he was thirsty for still more blood. "I have fixed two of them," he said, aiming the revolver at Manilla, Cora, and Mary, "and the rest of you might as well get ready." He squeezed the trigger, but to the women's relief, the weapon didn't fire. It was empty. While Hensley clumsily reloaded, the women fled to another room and bolted the door.

Determined, Hensley shot off the lock and stormed into the room, where the surviving McClintocks hunkered. But, as the *Ledger* reported, "The women fought for their lives. They struggled about the room for several minutes and, finally, the combined strength of the women triumphed, and they obtained possession of the revolver. Hensley then became stupefied, lay down and dozed off. About five o'clock, he drove away in his rig."

The Friday, October 11, edition of the *Enterprise*, a weekly newspaper that served the Noblesville area, made no mention of the women's victory over Hensley, explaining only, "After Hensley had tried to get into the room where the women had hid for protection, he lay down and seemed to sleep off the maniacal spell and then got up and started to Noblesville."

Regardless of which portrayal was closer to the truth, Hensley departed the McClintock house under his own power—bruised, scratched, covered in blood, and loopy as a polecat.

Arrest and Indictment

Noblesville police received word of the shootings from the McClintocks' neighbors shortly before 6:00 p.m. and posted guards on every road into the city from the northeast. Two deputies soon nabbed Hensley near Potter's Bridge. The *Hamilton County Ledger* reported that Hensley was in a dazed condition, requiring one of the deputies to jump into the rented rig and drive it to the city.

At the police station, Hensley talked little, although he insisted he had shot the McClintock men in self-defense. A doctor was called to dress Hensley's wounds—a gash on the left side of his head; cuts on his left wrist, back, and chest; and bruises all over his body. The *Enterprise* reported that Hensley was "the picture of a *demoniac*."

The next day, Friday, October 4, Walker and Enoch McClintock were laid to rest in Carey Cemetery near their home. Throughout the day, their farm was flooded with family, friends, and neighbors as well as strangers who wanted a firsthand look at the crime scene.

The *Indianapolis News* spoke with several of Hensley's acquaintances to help flesh out a compelling portrait of a double-murder suspect, whose "queer" behavior often morphed into "fits of anger." The newspaper's report stated, "Mrs. John Jones, at whose home he formerly boarded, said he had given evidences of unsoundness of mind. Sometimes in his efforts to be amusing, he would act like a silly man. At other times, when angry, he seemed insane."

The *Indianapolis News* also spoke with Indianapolis police captain Adolph Asch, who had arrested Hensley and Mary after their attempted elopement the previous year. Asch was another who regarded Hensley as not strong mentally. The paper quoted Ashe as saying, "The young man seemed entirely without nerve. I didn't suppose he'd ever kill anybody.... As I remember it, he had been a dancing master."

The following Thursday, a grand jury indicted Hensley on two counts of murder in the first degree, a charge punishable by either hanging or life in prison. The *Fort Wayne News* reported that talk of a mob lynching forced Noblesville authorities to transfer Hensley to the Marion County jail. Prisoners charged with murder were not eligible for bail, so he would remain there until the trial, which was set to begin on Monday, March 2, 1908.

Trial

Five months after the shootings, a paler, thinner Hensley walked into Judge Ira Christian's Hamilton County courtroom and pleaded not guilty to murdering Walker McClintock. Hensley had retained the legal services of W. A. Kittinger of Anderson, who would claim his client fired the shots in self-defense. Kittinger knew the scenario would depend on how well he could justify the killings after the victims' repeated demands that Hensley leave their property.

Hamilton County prosecutor Cassius M. Gentry would seek a conviction only for the elder McClintock's murder, which was considered the stronger of the two cases because of the younger McClintock's lethal use of a wooden stick. Whether Enoch's murder would ever be tried in a court of law depended on the outcome of the first trial.

During Gentry's nearly hour-long opening statement, he stressed that the day of the shooting, Hensley had been persona non grata at the McClintock homestead. One of the first witnesses Gentry called to the stand was the victim's sixty-eight-year-old widow, Manilla McClintock. The *Hamilton County Ledger* wrote that for a woman past sixty, Mrs. McClintock "showed remarkable strength" during the examination and the rigid cross-examination by the defense. Manilla told the jury about the events leading to the murder of her husband and son.

"My husband told him to leave," she said, "but the defendant insisted that Walker McClintock had no right to tell him to go away."

"What did you say to Mr. Hensley?" Gentry asked.

"I told him my husband most certainly *did* have the authority to order him off the premises."

Cora followed her mother on the stand and corroborated her testimony. Mary McClintock, the object of Hensley's passion, testified the next day.

Mary had met Hensley a year and a half before, while she spent the summer with relatives in Indianapolis. Although the *Indianapolis News* stated, "The girl was not one that you'd expect a man to commit murder for," Hensley fell for her almost at first sight, and when he proposed, she accepted. However, as soon as Mary learned Hensley was married, she broke the engagement.

From the witness stand, Mary's black ensemble—a long cloak, a large hat, and checkered waistcoat—contrasted with her porcelain skin. She appeared nervous but resolute as she spoke of her relationship with Hensley and the awful day he wreaked terror in the McClintock home.

"The day Hensley murdered my father and brother," Mary told the court, "he came into my room, where I was sick in bed, and said, 'Hello, love. You ready to marry me? I'll give you fifteen minutes to decide.'"

"How did you respond to that?" Gentry asked.

"I said I would not marry him under any circumstances," she answered sternly to quell her tears. "He then took a revolver from his pocket and snapped it several times in my face."

"Is that when you screamed for help?" Gentry asked.

"Yes," Mary said, "and my mother and father, Cora, and Enoch came to my assistance."

Guided by Gentry's gentle questions, Mary's portrayal of the events leading to the murder of her father and brother aligned perfectly with her mother's and sister's. The cross-examination by Kittinger, however, was designed to make Mary stumble, to get her answers tangled. But as the *Hamilton County Ledger* reported, "She adhered strictly to the story she told in her evidence in chief and made a remarkably good witness for one so young. She was cool and collected during the entire examination."

According to the *Hamilton County Ledger*, Hensley's trial drew more spectators than any other trial held in Hamilton County. "Not only is every seat taken," the paper reported, "but people crowd the aisles and flock to the corridor to get a glimpse of Hensley as he is taken to and from the jail by the sheriff."

The prosecution wrapped up its case Wednesday afternoon, March 4, leaving enough time for Kittinger to present his opening statement for the defense. Kittinger laid out his case, emphasizing how much Hensley regretted killing Walker and Enoch McClintock and insisting that Hensley had shot them only to save his life. Kittinger was adamant he would prove Hensley was not the aggressor but rather the victim. He said he would prove his theory of self-defense by establishing that it was Walker, not Enoch, who assaulted Hensley with intent to kill.

The first witness for the defense took the stand on Thursday morning. Alonzo Stubbs, a member of the grand jury that indicted Hensley, testified that Manilla told the jury that it was Walker, not Enoch, who struck Hensley with a stick of stove wood and precipitated the shooting. The next witness, court reporter Gus Baker, said his shorthand notes indeed showed that Mrs. McClintock had told the grand jury that her husband struck Hensley.

Kittinger also hoped to convince the jury that Hensley was insane and called Dr. Abner T. Wells to give testimony concerning Hensley's mental acuity. Wells examined Hensley two days after the murders and found him "flighty and irrational," which he attributed to the blow on the head.

Hensley took the stand next. He swore he'd been invited to the McClintock home the morning of the shooting but declined to say who had extended the invitation. He said he made every effort to comply with the McClintocks' order to leave the house but was unable to because Walker and Enoch wouldn't release their hold on him.

The prosecution's cross-examination of Hensley early Friday, March 6, threw no additional light on the double tragedy, so Gentry and Kittinger spent the balance of the day and part of the next morning presenting their summaries. The case went to the jury around 1:00 p.m. Saturday. Six hours later, the twelve-man panel announced that it had reached a decision, and Hensley was hustled into the courtroom to learn his fate.

Anticipating that he would spend the rest of his life in the Michigan City penitentiary, he appeared tense and nervous until the clerk turned to the courtroom and read the verdict aloud.

"We the jury," the clerk said, "find the defendant guilty of manslaughter."

Hensley's apprehension suddenly lifted. Manslaughter carried a penalty of only two to twenty-one years. Smiling, he rose from his chair and stepped up to the jury box and shook the hand of each man, thanking them one by one. He even grasped Prosecutor Gentry's hand.

Although he made no formal statement, Hensley figured he would be free in two years. However, the indictment charging him with the murder of Enoch McClintock was still hanging over his head.

Epilogue

Hensley had served two years in prison when the *Indianapolis News* reported on Wednesday, April 27, 1910, that he would be brought to Noblesville the following Saturday to be tried for the murder of Enoch McClintock. Having served the two-year minimum sentence for Walker McClintock's murder, Hensley was eligible for parole. It was highly unusual for an Indiana prison inmate to simultaneously be eligible for

James Hensley spent four years in the Indiana State Prison after he shot and killed the father and brother of the woman he loved in a skirmish in Strawtown in 1907. *Photo courtesy Indiana State Archives.*

parole and face a new conviction. As the *Indianapolis News* explained, "In the event he is acquitted at the trial next week, he may be returned to prison and held there until the [state board of pardons] recommends his release. Should he be convicted, he will serve the two terms concurrently and remain in custody during the shortest period of the longest sentence."

When Hensley appeared before Hamilton County judge Meade Vestal on Monday, May 2, 1910, he pleaded not guilty on the grounds of self-defense, alleging that Enoch McClintock had struck him over the head with a stick of wood. It was basically the same story he had told two years before, except in the earlier version, he blamed Walker as the instigator.

The trial, which lasted all week, brought Mary McClintock back to the witness stand. Her testimony mirrored the damning testimony she had given at Hensley's original trial.

On Friday, May 6, after deliberating thirty hours, the jury reported to Vestal that it was unable to reach a consensus. The judge had no choice but to discharge the jury and declare a mistrial. Hensley was returned to Michigan City to await the parole board's decision.

The following week, the case took one more peculiar turn. On Tuesday, May 10, Mary McClintock walked into the Noblesville jail and asked to visit her former lover. Her request was granted, and she and Hensley engaged in a long, private conversation. When she left, she walked directly to the office of George DuBois, a notary public, and made a statement. She had followed her mother's directive to lie on the witness stand, she swore. Thus, her testimony the previous week at Hensley's trial had been false. In the statement, she also swore that before the shooting, Hensley had begged Enoch several times not to strike him. According to the *Indianapolis News*, the state was certain Hensley could not be convicted of Enoch's murder without Mary's testimony.

Whether it had been Walker or Enoch who delivered the blow to Hensley's head was never clear. If Hensley and Mary had changed their stories to effect a lesser sentence, their ploy was successful. But one detail of the case would forever remain irrefutable: two men were dead, and Hensley had been the only man with a gun.

Even with Mary's retraction, Hensley served another two years before his appeal for parole was next heard. An article in the December 23, 1912, *Fort Wayne Daily News* under the headline, "Four Murderers Granted Pardons as Were a Bunch of Thieves and Cutthroats," reported that Hensley had been paroled by Indiana governor Thomas R. Marshall.

Unfortunately for Hensley, he was released from Michigan City only to be jailed in Tipton County, the new venue for the case against him for killing Enoch. Fortunately for Hensley, on January 8, 1913, because the state had failed to prosecute the second charge in a timely manner, Tipton circuit court judge James Purvis set him free.

After Hensley was released, he lived the life of a quiet, ordinary man. He remarried, made his home in Indianapolis, and earned his living as a carpenter. His name was never again splashed across a newspaper's front page. He died in December 1965 at the age of eighty-nine.

14

MURDER UNBECOMING A HERO

KOKOMO, 1869

Thanksgiving 1869 was supposed to have been a glorious and unforgettable day for the Daughertys of Kokomo. US Army lieutenant William W. Daugherty, twenty-nine, was home on furlough to visit his parents, Joseph and Maria, and his siblings.

However, that morning, Lieutenant Daugherty's mood darkened when his mother told him that a common laborer named Joseph Van Horn was spreading a vicious lie about one of the Daugherty daughters. The alleged lie claimed that the young woman had given birth to a "negro young one," an assertion the Daughertys believed had sullied her honor and tarnished the family's sterling reputation.

Shortly past noon, Daugherty suggested to his father that the two of them take a stroll uptown and seek out this Van Horn fellow. Their destination was the barroom at the Sherman House, a popular hotel that occupied the northeast corner of the courthouse square.

The Thanksgiving service at the Mulberry Street Methodist Episcopal Church, at the corner of West Mulberry and North Washington Streets, had ended only minutes before, and the churchgoers filled the streets of the busy downtown. As they passed the Daugherty men, the ladies nodded their hellos and the gentlemen tipped their hats.

On entering the hotel bar, the younger Daugherty immediately spotted a man he thought was Van Horn seated at a table on the opposite side of the room. He took a moment to focus before starting across the hardwood floor in the man's direction. "Is your name Van Horn?" he said as he stepped up to the table.

Van Horn gazed up at the man who had spoken to him. "It is," he said with a tentative smile.

"The woman you've been slandering is my sister," Daugherty said, "and you will retract your lie or take the consequences."

Van Horn's smile flattened, and he stood, his body rigid, his demeanor slightly more so. "Your sister?" he said. "I have not slandered your sister, or *anyone's* sister. Therefore, I will retract nothing, and you, sir, cannot make me." Van Horn glanced around the barroom. It had grown still, and all eyes were on him. "Furthermore," he continued, infusing his tone with defiance, "you need not come blustering about me that way."

The two men faced each other, separated by mere inches. The tension mounted, but neither appeared ready to back down. After a long moment, Daugherty lowered his right hand to his side. "I will see whether you will or not," he said and proceeded to unholster his revolver and cock it.

Seeing what was coming, Van Horn dove to the floor a split second before Daugherty fired. The bullet blazed past his head and tore into the plank an inch from his right leg. Van Horn scrambled to his feet and bolted for cover behind a wooden partition. Daugherty was quicker and met Van Horn on the other side.

With no time to lose, Van Horn grabbed hold of Daugherty's left shoulder and tried to wrestle the gun from his hand. But Van Horn was no match for the lieutenant's fervor, and the gun discharged, its fiery ball ripping a path through Van Horn's left breast.

As the bright-red splotch of warm blood spread across the front of Van Horn's white shirt, he threw himself at Daugherty, shoving him off balance. Van Horn seized the opportunity and attempted to escape the barroom before Daugherty could regain his footing and squeeze off another bullet.

Unfortunately for Van Horn, his maneuver failed, and he took a direct shot to his right breast. The instant it hit, he doubled over and stumbled toward the hotel office. He had managed a few wobbly steps when Daugherty's final shot pierced his back. Blood gushing from his mouth, Van Horn cried out. He stubbornly staggered onward through the dining room and into the corridor before his will to survive betrayed him. Dropping into a bloody heap, Van Horn weakly groaned, "I am killed," gasped once more, and died.

Mission Accomplished

With the slanderous denigration of his sister's honor avenged, Daugherty's aggressive demeanor suddenly morphed into the epitome of refined civility. Several members of the Mulberry Street church who had witnessed the shooting rushed to apprehend him. He offered no resistance as they escorted him to Mayor John W. Cooper's office.

"I regret most sincerely the necessity for the occurrence," Daugherty confessed, according to that evening's *Kokomo Tribune*, "but under the same circumstances, I could not but repeat the same thing tomorrow or at any future time."

He then turned himself in at the jail to await action by the grand jury, scheduled to meet the following Monday.

The Making of a Hero

William Wert Daugherty was born in 1840 in Boone County, Indiana. He graduated from North Western Christian University, predecessor to Butler University, in 1861. In the summer of that year, just three months after the start of the Civil War, he enlisted in the Twenty-Seventh Indiana Infantry. Daugherty served for a while in the Army of the Potomac under Major General George B. McClellan. He later fought in the battles of Antietam, Chancellorsville, and Gettysburg, among many others, including the campaigns leading to the siege and fall of Atlanta. In 1867, he joined the Regular Army and was sent to the western frontier, where he protected isolated forts and the expanding railroads while maintaining peace between pioneer settlers and native peoples.

By 1869, Daugherty's military service record preceded him. Many people—military and civilian—considered him a hero. However, the conduct he demonstrated that Thanksgiving Day was unbecoming a hero.

The Long Wait for Justice

After Daugherty turned himself in, news of the murder spread through Kokomo, sparking anger that incited a mob to gather outside the Daugherty house, hurling stones and bricks that shattered windows and terrified the family.

The grand jury met the Monday after the killing. The panel first mulled over the slander allegedly spread by Joseph Van Horn and his ex-wife,

Civil War hero Lieutenant William W. Daugherty found himself in trouble in Kokomo on Thanksgiving 1869, when he shot James Van Horn in the back for allegedly spreading rumors about Daugherty's sister. *Photo courtesy Michael Belis, First Battalion Twenty-Second Infantry website, www.1-22 infantry.org.*

Sarah, and declared them innocent of any wrongdoing. It then indicted Daugherty for murder. His trial was set for the following May. Ineligible for bail, Daugherty spent the ensuing months in the Howard County jail.

Public opinion, in the meantime, congealed around one of two sides: (1) Daugherty acted admirably to avenge his sister's honor, or (2) Daugherty killed an innocent man in cold blood.

The press, from all parts of Indiana and the nation, had a heyday. Many weighed in on the "barbarian lawlessness," while others called Van Horn's murder "justifiable."

The *New York Daily Tribune* was among the news organizations that forgave Van Horn for spreading the rumor because, as the paper noted, he had heard about the Daugherty woman's supposed indiscretion from his "busy, mischief-making gossip" wife. In addition to vilifying Mrs. Van Horn, the newspaper condemned Daugherty's action and wrote, "Society is established, laws are enacted, and executive power is delegated simply and expressly to prevent the ready revenge of the barbarian." The same newspaper also expressed concern that the day might come when no man's life could be considered safe. (Apparently, the *New York Daily Tribune*'s concern for women's lives was still evolving.)

At the other end of the spectrum, the November 30, 1869, *Daily Milwaukee News* quoted part of a *Cleveland Plain Dealer* editorial that chastised men who defiled a respectable woman's reputation. "There are some men in this world who seem to delight in slandering women," the piece stated, "forgetting the sex of their mother. . . . If we were disposed to be charitable toward these dealers in moral slime, we should call their propensity to slander the weaker sex monomania [i.e., an obsession]. . . . Society recognizes this meanness as one of the most detestable that man can be guilty of and is disposed to consider few punishments too severe for its perpetrator."

Thanks to the many press pontifications about the Thanksgiving Day murder, Sarah Van Horn could not separate herself from the shocking story. She was being blamed for her ex-husband's alleged verbal indiscretion while being held responsible for Daugherty's inexcusable reaction.

The newspapers' sensational headlines, scathing editorials, and sanctimonious letters to the editor about Daugherty's case were tantamount to a public trial. But Daugherty wasn't their only target. They had also dragged Sarah Van Horn through the mud, diminishing her value and soiling her respectability. Although Sarah was humiliated by the assaults, what she cared about most was protecting her fourteen-year-old daughter and preserving the Van Horn name.

In her January 21, 1870, letter to the editor of the *Kokomo Journal*, Sarah reminded the community that the grand jury had cleared her as well as her late ex-husband of committing any crime. "To my friends and neighbors who are cognizant of the fact and know something of my character," she wrote, "this publication and denial will be wholly unnecessary. But in justice to the good name of my daughter, I here pronounce the charge as made against me and my late husband as utterly untrue. . . . I honestly believe before God that Joseph Van Horn died without knowing for what and by whom he died—died like a dog shot down by a brutal master. And while God gives me life and ability to speak, I will vindicate his memory from this charge."

It was a vow she would do her utmost to keep.

Run-Up to Trial

Because of the heated public opinion and continued rumbling about a hanging, Daugherty's attorneys believed their client would not receive a fair shake in Howard County. On May 12, 1870, what would have been day one of Daugherty's murder trial, his attorneys asked the judge for a change of venue.

Well aware of the anger permeating the community, the judge moved the case to Tipton County. Daugherty was transferred at once to the Tipton jail, where his bail was again denied and his trial scheduled for late October.

Following Daugherty's transfer out of Kokomo, interest waned and newspaper ink was reallocated to the next shiny object. Daugherty's name was absent from local newspapers until shortly before the start of his trial. A tiny article in the October 14, 1870, *Kokomo Journal* left no question about its view of Daugherty's innocence or guilt. "The trial of Lt. Daugherty for the murder of Van Horn will begin the last week in this month at Tipton," it wrote. "Every effort will be put forth to save him from his richly deserved punishment."

To Daugherty's benefit, however, Laura Ream, a traveling correspondent associated with the *Cincinnati Commercial*, interviewed him in his Tipton jail cell and produced a sympathetic portrait. The *Kokomo Tribune* ran the piece on October 20, 1870, on page one. "I visited the jail," Ream wrote, "which is at the outskirts of the town. The only occupant is Lieutenant Daugherty . . . a very sprightly and intelligent gentleman, singularly possessing in manners and conversation. He has a sweet, low voice that is quite winning, and in happier hours, he must have been a charming companion. For the present, he is exceedingly depressed, looking forward to his approaching trial with considerable uneasiness. One cannot help feeling that it was never born in his heart to take a human life and even deplore the mistaken confidence of family troubles which drove him to the fatal act."

Ream's thinly veiled infatuation referred to Daugherty as "faultlessly neat with a strong Milesian face, well-turned nose, blue eyes, thick brown hair, fair forehead and handsome teeth." It didn't stop there. She went on, "It was altogether a frank, manly face and a plain index of a healthy mind and heart."

Ream's highly favorable fluff piece caused many to wonder whether it would influence the outcome of the trial.

The Trial at Last

The trial was supposed to begin October 31, but the judge's last-minute cancellation caused a slight delay. A replacement judge, John W. Robinson of Kokomo, was secured, and the trial got under way on Thursday, November 3, 1870.

Details of the trial are sketchy today. Most of the local papers and court records have long vanished, but the few news articles that remain portray a trial that was rushed, thanks to the judge, who, according to the *Kokomo Tribune*, "shut out a very large number of witnesses." It also reports that the few witnesses who did make it to the stand were physicians who validated the defense attorney's claim that Daugherty was temporarily insane when he killed Van Horn, or they were Daugherty's army friends and associates who spoke glowingly of his good character.

The state also planned to call several physicians as witnesses, who, contrary to the defense's stance, were to testify that Daugherty was perfectly sane. Unfortunately for the state, the strategy failed. The *Kokomo Tribune* explained why: "By decision of the court, no physician was allowed to testify unless he would state under oath that he was an expert—that is, that he had made the subject of insanity a special study. By this rule, nearly every physician summoned by the state was shut out."

The defense team's key witness was Dr. G. V. Woollen, a surgeon from Indianapolis, who claimed to know Daugherty better "than any other living man." Woollen had been a surgeon in the Twenty-Seventh Indiana Infantry during the winter of 1861, when he had treated Daugherty for malarial congestion. "The disease attacks different organs in different people," Woollen explained from the witness stand late in the afternoon of Monday, November 7. "In Lt. Daugherty's case, it was his brain and nervous system that were under attack. At the time I treated him, I observed in him a tendency of violence."

Woollen was the last witness, and final arguments started the next day. According to the *Waterloo Press*, the lead on the defense team, former Indiana senator Thomas A. Hendricks, gave such a powerful argument that when he finished, the courtroom cheered. The case went to the jury at noon on Thursday, November 10.

The *Kokomo Tribune* wrote, "After thirty minutes of deliberation, the jury returned the verdict of acquittal. Indeed, the verdict might have been made without them leaving the box."

The *Indianapolis News* reported that "the verdict was received with great rejoicing by the prisoner's friends."

The mood in the courtroom may have been overwhelmingly supportive of Daugherty, but at least one person in attendance was not happy about the trial's outcome. Sarah Van Horn had been present for all the court proceedings, and when she heard the jury's decision, she followed through on a promise she had made to herself months before: If the state wouldn't avenge her husband's killing, she would do it herself.

Sarah's attempt to assassinate Daugherty was reported on the front page of the November 11, 1870, edition of the *Indianapolis News*. "As Lt. Daugherty was leaving the courtroom at Tipton after his acquittal," the article stated, "Mrs. Van Horn attempted to visit summary vengeance upon him in pursuance of a threat she had made long ago in case of his acquittal. But after one shot from a revolver, which did no harm, she was disarmed by the sheriff."

Whether Tipton County sheriff Alexander McCreary arrested Sarah Van Horn after her attempt to kill Daugherty or simply gave her a stern talking to was not reported.

Statewide, the press's reaction to the acquittal ranged from sympathy for Daugherty losing a year of his life in jail, to condemnation of Van Horn for slandering a righteous woman's character, to complaining that the trial had been "the most disgraceful on record."

In the final analysis, Daugherty's blind wrath had taken the life of an innocent man—and for what purpose? To save his sister's good name? Aside from that being a ridiculous rationale, before Daugherty had killed Van Horn, few people knew of the rumor. But after Van Horn's death, everyone knew it. Furthermore, Daugherty's despicable, misplaced chivalry ensured that the very rumor he sought to quash with his bullets would still be spoken of and written about 150 years later.

Epilogue

Daugherty proceeded directly from the Tipton County courtroom to Indianapolis. From there, he quickly boarded a train to Washington, DC, where he reported for duty with the Regular Army. Throughout Daugherty's yearlong incarceration in the Tipton jail, the War Department had continued to issue him his monthly pay. The government's generosity enabled him to resume his life after his acquittal with little difficulty.

Daugherty was promoted to commander of the army's Twenty-Second Infantry, a position he held until he retired in 1893. Having attained his commission as major, he married Mathilda Anderson. The Daughertys lived the rest of their lives in Indianapolis, where he was a distinguished member of the Loyal Legion and in 1918 served as its state commander. In

September 1910, he accompanied then governor Thomas R. Marshall and a party of Civil War veterans to the battlefield of Antietam in Maryland for the dedication of Indiana's war monument. Daugherty was a prominent figure at numerous national encampments of the Grand Army of the Republic and served on the national commission at the Gettysburg celebration in 1911.

According to the *Kokomo Tribune*'s November 27, 1929, retrospective about the Daugherty–Van Horn incident, Daugherty returned to Kokomo only once, long after he had become a white-haired old man. The occasion was the state Grand Army of the Republic encampment held there in 1908.

Daugherty died at the age of eighty-one on February 4, 1922, in his home. He is buried in Indianapolis's Crown Hill Cemetery.

PART VI
WORST OF THE WORST

15

THE AWFUL CRIME OF JESSE McCLURE

POINT ISABEL, 1903

Late October is harvest time in Indiana—the time of year when folks reap the fruits of their labor and prepare to settle in with family for the coming winter. But for Jesse McClure, thanks to a quick, brutal temper and love for liquor, life at home had deteriorated to cruelty and insufferable hostility. It was a deadly combination—liquor and rage—impelling him to reclaim what he perceived as his personal property: his wife and sons. If they resisted, he'd show them who was boss.

McClure was a skinny, ashen-complected five-foot-seven, forty-two-year-old laborer with bloodshot eyes that peered angrily beneath his low-set brow. A bad haircut revealed two large cysts that looked like broken-off horns and made him appear all the more sinister. He had held a steady job at the planing mill in the tiny southeastern Howard County town of West Liberty. But his wife, Sarah (whom he called Sallie), had left him several weeks before, and since then he'd been working and bunking with a buddy in Frankton over in Madison County. McClure not only had lost the respect of his family, his self-esteem had taken a hit—both of which set his perpetual bad mood on fire. By Saturday, October 24, 1903, McClure needed some space for a couple of days. And some time to think. He rented a room in an Elwood boardinghouse, where he found both.

By the next morning, he had a plan. He rented a rig at the Newkirk Livery and began to drink. At noon, after consuming enough whiskey to muddle his judgment, he climbed into the buggy and stashed a bagful of sweet cakes and stick candy under the seat next to the .22 caliber revolver he had purchased the day before. Heading north, McClure drove the eleven miles to Point Isabel, a small rural community situated where the counties of Howard, Grant, and Tipton converge. It was there his estranged wife and children had taken refuge at the home of Robert Hall, the future brother-in-law of Sarah's sister, Emma Kilgore.

When McClure arrived at the residence shortly before one o'clock, he was greeted at the kitchen door by Hall. No love was lost between the two men.

"Jesse," said Hall. He pushed the screen door open no more than a few inches and propped it in place with his foot, blocking the entrance with his leg. He wasn't about to invite Sarah's no-account husband inside. "Sarah don't want to see you."

"Tell 'er to git out 'ere," McClure demanded, slurring his words. "I wanna talk to 'er."

"Go home, Jesse," Hall said, disgusted that McClure was inebriated on this, the Lord's day. "Yer drunk."

Ignoring the suggestion, McClure shifted his focus past Hall and peered into the house. "Sallie!" he shouted.

At once, Emma called out from a safe distance behind Hall. "I have a message from Sarah," she said. "She don't want to see you—not now or any other time. She says to tell you it's over and nothing good can come from discussing your troubles."

McClure curled his lips into a mirthless grin. "She's goin' to regret that decision," he muttered. Turning away, he sauntered a few steps, stopped, and looked back at Hall. "Tell Sallie to send out my boys. I wanna take 'em fer a buggy ride." Furious, he stomped back to the rig. He figured he could have handled things differently if Hall hadn't been there. Instead, McClure was forced to wait for his wife to give him the boys, and he wasn't sure she would.

The wait ended sooner than he expected, when the back door opened and McClure's two sons—Homer, age three, and Dee, age two—strolled hesitantly outside. A surge of malevolence coursed through his veins.

At first, the boys seemed unwilling—or perhaps afraid—to get close to their father, but when McClure showed them the cakes and candy he had brought, they ran to him. As Homer and Dee relished their treats, he lifted the boys into the buggy and drove away, calling out to his wife that he would return with the boys in a little while.

But that was not the way the visit would turn out. When Sarah McClure next saw her children, one would be dead and the other would be fighting for his life. What happened in between is accounted for only by the story McClure told—first to the Grant County sheriff when he turned himself in, and later to the authorities in Indianapolis and Tipton.

The Awful Crime

According to McClure, after the boys settled into his buggy, he drove up and down the road, passing the Hall home repeatedly, each time yelling for Sarah, begging her to join him. When he became convinced his efforts to rouse his wife were futile, he proceeded up the road about a quarter mile from the house, two miles west of the Tipton County line, and stopped the buggy. By then, both children had fallen asleep. McClure plucked his pistol from under his seat and, cradling little Dee in his arms, climbed out of the buggy and laid the boy on the grass beside the road. McClure gripped his pistol in his rough, chapped hand, curled his finger around the trigger, and fired a ball into the child's head.

Startled by the noise of the gunshot, Homer sat upright and asked, "What are you going to do, Papa?" McClure ignored the question as he whisked the terrified youngster from the rig and made him lie down next to his mortally wounded brother. Confusion and fear shone in Homer's tear-filled eyes, prompting McClure to cover them with his free hand before firing a bullet into the boy's skull.

McClure was unaware that although Homer apparently died instantly, Dee, the younger child, was still clinging to life. Believing that both of his sons were dead, McClure awoke to a moment of clarity. He suddenly realized that as soon as folks found out about the abhorrent act he had committed, they would surely lynch him. He figured he had one chance to escape an angry mob. He hightailed it to Marion to turn himself in to Grant County sheriff Clark Mills.

John Tygart, a resident of nearby Phlox, discovered the McClure children lying alongside the road within minutes of McClure's departure. Tygart would testify during McClure's trial that when he found the boys, Dee's tiny fist was still gripping a stick of hard candy, and both boys' lips

Angry and drunk, Thomas Jesse McClure took his two small sons for a buggy ride one Sunday afternoon in October 1903. Inexplicably, after he gave them candy, he shot and killed them. *Photo courtesy Indiana State Archives.*

were edged with traces of the cakes their father had used to lure them to their deaths.

McClure arrived at the Grant County jail at 4:30 p.m. In his shocking confession, he revealed that he had intended to kill himself after murdering his children but lost his nerve. He admitted that he would have killed his wife, too, had she gone with him. He expected to hang for his crime but said he hoped to live long enough to see his boys buried. Wringing his hands while making his statement, he frequently broke down and cried, "My God! What have I done? What have I done?"

Some thirty minutes later, word reached the Grant County sheriff that a mob was forming. Mills had learned that folks had worked themselves into a frenzy for McClure's blood and were bent on a lynching. As a preventive measure, the sheriff and his deputies escorted McClure to the railroad depot, where they boarded a train for the jail in Indianapolis.

"God Told Me to Do It"

On Monday, October 26, Tipton County sheriff George Schulenberg transported McClure to Tipton and locked him up to await a trial in the Tipton Circuit Court. News of the case shocked all of Indiana, and rumors swirled that an unruly mob would storm the jail to take the law into its own hands. Tipton County authorities were ready, but as it turned out, there were no mob demonstrations and no further serious threats.

The *Indianapolis News* reported that McClure talked quietly about what he had done and showed little regret. "I wish I could have killed my wife, too," McClure said. "She was the cause of all my troubles."

The reporter asked McClure how long he had been planning to kill his sons.

"I had it in mind for about a week," McClure replied as he wiped a tear that had slid onto his mustache. Admitting that he had purchased a revolver the Saturday before the shooting, he lamented, "It was a terrible thing to have to kill them, but I knew I had to do it to keep that woman from having them. . . . I'm glad it is all over."

Edward Daniels, Tipton County prosecutor, promised that a grand jury would quickly indict McClure and the circuit court would hear his case immediately, giving it priority over all other cases on the docket. "Within two weeks at the most," Daniels told the *Kokomo Daily Tribune* on Tuesday, October 27, "I expect to have Jesse McClure tried, convicted, and probably sentenced to be hanged for the diabolical crime he committed."

Defending McClure were court-appointed pauper attorneys Oglebay and Oglebay, also of Tipton. Anticipating that the defense would offer the so-called insanity dodge on behalf of their client, Daniels called in three Tipton doctors to examine McClure's mental state. Afterward, Daniels said the doctors were unanimous in their belief that there was "absolutely no doubt that the prisoner is perfectly sane."

The next day, however—Wednesday, October 28—demonstrating his ignorance as well as his attorneys' failure to muzzle their client, McClure spoke to the *Kokomo Daily Tribune* reporter and scoffed at the doctors' decision. "I am *not* crazy," he said. "I knew what I was doing all the time. I killed my boys because I loved them and did not want my wife to have them. God told me to do it, and He will take care of me."

Homer's funeral was held Tuesday, while his younger brother, Dee, remained unresponsive amid doctors' assurances that he would recover.

The next evening, after learning of Homer's burial, McClure broke down in tears and, for the first time, declared regret for what he had done to his children. He implored his lawyers to send for his wife so that he could beg her forgiveness.

Within the next two weeks, the grand jury would return a first-degree murder indictment, and Dee would be dead and buried during a blinding rainstorm next to his brother in Grant County's Knox Chapel Cemetery.

Prosecuting Attorney Daniels announced that he would not seek a revised indictment to charge McClure with the double murder. He would try the case according to the indictment the grand jury returned for Homer's death alone. "If the jury brings back an unsatisfactory verdict," Daniels said, "I'll have another murder charge for Dee McClure, and I'll try the case again."

The Trial

McClure's trial got under way on Monday, November 23, 1903—not quite as quickly as Daniels initially vowed but quick by today's standards. In the court of public opinion as well as the press, the trial was unnecessary. The public had decided McClure was destined for the gallows.

The *Kokomo Daily Tribune* reported that by sunrise, Tipton's downtown was bustling with people from all parts of the county, all of them eager to nab a seat in the courtroom. At 9:00 a.m., Judge J. F. Elliott entered, and the bailiff announced, "Hear ye, hear ye, hear ye."

Tipton Circuit Court was in session. The courtroom was packed.

The prosecutor had barely begun to make his brief preliminary statement when Sheriff Schulenburg ushered McClure into the courtroom and seated him at the defense table. The *Kokomo Daily Tribune* reported, "There was a rustle throughout the courtroom when the accused man's face appeared in the doorway, and there was a simultaneous tiptoeing and craning of necks in order to get a glimpse. McClure was dressed in plain, cheap clothing, probably the suit he had on when he killed his little boys. Shuffling in, he looked every day of his forty-two years. His face was pale and haggard, and he was nervous and ill at ease under the curious regard of so many eyes."

Continuing his opening statement, Daniels said the state would prove McClure had thoroughly premeditated his crime. Daniels vowed to prove that the defendant drove from Elwood to the Hall house in Point Isabel, where Sarah and the children were guests, for the sole purpose of killing them all.

The state called some two dozen witnesses, including Sarah, who was the principal witness against the defendant, and several doctors who testified about McClure's mental state.

Sarah McClure offered details of the murder, while the courtroom spectators sobbed. She said her marriage to McClure was awful. She claimed he drank heavily and often abused her, adding that two days before Homer was born, he knocked her down with a chair and kicked her. On another occasion, she said, he became enraged over some trivial matter and broke a washboard over her head. McClure had threatened many times to kill her and once broke her arm with a stick, caused a gash in her head, and whipped her with a strap.

The prosecution presented as evidence the strap and the bloody cloth that Sarah had used to bandage her head.

Sarah said that having experienced her husband's abuse, she would never forgive herself for allowing the children to go with him the day he called for them at the Hall home. She testified that, while McClure had been driving back and forth in front of the house, she escaped out the back door. She ran through the cornfield to a neighbor's home and telephoned other neighbors for help in stopping her husband from taking the boys. But she never dreamed he would seek revenge on her by slaying them.

McClure assumed an attitude of indifference when his wife began her testimony, but as she went on, he broke down and wept.

The state closed its case shortly before noon on Wednesday, November 25. The defense opened its case immediately after. Oglebay and Oglebay had entered their plea of not guilty by reason of insanity on Monday. Now, standing before the jury, they explained why. Their client was so distressed since separating from his family, they said, "that his reason had failed him, that he had indulged in intoxicants, and finally had become afflicted with homicidal mania, the result of which had been his unprovoked and most unnatural assault upon his innocent little children."

Court adjourned late Wednesday and resumed early Thursday, November 26—Thanksgiving Day. Anticipating that jurors might need further proof of McClure's mental impotence, Oglebay and Oglebay played an additional insanity card and then another. The man had been "crazy" for eight years after being thrown from a horse, the defense team proclaimed.

They hypothesized that McClure's resulting head injury had permanently rendered him unaccountable and, therefore, not responsible for his reprehensible conduct. In addition to their crazy-by-head-injury theory, the defense team called witnesses who swore McClure was "afflicted with a hereditary taint of insanity." They testified that a number of McClure's nearest relatives had gone insane and others were complete imbeciles.

The trial concluded at 11:00 a.m. on Friday, but it was 3:00 p.m. before both sides finished their closing arguments. At that point, Judge Elliott informed the twelve men of the jury of the possible verdicts—first-degree murder, second-degree murder, and manslaughter—and then handed McClure's fate over to them.

Deliberation and Verdict

On the first ballot, nine members of the jury found McClure guilty of murder in the first degree and favored hanging him, while three argued that he was insane and should thus be acquitted. The jury carried on with its deliberation until past midnight, but with three of the men holding firm for acquittal, they broke for the night without a unanimous decision. Finally, the next morning, Saturday, November 28, the twelve men reached a compromise.

Resuming at 9:30 a.m., the court learned the jury's verdict: guilty of first-degree murder with the punishment fixed to life in prison. For those invested in the trial, the penalty was a disappointment. The community was outraged by the leniency, and many expressed regret that McClure had not been hung in Tipton the day he arrived at the jail.

Surprisingly, McClure's reaction to the sentence was not unlike the community's. Throughout the weeks leading up to the trial, he often told his jailers and attorneys that he longed for his execution. "If only the court would have permitted me to kneel down on my knees and pray to the jury that the death penalty would be inflicted upon me," McClure reportedly said to his attorneys, "it would have granted me a great favor. Now, I am compelled to go to prison and die by inches."

Despite the widespread contempt for McClure, members of the Windfall Holiness Church gathered at the jail Sunday morning with forgiveness and kindness in their hearts. The congregation prayed for McClure, presented him a Bible, and urged him to serve the Lord at the penitentiary as a force for good.

By Wednesday, December 2, when McClure and Sheriff Schulenberg boarded a Michigan City-bound train at the Tipton depot, McClure espoused renewed faith and belief that God had forgiven him. Consequently, he and his newly acquired Bible were inseparable until the day he died.

After the Lake Erie and Western train pulled out of the station, Elwood's *Daily Record* summed up area residents' feelings: "Tipton officials are glad to be rid of McClure, for he was one of the most thoroughly detested criminals ever confined there."

Similarly, the *Kokomo Daily Tribune* reported, "McClure was the object of much interest on the northbound LE&W train this morning, all the people aboard being anxious to get a glimpse of the man who had been guilty of such a monstrous crime as the cold-blooded slaughter of his own children."

Epilogue

In early August 1905, several Indiana newspapers ran a small, inside article informing readers that the Tipton County convicted child killer, Thomas Jesse McClure, was a mental and physical wreck. Confined to the penitentiary infirmary, he was not expected to live. Another tiny news article in mid-January 1907 reported his death on January 12 due to tuberculosis.

The same day, the prison warden, James D. Reid, sent a telegram to McClure's only known relative—a cousin residing in Elwood. The message read: "Jesse McClure died this morning. Has he relatives that will pay funeral expenses?" A reply came back stating simply, "Cannot pay expenses." Consequently, McClure's body was delivered to Stinchfield and Peters Mortuary in Valparaiso. As an agent of the Indiana Anatomical Board, which was charged with securing cadavers for dissection in the state medical colleges at Bloomington and Indianapolis, the mortuary undoubtedly shipped McClure's body to the Indiana University School of Medicine.

Looking back with today's perspective, it's ironic that despite the jurors' compromise to spare McClure's life, their relative leniency gave him nothing but time to carry the weight of his awful crime, grieve for his boys, and stew in his self-loathing.

Ultimately, the jury's life sentence dealt McClure a death that proved far less merciful than the hangman's noose.

16

MASSACRE ON LAUGHERY CREEK

AURORA, 1941

> I left home about 10 o'clock and got there [the Agrue farm] about noon and walked in the house. I said hello to Mrs. Agrue and asked her where the boys was. She said they was up on the hill planting corn. I walked up on the hill where they was and said hello to Leo and asked what he was doing. He said, "By God, ain't doing much of nothing." His kid brother stepped back, and he dropped his gun. . . . I hit [Leo] with my fist and took the gun away from him, whirled around and shot him.

So begins the confession of Virginius "Dink" Carter, whose murder of five members of the Johnson Agrue family—a massacre by any other name—on Friday, May 16, 1941, six miles south of Aurora, Indiana, on Laughery Creek Road, is among the bloodiest, most perplexing sagas in the state's criminal history.

Two of the killings were reported the next day by Dearborn County farmers Harvey Sellers and his son, Bill. The two had been up since dawn that chilly, damp Saturday, working outdoors and tending to chores. They dipped sheep until about 10:30, when they stopped and hiked to their alfalfa field. A hard rain had hammered the area the night before, and Harvey and Bill wanted to see if the crop was dry enough for them to cut after their noon dinner.

"But when we got down to the field, we found Mr. Agrue's cows in there," Harvey would testify five months later.

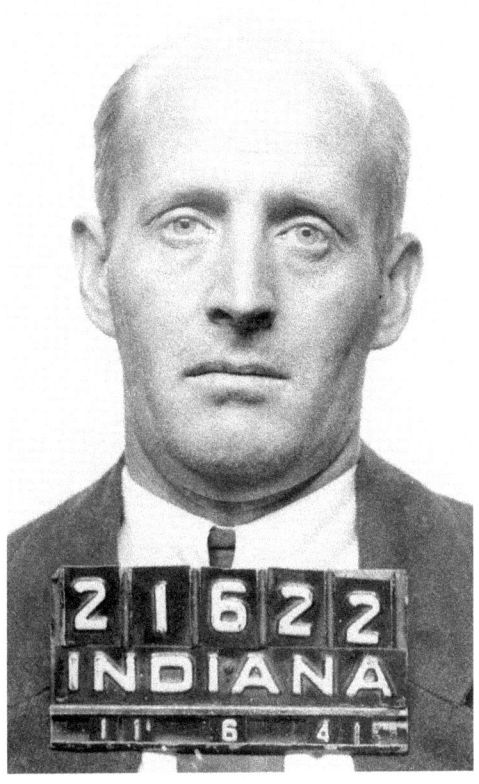

Virginius "Dink" Carter was tried and found guilty of the execution-style murder of five of his in-laws on May 16, 1941, near Aurora, Indiana. He was executed the following February at the Indiana State Prison. *Photo courtesy Indiana State Archives.*

The Sellers men thought it odd that their closest neighbor, fifty-nine-year-old Johnson Agrue, had left his milk cows out overnight. Even more curious, based on the size of the cows' udders, they hadn't been milked since two days before.

"We drove them out," Harvey continued, "and that was when we found Mr. Agrue's body laying across the path."

At first, the two men didn't realize Agrue was dead. But when they saw the gaping, bloody hole in the back of his head, they rushed down the path toward the two-story farmhouse for help. Upon reaching the barnyard, they were unsettled by an eerie stillness. Nothing stirred. No one greeted them.

"When we got close to the barn," Harvey said, "we seen the little girl laying in the barn door on her face."

The girl was Agrue's eleven-year-old granddaughter. She had been shot in the face and back at close range.

The evening before, Bill Sellers had given Agrue a two-mile ride from US Highway 50 to the Agrue farm lane on Laughery Creek Road, where he dropped him off at about 5:30.

Thinking back, Sellers recalled that about thirty minutes later, he had heard a pair of cracking sounds coming from that direction. They sounded like gunshots, although at the time, he thought nothing of it. Gunshots were not unusual for Dearborn County.

The discovery was gruesome. Fearful for their own lives, Sellers and his son hightailed it to the nearby farm of friend and county commissioner Joe Schmidt. He was one of the few area farmers with a telephone.

Tragedy Times Five

Deputy Arthur Voit responded to the call in lieu of Dearborn County sheriff William Winegard, who was out of town. When Voit and his officers arrived at the Agrue house, they fired tear gas inside. It was a precaution in case the killer was waiting for them. He wasn't. After the fumes cleared, the officers rushed inside. Entering the kitchen, they found Agrue's sixty-year-old wife, Nina, on the floor. She had been shot in the chest, her body surrounded by blood and pieces of the dinner she had been preparing.

From there, law enforcement officers, with the help of neighbors, set out searching the grounds of the farm for the Agrues' two sons. They found the body of twenty-three-year-old Leo at 2:00 p.m. in a field about a quarter mile from the farmhouse. Like his father and niece, Leo had suffered a fatal bullet in the back of his head.

When Sheriff Winegard arrived at about four o'clock, he observed that the kitchen table had been set for six, leading him to deduce that the Agrues had expected a guest for dinner. If that were the case, the suspect would likely turn out to be a relative or family friend. Initially, that assumption was the only clue the investigators had to go on. No spent cartridges were found anywhere on the grounds, the heavy rainstorm the night before had washed away possible evidence, and the killer left no clues.

As word about the tragedy spread throughout the county, a large crowd of concerned friends and neighbors converged at the farm. Among them was Dink Carter watching quietly when the body of Leo's brother, thirty-three-year-old William, was located at around five o'clock on a sloping hillside just three hundred yards from Leo. William also had been shot in the back of his head.

While onlookers reacted with shock and grief, Carter showed indifference.

Winegard noticed. He made some inquiries. After learning that at least three neighbors had seen Carter near the farm the previous evening, he took Carter into custody on the spot.

Suspect Nabbed

The next morning, Sunday, May 18, newspapers were reporting that the sheriff had a "hot suspect" in his custody. "This fellow," Winegard said, "has been telling us so many conflicting stories, but I know he will help us out if he really talks."

By the next day, the suspect was revealed as Virginius "Dink" Carter, Johnson and Nina Agrue's thirty-three-year-old son-in-law.

An unsavory character, Carter first married one of the Agrue daughters, Mary. After that marriage ended, he married another Agrue daughter, Leona—Leo's twin. Prior to his marriages, Carter had served two years at the Indiana State Farm for automobile theft and two more years at the Kentucky State Reformatory for sexual assault of a minor.

As of Sunday, Carter hadn't admitted anything, despite rigorous interrogations by the Dearborn sheriff and the Indiana state police. In addition, several witnesses had spotted Carter in the vicinity of the crime scene on Friday. Trucker Charles Campbell had driven Carter from Aurora to the Agrue lane shortly before noon; neighbor Charles Elliott had spoken with Carter in the vicinity of the Agrue home around 1:30 p.m. and again between 6:00 and 7:00 p.m.; and Aurora resident Paul Chase had seen Carter thumbing a ride that evening on the state road near the Agrues' farm and had given him a ride to town.

Regardless, Carter stubbornly remained tight-lipped.

Thanks to the prolonged questioning by the state police, however, Carter's steadfast denial was short-lived. Within forty-eight hours, he was singing like Deanna Durbin.

Carter Breaks His Silence

The Tuesday edition of the *Indianapolis News* reported that the Indiana state police had questioned Carter at its headquarters in Indianapolis for hours on Monday and into the wee hours of Tuesday. Carter initially insisted he had been in Aurora the day of the shootings, but when asked for specifics, his answers had been hazy. Police subjected Carter to a lie detector test but still got nowhere. At daybreak Tuesday, Carter was transported back to Dearborn County, where he soon had a change of heart.

A story in the May 23, 1941, edition of the *Lawrenceburg Press* credited Sheriff Winegard's interrogation skills for Carter's confession. The paper reported that Winegard told Carter, "You know we've got you on the spot. You'd just as well tell me everything."

After that, displaying not an ounce of remorse or emotion, Carter dictated his confession to court reporter Edgar Kurtzman. The statement included a complete description of when and how, one by one, he killed the members of the Agrue family. "Leo and Willy Agrue hated me and I killed them," his confession stated. "I later shot their father, Johnson Agrue, then the mother, and lastly, the granddaughter, Mary Elizabeth Breeden."

"Without any emotion," wrote the *Lawrenceburg Press*, "the stocky Auroran recounted how he left the body of an innocent girl laying sprawled at the entrance to the barn, where she fled, hoping for safety. Mary Elizabeth fell face down, her little hands clutching dirt and straw as she dragged herself on the ground before death gripped her."

According to his written confession, Carter had hitchhiked to the Agrue farm on Friday morning and found his brothers-in-law, Leo and William, on a hillside planting corn. The conversation grew heated, and Carter seized their shotgun and fired a round into each of their heads. From there, he hiked down to the farmhouse, where he carried on a friendly visit with Nina and her granddaughter—his niece—Mary Elizabeth, for about three hours. Knowing it was time for Johnson to return home from his job at the Madison Ordnance Proving Ground, Carter excused himself, retrieved the shotgun from where he'd left it, and took a hike along Laughery Creek. When he met his father-in-law coming down the hill, he shot him twice. After that, he returned to the house and shot Nina, and when Mary Elizabeth fled into the barnyard, he chased after her and shot her too. Having killed all the Agrues, he hid the gun and hitchhiked back to his home in Aurora, where he crawled into bed.

Unable to read or write, Carter scribbled his illegible signature across the bottom of his printed confession.

Asked to explain why he did it, Carter could not articulate a single reason for his deadly outburst—only that he had gone to the Agrue farm to reassure his father-in-law that he would pay back the ten dollars he had borrowed two weeks before as soon as he was rehired at the munitions plant in Charlestown. But when he got to the farm, something snapped. Carter admitted that he had always had "a grudge" against the Agrues, and after he killed Leo and William, he figured he might as well "wipe out" the rest of the family.

Carter led authorities to the murder weapon after he confessed on Tuesday. He had stashed the gun in a wooded area on the Agrue farm in a hollow tree that the investigators might have overlooked had he not shown them.

Ten days later, Friday, May 30, a Dearborn County grand jury charged Carter with five first-degree murder indictments, and Judge William Ricketts appointed Willard M. Dean, former Dearborn County prosecutor, as Carter's pauper attorney. At the arraignment on June 18, Carter pleaded not guilty. Dearborn County prosecutor Lester Baker announced that he would try Carter first for the murder of Mary Elizabeth, and he made it clear he would seek the death penalty, which, in Indiana, meant the electric chair.

Ricketts set the trial for June 30, but when he died suddenly and unexpectedly, the trial was postponed to Monday, October 13.

Order in the Court

The newly appointed judge, Morris W. McManaman, entered the Dearborn Circuit Courtroom on October 13, 1941, took the bench, and called day one of the Carter trial to order. The attorneys spent the first two days wading through the pool of potential jurists in hopes of finding twelve men who hadn't already formed their opinion of Carter's innocence or guilt and wouldn't oppose the death penalty. When the trial started Wednesday, Carter stepped into the courtroom appearing gaunt and pale but unusually dapper in a new suit and tie. As the court proceedings unfolded, Carter maintained a solemn, engaged demeanor that was betrayed when the occasional smile tugged at his thin lips. At his side sat his young wife, Leona, donning an artificial red flower in her black bobbed hair and holding his hand. If she fully comprehended what her husband was being tried for, she didn't show it. Next to Leona was Carter's white-headed farmer father, Tom Carter. Clad in a blue suit and resting his

Leona Carter is shown here with her daughter shortly after her husband, Dink, murdered five members of her family. *Photo courtesy Jenny Awad of the Dearborn County, Indiana, Historical Society.*

black hat on his knees, Tom Carter leaned forward with a cupped hand behind an ear to improve his hearing. Watching from behind him in the front row was Mary Elizabeth Breedon's mother, Bessie Wiant of Chicago.

During his opening remarks, Prosecutor Baker claimed that Carter had been observed on the Agrue farm the day of the massacre, and the next day, he had joined a mob of outraged area residents and coolly participated in a discussion about what may have happened. Less than two days later, Baker continued, Carter provided a totally voluntary confession.

Defense attorney Dean, in turn, told the jury that evidence and witnesses would prove Carter was nowhere near the Agrue farm that day and, thus, could not possibly have shot and killed the young girl or any of the other victims. As for the confession, according to Dean, his client had made it under the duress of fifty-plus hours of continuous, heavy-handed police interrogation. Casting doubt on the veracity of the confession as well as on Carter's intelligence was Dean's strategy. "We expect the evidence to show also," Dean declared, "that Carter is illiterate, has had no education, and can barely sign his name. We expect it to show that he could not read the confession or know what was in it."

If the jury were to buy Dean's arguments and reject the confession, the state's case would be largely circumstantial, a distinct advantage for the defense.

Damning Testimony Mounts

Over the next seven days, the courtroom was packed. Spectators filled all 150 seats, while dozens more sat on the windowsills and crammed into every inch of standing room. In addition, hundreds of people gathered on the courthouse lawn, where they awaited updates about the proceedings and a glimpse of Carter with his state police escort on his way back to the jail.

Every day of the trial, the jury heard from numerous witnesses who offered testimony that both persecuted Carter and vindicated him. One of the most emotional testimonies was given by Bessie Wiant. Through her tears, Wiant told the jury that Carter's relationship with his wife's family was dicey, and he never had a kind word for any of them.

Beatrice Agrue, widow of William Agrue, gave a heartrending testimony. She described an argument between Carter and her husband over the sale of pickles. Carter believed William had cheated him and

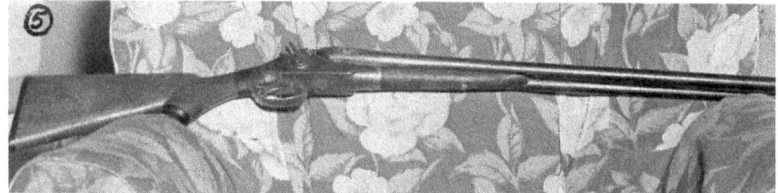

Pictured is the double barrel, twelve-gauge shotgun Dink Carter used to kill five members of the Agrue family, including eleven-year-old Mary Elizabeth Breeden. *Photo courtesy Jenny Awad of the Dearborn County, Indiana, Historical Society.*

threatened to "get even." He had told her husband, "I'll cut your guts out," she said.

Conversely, Agrue neighbors Harvey and Bill Sellers, who had discovered the bodies of Johnson Agrue and Mary Elizabeth, testified that Carter occasionally worked for them and hadn't given them a moment's trouble. If Carter's relationship with the Agrue family was stormy, the Sellerses had no knowledge of it, they said.

On day three, the Dearborn County sheriff William Winegard testified that within twenty-four hours of the brutal killings, Carter had confessed to him, laying out the details of his unthinkable acts and blaming the shootings on a grudge he had carried against the Agrues ever since they forced him to marry Leona after he had divorced her sister, Mary.

When the judge dismissed court, Carter kissed his clueless wife and slunk away with Deputy Voit.

The next day, Thursday, October 16, the prosecution won a major victory when it convinced the judge to admit Carter's confession as evidence of guilt, thus clinching the state's demand for the death penalty.

Carter's public defender fought admission of the confession, claiming his client had been deprived of his constitutional rights, coaxed, exhausted, and unable to read the statement to which he affixed his scrawling signature. Despite Dean's perseverance, however, he was unable to overshadow the strong case of circumstantial evidence the state had built. From that point forward, his best hopes were acquittal or life imprisonment.

That afternoon, while court was in session, the jail's janitor entered Carter's third-floor cell to sweep it out and discovered a stash of escape paraphernalia—an eighteen-foot rope, three hacksaw blades, and a skeleton key. Further investigation revealed that three of the inch-thick bars in Carter's cell window had been sawed through and the seams concealed with soap.

When the sheriff demanded an explanation, Carter admitted that he had planned to slide through the fourteen-inch-wide opening in his window and lower himself to the ground using his makeshift rope, crafted from the canvas straps supporting his mattress. The Baltimore and Ohio Railroad tracks were less than a block from the jail, and he voluntarily handed over a handwritten train schedule that he also had hidden in his cell. Once outside, he had planned to jump a freight car as the next train rolled through town.

Carter told Winegard that he had been working on his escape plan for a week. And although the plan was foiled, he vowed he would try again. "I would rather die by police guns than by the electric chair," he told the sheriff. Because of the stunt, the sheriff had Carter moved to a windowless, solitary-confinement cell with a guard posted at the door round the clock. Leona was no longer allowed to visit her husband without an officer in the room.

The State Rests

While Friday's news of the derailed escape caused a sensation, the trial progressed unimpeded. But by Saturday, the public's interest had become so frenetic that when the doors to the courtroom swung open, the throng of spectators tore off one of the hinges.

That day, the prosecutor called Carter's friend Francis Graves to the stand. The two had joined up the evening of the Agrue murders, and he admitted to forging Johnson Agrue's signature on the payroll check Carter had plucked from his dead father-in-law's pocket. After cashing it, he said, they had blown the fifty-one dollars on an overnight drinking spree in Cincinnati and Newport, Kentucky—not at a movie, as Carter maintained.

The prosecution next called Carter's first wife, Mary Agrue Carter, to the stand. The courtroom was shocked when Mary testified that she and Carter had never divorced, and technically she was still his wife. Wives cannot be coerced to testify against their husbands, but Mary did so with great relish, referring to Carter repeatedly as "that thing." She left him in 1933, she said, after one year of marriage. He once threatened to kill "the whole damned Agrue bunch," she added. After Mary stepped down, the state rested its case. A total of thirty-nine witnesses had testified on behalf of the prosecution.

The defense's turn came Monday afternoon. Dean called four witnesses to the stand, saving his client for the end. He first called on Thomas and Barbara Carter, the defendant's parents, to testify. They told the court their son had always been a good boy despite his questionable choices. They blamed his illiteracy on poor health as a young child, which prevented him from attending school regularly and kept him from advancing beyond third grade.

Following the Carters came an impassioned testimony by their son's adoring, current wife, Leona, whose family he literally had exterminated five months earlier. She defended him, telling the court she believed her husband's alibi for the day of the massacre and wasn't at all bothered by his occasional infidelity. "If all marriages were as happy as mine," she said glowingly, "there would be no divorces."

Under cross-examination by the prosecution, Leona disclosed that, according to her husband, Francis Graves was her family's killer. Carter begged her to keep it quiet for fear Graves would fulfill his threat to harm her and the children.

Dean thanked Leona and dismissed her from the stand. Turning to his defendant, he nodded at Carter. It was his turn.

Carter Testifies

When Carter took the stand, gone was his carefree swagger and impish half smile. Slumping in the witness chair, he avoided eye contact as he answered his attorney's questions in a voice that was sometimes flustered, sometimes defiant. Yes, he admitted, he had been on the road to the Agrue farm that day, but he denied setting foot on the Agrue property. Conveniently, he couldn't quite remember where exactly he had been going.

In the state's cross-examination, the prosecutor asked Carter to explain his whereabouts between noon and suppertime that day. Carter got huffy and sniped, "That's for me to know, and I ain't telling nobody."

What Carter didn't seem to mind telling, however, was that his buddy Francis Graves told him he was the one who killed the Agrues. The prosecutor pressed Carter, asking how he could know the intricate details of the shooting if he hadn't been there. Appearing flustered, Carter blurted out that Graves had laid it all out to him during their outing that Friday night.

Then why had he confessed?

"I was going crazy from the grilling," Carter said. "No rest, no sleep, nothing to eat."

And how, asked the prosecutor, did Carter know exactly where the gun had been hidden?

"I only knew what I was told," Carter answered.

"Well, I believe you said you couldn't tell [Sheriff] Winegard where it was," the prosecutor said. "You figured that he couldn't find it from Graves's directions, but *you* could?"

"I know all them hills out there."

We, the Jury, Find the Defendant . . .

On Tuesday, October 21, 1941, the eighth and final day of the trial, both the prosecution and the defense made their final arguments—Baker weaving together the pieces of evidence that pointed to an almost certain conviction; Dean asking only that the jury follow their God-given wisdom in making their decision.

The case was given to the jury at 11:59 a.m. After only two hours, which included an hour-long lunch, the jury reached a verdict. At 2:30 p.m., the foreman handed the slip of paper to the court clerk.

"We, the jury," the clerk read, "find the defendant, Virginius Carter, guilty of murder in the first degree."

Before Judge McManaman pronounced the sentence, he asked Carter if he knew of any reason why his sentence should not be pronounced. Carter's nearly inaudible reply was, "I'm not guilty."

The judge then advised Carter that the punishment would be death, to be carried out before dawn on February 10, 1942.

Leona immediately rushed to her husband's side, where she promptly collapsed. As she was carried out of the courtroom for medical attention, she continually blubbered, "I want Dink . . . I want Dink." Carter's father sobbed loudly, repeating several times that he would "care for the babies." Carter, shackled to a police officer and a deputy, shuffled out of the courtroom amid the confusion. Tears streaming down his pale, hollow cheeks, he could be heard moaning, "They'll give me the chair."

In the coming days, Carter was moved to the Indiana State Prison in Michigan City, his attorney asked for and was denied a new trial, and Carter's wife visited the Indiana governor twice to plead for her husband's life. He said no. Twice.

Execution Day

In the waning hours of Virginius Carter's time on earth, a tiny debate concerning the timing of his execution arose: Should he be electrocuted at midnight standard time or midnight war time (later termed daylight saving time)? The decision was Warden Alfred F. Dowd's. At stake was sixty minutes of Carter's life.

The question arose from the scheduled time change, meaning that, at the stroke of midnight on Monday, February 9, 1942, the nation's clocks would spring forward one hour. If Carter's execution were performed at midnight Standard Time, he would lose an hour. Citing a desire to avoid legal problems, the warden postponed the execution until 1:00 a.m.

Prison guards said Carter had been resigned to his execution from the day of his arrival at the prison in November and spent much of his time talking quietly to them when not staring into space. On Carter's last day, he had an hour with Leona, who had traveled by bus to Michigan City with their four-year-old daughter. They were the last people from home to see him alive. For his last meal, he asked for a home-style fried chicken dinner with peach pie à la mode, followed by cigars, cigarettes, conversation with the guards, and prayers with the prison chaplain.

Reportedly, Dink Carter started his stiff-legged walk to the chair without resistance at 1:02 a.m. and received his first zap of electricity two minutes later. The prison doctor pronounced him dead at 1:13.

Within hours, the prison had prepared Carter's body for burial and shipped it to Lawrenceburg via the Baltimore and Ohio, the same train he had hoped to hop after his attempted jailbreak back in October. Private services were conducted for him the next day in Aurora. Burial followed in Riverview Cemetery, a stone's throw from the graves of the five people he had massacred nine months before.

Three days later, the Dearborn County auditor received a bill from the Indiana State Prison. It wanted fifty dollars for carrying out Carter's execution. That was the first time the state had electrocuted one of Dearborn County's citizens, and receiving a bill for it was a tad jarring. But all things considered, fifty dollars was a bargain.

Murder in the Killer's Own Words

Following is the confession Virginius Carter dictated on May 18, 1941, to former Dearborn Circuit Court reporter Edgar Kurtzman, who wrote down the confession in shorthand. After the confession was typed, Carter scribbled his illegible signature at the bottom, vouching for its veracity.

    I, the undersigned, Virginius Carter, do hereby make the following statement in the presence of Lester Baker, William Winegard, Arthur Voit, and Ted Cook, and I do hereby make the statement of my own freewill and accord and under no duress:

    I left home about 10 o'clock [Friday morning] and got there about noon and walked in the house and said hello to Mrs. Agrue and asked her where the boys was. She said they was up on the hill planting corn. I walked up on the hill where they was and said hello to Leo and asked him what he was doing. He said, "By God, ain't doing much of nothing." His kid brother stepped back, and he dropped his gun, and I ran underneath the gun and threw the gun in the air and I hit him with my fist and took the gun away from him, whirled around and shot him.

    His brother started running and I shot him. I ran after him a little piece and came back down to the house and was there about three hours I imagine. I walked up the creek with the gun and I met Mr. Agrue coming down the hill and I shot him twice. Came on back to the house and Mrs. Agrue asked me what was the matter, and I said "nothing." She whirled around to me and I shot her. I picked up the gun and started to the door and told the girl, little girl, to come with me. She got to the barn and went to screaming and said she wasn't going and I shot her. I went up the hollow and hid the gun in a hollow log.

    A half mile. I walked on up the hollow and hid the gun, walked on out to the state road and walked about two miles and got a ride into town and stopped at a filling station. This fellow got three gallons of gas. I offered to buy him a bottle of Coke and he let me out at Ullrich's Drug Store point.

    I went up home, took off my clothes, put on some more clothes and had my supper and came downtown. Went to Battle Hulbert's and drank one shot of whiskey and I guess that is all. My daddy told me the Agrues got killed. We got in the car and went out there, walked down the creek, and walked over the hill, walking around the pasture field some back down the hill by the house and walked up the hollow and got in the sheriff's car and put in jail. That is all.

—Virginius Carter

PART VII
LOCAL LEGENDS

17

THE LEGEND OF KOKOMO MAYOR H. C. COLE

KOKOMO, 1881

Was the shooting death of Kokomo Mayor Henry C. Cole in 1881 due to the fatal blunder of a bungled burglary, or was he the victim of an assassination conspiracy? Nearly a century and a half after a posse of Kokomo officials and businessmen gunned down Cole on a starry autumn night on the secluded grounds of a north-side flour mill, local history buffs are still scratching their heads. It's the stuff of which legends are made.

The Crime

Howard County sheriff J. W. DeHaven never revealed who had warned him about the mayor's plan to burglarize and torch the Spring Mill on the night of Monday, September 19, 1881. Acting on the tip, the sheriff called together a posse—Deputy Sheriff J. W. Learner, William Styer, who ran the mill; Asher C. Bennett, an attorney; and Constable George W. Bennett—all of them Cole's ardent adversaries.

According to the statements they gave the coroner two days later, the men met at the mill, situated near the southeast corner of Indiana Avenue and Jefferson Street in Kokomo, at about 9:00 p.m. and took their assigned posts. Nothing unusual happened, they said, until shortly before eleven o'clock, when they spotted two men creeping about the facility.

Kokomo's notorious mayor, Henry C. Cole, was shot and killed in 1881 by a posse while, they claimed, he was stealing flour from an area mill. *Photo courtesy Howard County Historical Society, Kokomo, Indiana.*

The posse alleged that one of the intruders picked up four sacks of flour, each weighing twenty-five pounds, and carried them to a window. There, his accomplice, whom they said turned out to be Mayor Cole, took a bag in each hand, dragged two of the sacks several yards to an outhouse and returned for the two remaining. While the mayor was hauling away the second pair of bags, Deputy Sheriff Learner called out, ordering him to halt. Cole bolted instead, emboldening the deputy to start shooting. Amid the gunfire, Cole ran about a hundred yards, shouted, "Goddamn you!" and dropped to the ground.

The men said they rushed to Cole and found him dead—blood trickling from his nostrils, one knee bleeding, and each hand clenching a five-chamber Smith and Wesson. The *Kokomo Dispatch* heralded the posse as heroes, claiming, "The doctor would have made his assailants bite the dust if his thread of life had not been so suddenly snapped in twain." Within an hour of the incident, news that the city's charismatic forty-three-year-old mayor had been shot dead at the mill was spreading and curiosity seekers were swarming the scene.

While Cole's shooting death rocked the Kokomo community, its coverage by the local press was dwarfed by the news of President James A. Garfield's passing that same night. Due to Garfield's national significance, the *Kokomo Dispatch* couldn't carry the entire story of Cole's death until Thursday, September 22. The delay allowed reporters to thoroughly question witnesses and recount their stories in dramatic detail, including the complete statements of each member of the sheriff's posse. However, the degree of sensationalism and biased conjecture in the *Dispatch*'s coverage made it nearly impossible for readers to separate fact from fiction. Headlines read like twenty-first-century citizen-journalist tweets: "Mayor Cole Shot Dead While Committing Felony," "Riddled with Bullets by the Sheriff's Posse," "He Died With His Boots on and a Revolver in Each Hand," and on they went. Fact or fiction, the stories were a fitting end for a man whose controversial exploits had already catapulted him into the legendary echelon years before he died.

Cole's Paradoxical Past

When Dr. Henry C. Cole was elected mayor of Kokomo in 1880, he had been in the public eye for most of the fifteen years that he had resided in the city. His stubbornness, independence, and checkered past were notorious. Although his eccentric personality troubled many Kokomo citizens, it was of little concern to the majority of voters who elected him to shake things up. And did he ever. During Cole's nine months as the city's chief executive officer, he repeatedly challenged his political opponents, adhered to his principles, refused to compromise, and generally rubbed Kokomo's old guard the wrong way.

Part of Cole's challenge with his malcontents stemmed from the city's soaring crime rate. It was off the chart and compounded by an ineffective police force that couldn't keep up. During his mayoral campaign, Cole promised to clean up crime, but to his enemies' ears, the vow was a call to arms.

Few knew that Cole was not so squeaky clean himself and may have taken part in some rather nasty shenanigans. Heading into the election, a whisper campaign linked him to the notorious band of hoodlums known as the Mollihan gang, who had imposed a reign of terror throughout Howard and Tipton Counties during the 1870s.

An October 30, 1950, *Kokomo Daily Tribune* retrospective said of Cole's alleged criminal ties: "His name has been connected with many daring and elaborate schemes of revenge and with criminal enterprises of various kinds—murder, arson, abortion, counterfeiting, and larceny among them. Had some of the things of which he was accused been established by legal process, he would have landed behind prison bars or wound up on the gallows."

Luckily for Cole, there was no tangible evidence of his participation in the alleged crimes, and his cavalier behavior continued to endear him to his loyal supporters.

The only child of Jesse and Elizabeth Cole, Henry was born in 1838 in Ripley County, in the southeast corner of Indiana. Information about his life is sparse until the Civil War, when he joined the Union Army's medical corps, serving as a surgeon. Cole moved north after the war, settling in Kokomo, where he established a successful medical practice as well as a double-edged reputation. To some, he was a larger-than-life, kindhearted, Robin Hood–like hero. Tall, graceful, and handsome with lustrous blue eyes and a silky beard, Cole was a charismatic character whom women fawned over and men shunned. Perhaps it was his complicated, multifaceted persona that caused many Kokomo residents to view him as a celebrity. It was a distinction he seemed to relish. On the flip side, he could easily become an unpredictable, erratic hothead prone to fits of rage.

An October 1866 incident illustrated the depth of Cole's reckless temper and subsequently claimed a place in the annals of Kokomo folklore. The event sprang from his relationship with his stunning wife, Nellie. The marriage had taken a downward turn after she took up with a new love interest, Chambers Allen, a well-known Kokomo businessman. Nellie's infidelity both infuriated and embarrassed Cole, spurring him to write Allen a letter in which he promised to kill him if he got the chance. Allen foolishly dismissed the warning and continued his affair with the estranged Mrs. Cole—that is, until the day he met Cole by chance at the Buckeye Street post office.

Allen didn't expect Cole to follow through on this threat, and certainly not in a public venue with witnesses all around. But underestimating Cole's vehemence was Allen's downfall. Without uttering a word or blinking an eye, Cole drew his revolver and coldly fired three rounds into Allen's chest, killing him instantly.

Cole was promptly arrested, hauled off to jail, and charged with murder. When his December court date rolled around, he demanded a change of venue to Tipton County, where he entered a plea of insanity—a common defense for murder at the time.

Cole retained US Representative Daniel W. Voorhees as his defense counsel, and, remarkably, he was acquitted. He walked away scot-free.

Cole's political ambitions were gaining momentum by then, and Mayor N. P. Richmond appointed him chief fire engineer. It was a position Cole held until 1877, when he was elected to the Kokomo City Council to represent the city's third ward. Just three years later, he tossed his hat into the ring, vying for the mayor's seat that his old friend, Richmond, still occupied. While the prospect of a Cole victory caused his enemies list to grow, it excited his supporters.

Cole took office in January 1881, thanks to his enormous popularity among Kokomo's working class. Flaunting his affable personality and good looks when it was to his benefit, he also would easily slip into his menacing dark side to fend off adversaries when it suited him. Perhaps unintentionally, he alienated many of his constituents.

Among the disgruntled were the chief of police and a handful of cronies from the community's influential upper crust. Among that constituency was the posse that brought him down.

Investigation into the Incident

Coroner J. C. Wright was in Russiaville the night Cole was killed and couldn't make the trip back to Kokomo until the next morning. By then, hundreds of lookie-loos had flocked to the scene of the killing to gawk at Cole's dead body, of which the *Kokomo Dispatch* said, "presented a ghastly scene as it lay rigid and contorted on the open commons, where life's frail taper had gone out." On his return, Wright ordered Cole's remains removed to the mayor's Main Street residence, where he and a team of five local doctors performed the autopsy that day. They determined that Cole had been shot in his left knee, right index finger, right arm, his head just below the right ear, lower back, and his heart's right auricle. He had taken two pistol balls and twenty-one balls of bird shot. Cole's death resulted from the bird shot that entered his heart, resulting in an internal hemorrhage.

Wright convened an inquest the next afternoon at the courthouse to question the entire sheriff's posse as well as witnesses. According to the *Kokomo Dispatch*, the hearing was held in the presence of "a vast throng of citizens, some of whom were ladies!"

Asher C. Bennett spoke first. "I have been acting in connection with U.S. authorities," he said. "I had knowledge of the contemplated robbery and knew there was a scheme on foot to steal flour and burn that mill." Bennett said he fired his .38 caliber Smith and Wesson revolver only once.

Howard County sheriff J. W. DeHaven told the panel that he learned of Cole's scheme the Saturday before from a confidential informant. Pursuant to that, he said, he appointed the four-man posse and told them what to do.

William Styer testified that when the shooting had subsided, he joined the rest of the men gathered around Cole and lit a match to illuminate the face of the vandal to positively identify him. When asked whether he had fired his gun, Styer replied that his pistol had discharged only once, accidentally, while he was climbing off his assigned post atop the woodpile.

Constable George W. Bennett stated that the sheriff had ordered the deputized posse to capture the perpetrators of the burglary—dead or alive. Bennett later took credit for firing the fatal shot. It was a distinction he carried with pride for the rest of his life.

"Someone hollered 'halt,' and a shot was immediately fired," Bennett told the coroner. Continuing, he said:

> In an instant, another shot was fired and there was another call of "Halt." That seemed to bewilder [Cole], and he started to run. I got a glimpse of him around the privy, and I fired both barrels of my shotgun. I saw him running and took after him and called him to halt. He didn't halt, and I fired again. I told him he'd as well surrender because we had him. I believe he said, "Dokey," and he fell. I said to the other boys, "We've got him," and they came running up. Cole had a revolver gripped tight in each hand. I laid down my shotgun and took hold of his left-hand pistol to twist it out of his hand. He had a death grip on it, and I discovered life in the body. But it was only a short time before he expired.

The last member of the posse to testify was Deputy Sheriff J. W. Learner. "I hallooed 'halt,' and Cole started to run. I attempted to fire, but I was not positive whether I discharged my gun or not. I was near Mr. Styer and thought it was his weapon that discharged instead of mine."

The deputy later admitted that he had been "somewhat excited" during the altercation. "It was the first case of the kind I was ever in."

There were many questions about Cole's revolvers. Was there one, or were there two? Were they in his hands? Where were they in relation to the body? Were they cocked?

Witness Dorsey Mahan said he saw Cole clenching a cocked revolver in his right hand, while a gun lay in his half-open left hand. His observation conflicted with the testimony of George Bennett, who said he had wrenched the gun from Cole's left hand. DeHaven said he observed Cole's right hand resting on his foot with a revolver barely in it, while his left hand was thrown back with a revolver lying up to a foot away.

DeHaven was asked whether he had had any contact with the posse's weapons. He replied, "I did not examine those revolvers any more than to look at them. I did not touch them, nor did I allow anyone else to touch them. I touched nothing, and no one else touched anything."

Styer's testimony substantiated the sheriff's recollection that Cole held a revolver in his right hand, while another weapon lay on the ground a few inches to his left.

The next day, Wednesday, September 21—despite the conflicts in the participants' testimonies, the posse's lack of law-enforcement experience, the excitement of the chase, the contamination of the crime scene caused by hundreds of thrill seekers, the sheriff's refusal to identify his unnamed informant, a flawed ballistics evaluation, and no real attempt to apprehend Cole's burglary accomplice—the coroner filed his verdict. It read: "I, J. C. Wright, coroner of Howard County, after examining the body and hearing the evidence of the witnesses at an inquest held over the dead body of Dr. H. C. Cole, in the city of Kokomo, county of Howard, state of Indiana, on the 20th day of September, 1881, do find that the deceased came to his death by being shot by officers of the law in the discharge of their duty, at or near the Spring Mill in the city of Kokomo, Howard County, Indiana."

Epilogue

Cole was buried September 21, following a funeral at his home and a procession to Crown Point Cemetery. The case was officially closed on October 18, 1881, when a Howard County grand jury returned an indictment of voluntary manslaughter against the sheriff's posse.

The *Fort Wayne Daily Gazette* reported on November 18, 1881, that the officers who shot Cole, while carrying out their duty, were arrested and "a terrible pressure brought to bear to prove that Cole was unjustly accused of the crime of stealing." The following March, the judge dismissed the case, stating that no evidence was found to sustain the indictment.

Kokomo-area residents spoke of Cole for years after his death, and rumors of conspiracy swirled for decades. As with most conspiracy theories, numerous questions and various scenarios surrounding Cole's shooting death were posed, but they were never answered.

For example, Cole's motive for entering the flour mill that fateful night was never established and always suspect. Had he intended to burglarize the mill and then burn it down to cover his tracks as the sheriff testified? The posse swore that they caught Cole in the act of stealing flour, but why would he steal flour? Flour sold for less than six dollars a barrel in 1881. Was it the safe he was after? If so, why were no tools or explosives found? These points naturally beg the question: Was Cole set up?

The October 30, 1950, *Kokomo Tribune* article reexamined Cole's death. The paper reported that many of Cole's friends refused to believe the charges against him. They insisted he had been killed elsewhere and his body moved to the mill.

It should not be overlooked that every member of the sheriff's posse, including the sheriff, had experienced run-ins with Cole. While the sheriff claimed he had received a tip, he steadfastly refused to reveal the identity of his informant. Assuming the turncoat even existed, some historians point to the leader of the Mollihan gang as a possible candidate.

Another of the conspiracy rumors theorizes that Cole went to the mill in response to an anonymous urgent call to treat an injured man. Although Cole likely would have been leery of such a request, he often provided free medical care to the poor, so it wasn't outside his character to answer the call. It's curious that no one ever stepped forward to confirm the claim. It's more curious that the owner of the livery stable where Cole had his buggy readied for the trip to the mill that night said the mayor had no guns.

The circumstances, contradictions, and controversy that define the life and death of Henry C. Cole are as vibrant today as they ever were. They elevate him to a place of distinction that probably would have eluded him had he simply been allowed to fade into obscurity and die of old age. They provide a fitting legacy for a man who lived a life full of lustful abandon. They are what made him a legend.

The Mollihan Gang

Fifty years before the Dillinger gang blazed a trail of murder and mayhem throughout Indiana, Kokomo was home base for a band of lawless cutthroats all its own. The Mollihan gang, which used the Junction Saloon as its operation center, wreaked havoc in Kokomo and its surrounding areas from about 1872 through early 1879, when the gang's chaos ended rather abruptly.

A Civil War veteran, Mart Mollihan was a likable fellow who cultivated many friends when he returned to Kokomo after the war. He was an enterprising entrepreneur and started a saloon at the railroad junction on the city's north side.

Initially, Mollihan and his band of thugs concentrated on burglaries and safecracking. They branched out to counterfeiting shortly after a convicted "shover of the queer" (i.e., passer of counterfeit money), Isaac Lang, returned to his Kokomo home following his release from prison.

Over the next several months, area residents began to notice the frequency with which mutilated bodies were found scattered about the train tracks on the northwestern outskirts of the city. Folks assumed that an inordinate number of men simply had gotten in the way of passing trains, until investigators became aware of signs of foul play.

For example, none of the victims possessed money, valuables, or identification, and most had been traveling aboard a night train. It was later determined that when they disembarked at the junction depot, they were lured into the Mollihan Saloon, drugged, robbed, murdered, and dropped through a trap door into the cellar. There they remained until the gang threw them across the track minutes before the next locomotive chugged around the curve.

Scores of bodies were sliced and diced. While most of the deceased were strangers, some were not. Some were high-profile Kokomo businessmen and law enforcement officials.

In early 1879, once the city and county finally decided to take action, police and a posse of outraged citizens captured fifteen of the gang's members in one swoop. Amid the raid's commotion, Mollihan crashed through a saloon window and disappeared. A month after the gang was jailed, eleven of its members escaped during a political rally. Without their leader, however, the gang's activity ceased.

Mollihan's whereabouts remained a mystery until July 1894, when he was recognized in Kansas City, Kansas, and brought back to Kokomo to be tried. However, as reported by the July 17, 1894, *Huntington Weekly Herald*, because all the witnesses to Mollihan's long-ago crimes had since died, his conviction was doubtful. A September 9, 1912, *Tipton Daily Tribune* article confirms Mollihan was never indicted. In fact, the article reports that he moved to Dallas, Texas, where he was "reputed to be living a quiet life and enjoying the fruits of a comfortable fortune."

During his years in Kokomo, Henry C. Cole was linked to both Mollihan and Lang, although no evidence to support the rumors was ever produced.

18

GUN GIRL

ELWOOD, 1933–41

Bold, beautiful, blonde (although sometimes brunette), and not yet twenty-one. It can be a recipe for trouble in any era. But in Depression-era America, when a young, attractive spitfire wielding not one but two guns demonstrates her spunk by taking down the Pittsburgh police with nothing but her "small feet and dainty hands," it's a recipe for selling newspapers.

And sell newspapers is exactly what Elwood's Isabelle Messmer did after the media dubbed her the notorious "Gun Girl" in 1933. For the next decade, she dominated headlines from California to Maine, generating almost as much publicity as her hometown's other media darling, Wendell Willkie.

Gun Girl Is Born

Isabelle dropped out of school in 1930 at the age of fifteen and ran away in search of a life that satisfied her intrepid spirit. She was good at catching rides and keeping on the move. The destination didn't much matter as long as it was far away from Elwood. She never had a steady job or a place to call home, but a resourceful, nice-looking woman could always get by.

It was October 19, 1933. Pittsburgh was her latest stop, but hotel rooms weren't free and finances were tight. Fortunately, she could count on her

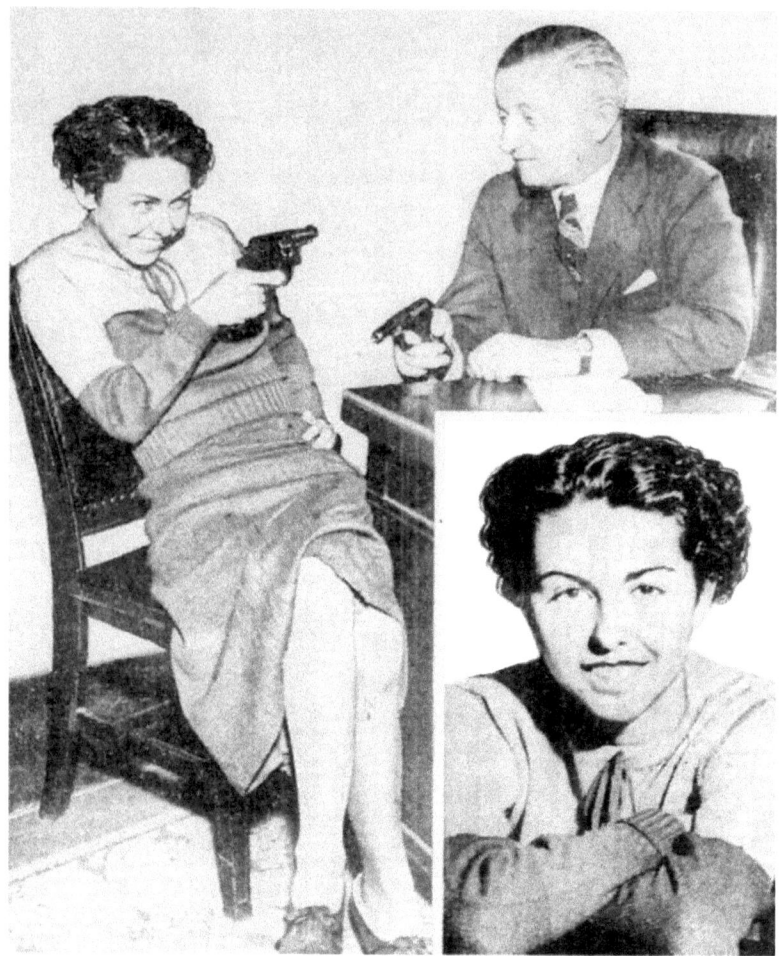

Isabelle Messmer, Elwood's notorious homegrown "Gun Girl," made her first coast-to-coast headline in October 1933 after she was arrested by Pittsburgh police detectives. Here, she and Pittsburgh police superintendent Franklin McQuaide take aim as they mug for the camera. *Photo courtesy the* Pittsburgh Post-Gazette, *Pittsburgh, Pennsylvania.*

feminine wiles to scrounge up a few bucks, and bus stations were loaded with willing gentlemen.

The day had been lucrative for her. After making a quick stop at the bus station locker in which she'd stashed her revolver, she dropped the gun into her pocketbook and trooped the few blocks down Seventh Avenue to her hotel. She was unaware of the two well-dressed Pittsburgh police detectives tailing her. No sooner had she entered her room than the door flew open and the two men burst in, demanding the gun in her purse as well as the one on her nightstand.

"Not so fast, boys," Isabelle snarled. Ignoring the detectives' demand, she lunged at them, landing a swift, hard kick to one officer's left shin and swinging a haymaker at the other officer's nose. Her relentless fight forced officers to pick her up, still kicking and punching, and carry her to their car. Even at the police station, she was "flinging kicks, right hooks and left jabs at all who approached her," according to the *Indianapolis Star*. She would not be subdued.

The persona of the feisty, fresh-faced "Gun Girl" was born the next day, when newspapers all over the nation carried an Associated Press photo of an amused Isabelle and a stone-faced Pittsburgh chief of police Franklin McQuaide pointing revolvers at each other.

Despite the apparent playfulness of the scene, the run-in earned Isabelle a sentence of two-years in the clink. But six weeks later, the Pittsburgh police chief set her free on the condition she leave the state and keep her nose clean. A grateful Isabelle agreed, but in January, despite her promise, Miami police hauled her to jail for allegedly stealing $900 in an armed robbery. However, for whatever reason—be it her sweet smile, her pretty face, her tiny stature, her Hoosier charm—she was quietly set free.

Eight months later, police in Washington, DC, arrested an eye-catching young woman attired in boys' clothing and armed with a pistol. Flummoxed officials were unsure what to make of her, so they handed her over to the Gallinger Municipal Hospital's psychopathic ward.

The August 15, 1934, *Elwood Call-Leader* reported, "The mite of a girl with rolling eyes and a sense of humor, as well as a pack of deviltry, was downright amused" when psychiatrists diagnosed her as a "psychopathic personality" and an adventurous, irresponsible "romancer" that enjoyed notoriety.

Displaying waifish innocence, Isabelle appealed to the maternal instincts of Washington's female police officers, who advocated for her release, provided she return home to her mother's care. She did return home but informed her mother, "Elwood is too small for the big-time excitement I crave." The reunion was brief.

Gun Girl Returns

Isabelle managed to operate under the radar for nearly three and a half years. But in late January 1938, she scored front-page headlines for resisting arrest in New Jersey. Gun Girl initially obeyed a pair of Newark traffic cops who ordered her to stop the LaSalle roadster she was driving. But when they approached on foot, she floored the gas pedal and ran one of them down.

A stunning ten-mile highway chase ensued at speeds reaching eighty miles per hour. Officers fired five shots before they managed to force Isabelle off the road and arrest her.

Guilty of "atrocious assault and battery," she told the judge she had mistaken the two officers for gangsters. The judge told her that her days of relying on a "pretty face and vicious personality" were over. Despite her tears, the judge sentenced her to seven years in the New Jersey Women's Reformatory, an unwalled, minimum-security facility.

Isabelle stayed put at the reformatory without incident for almost a year. And then on the evening of January 20, 1939, after attending a movie on the prison grounds, she simply walked away.

The escape was highly publicized, but Isabelle remained on the run until a Saint Louis policeman arrested her on October 5 for packing a .38 in her purse. The next morning, after learning the New Jersey reformatory wanted her back, she staged a mini riot in her jail cell, stripping naked and leaping headfirst from her upper bunk onto the hard cement floor. Adamant that she would not return to New Jersey, she confessed to a crime that trumped running down a cop.

"I killed Buford Armstrong," she told Detective Sergeant Kenneth McGuire.

Armstrong, a twenty-five-year-old pitcher for the House of David semipro baseball team, had been found shot to death in an Odessa, Texas, tourist cabin on March 30, 1939. Isabelle told the Saint Louis police she had arranged to meet Armstrong for a fling, but when he attacked her, she shot him in the heart.

Isabelle begged the Missouri police not to send her back to New Jersey. She even threatened suicide, but she needn't have bothered. Three Texas officials—Ector County sheriff Reeder Webb, county attorney O. E. Gerron, and Texas Ranger Hugh Pharies—were on their way. When they reached Saint Louis on October 15, they escorted their murder suspect to Odessa to stand trial.

Two days later, she told *Elwood Call-Leader* reporter Tony Slaughter, "I'm glad to get back in Texas. I'd rather give my life to Texas in the electric chair than return to New Jersey."

The Odessa court arraigned Isabelle on December 6 on a charge of murder. She pleaded not guilty, claiming self-defense, and the judge set her trial for Monday, March 25, 1940.

Gun Girl on Trial

By the end of the trial's first day, the state had rested its case without a single eyewitness. The closest the prosecutor had come to credible witnesses were a justice of the peace that identified Isabelle as the woman who knocked on his door after the shooting and the taxi driver who had picked her up near the cabin.

The defense spent most of the next day, Tuesday, March 26, presenting its side. The star witness stuck to the statement she gave the Saint Louis police more than five months before. "Yes, I killed him," Isabelle said without apology. "He was trying to . . . um . . . attack me."

For clarity, the defense attorney asked her whether the term *attack* was code for rape.

"Yes," she said, "he was making advances toward me, so in defense of my honor, I shot him."

Having made the cause and effect obvious, the defense delivered closing arguments late that afternoon. The case went directly to the jury, which, surprisingly, returned its verdict before the clock struck midnight.

A police officer and a jail matron soon escorted Isabelle into the packed courtroom, where she took her place beside her attorney. Confident of an acquittal, Isabelle stood, facing the judge as the jury foreman handed him a folded sheet of paper bearing the panel's official statement.

The judge unfolded the paper and read it to himself. After a moment, he looked up at Isabelle and said, "The jury finds the defendant guilty."

The instant the judge's last word was spoken, even before he could draw his next breath, Isabelle leaped onto the courtroom railing and screamed at the jail matron, "You won't take me back! You won't take me back! I won't go back to the penitentiary!"

As she toppled forward, nearby spectators caught her and helped police constrain their prisoner. But she refused to go quietly, fighting her captors "like a tiger woman" all the way back to her cell.

Handing down what amounted to a mere slap on the hand relative to a murder conviction, the judge sentenced Isabelle to three years in the Texas prison system. As he explained, with no witnesses or hard evidence linking a suspect to the shooting, the court was forced to rely entirely on Isabelle's confession.

The press was mum on its cherished Gun Girl for the next ten days. With her securely locked up in Odessa awaiting transfer to the Texas penitentiary, there was nothing sensational to report. However, Isabelle rarely strayed from the limelight for long.

Ten days after the jury handed down its guilty verdict, an Ector County judge refused to grant her a new trial. The next day, Isabelle escaped.

The media pounced on the story, splashing headlines coast to coast—"Isabelle's on the Loose Again," among them. According to reports, the officer who brought Isabelle's breakfast forgot to lock her cell. So she cracked open the door of her cell block with a piece of metal broken from her iron cot, smashed a window in the hallway, and climbed down a lattice three floors to freedom. Rumor had it that she'd been helped, although an accomplice was never identified.

The escape was the cherry on her growing list of unlawful accomplishments and elevated her to the status of criminal legend. Some papers called her the "female Dillinger." Some ranked her Public Enemy Number One. If nothing else, the escape put her on the run like never before and ignited speculation that she was sneaking home to the comfort of her mother's arms.

Remember the Night

The Gun Girl's flight from justice finally came to an end the afternoon of May 29, 1940, after an anonymous tipster spotted her stepping off a bus at the Tipton traction station, ten miles west of Elwood. The tipster immediately phoned the Tipton County sheriff, and the search was on.

The pursuit was brief and came to an end at the Ritz Theater, into which Isabelle had ducked to wait for nightfall. The picture show that day was titled *Remember the Night*. She likely did remember the night for a long time, since it marked the end of her arduous eight-week journey from Odessa. Isabelle was apprehended when she walked into the theater's lobby to place a long-distance call to Elwood. Four local law enforcement officers were waiting for her. The next day's *Tipton Daily Tribune* reported that her quiet capture was "the model of cooperation."

"Sheriff C. D. Hobbs followed her out of the auditorium," the paper stated, "State Policeman K. A. Wines drew his gun and pressed it in her back, Deputy Burl Lilly grabbed her handbag, which might have held a deadly weapon, and Police Chief H. B. Richardson stood guard, watching her every move."

Isabelle was again placed behind bars, and the Tipton sheriff arranged to have her flown back to Texas, according to the *Tipton Daily Tribune*, as soon as the county health officer declared her healthy enough "to stand the trip."

Exactly what the health officer was waiting for was not clear, but during the delay, Isabelle staged a two-day hunger strike, threatened suicide, and hinted at murder, while her mother tried to have her declared criminally insane.

None of it worked, and on Tuesday, June 4, the doctor sedated her. Amid Isabelle's earsplitting objections, Sheriff Hobbs and State Trooper Wines handcuffed her wrists and ankles, carried her to the waiting squad car, and stuffed her into the back seat. From there, they headed for the Indianapolis Municipal Airport, where Sheriff Webb of Odessa, Texas, would meet them.

Isabelle may have arrived at the Tipton jail quietly, but she wasn't about to leave that way. The newspaper called her behavior "a blue haze of screeching fury," as she screamed vindictive threats of death at all officials and wailed for her mother. Her behavior had been even worse the day before, when she ripped off her skirt and strangled her mother with it for suggesting she was insane. When Sheriff Hobbs pulled her off her mother, Isabelle stripped off all her clothes, hurled dishes, and repeatedly swiped at him with a razor blade. "I'll kill someone before it's all over," she screamed.

She continued to scream from the back seat of the police car all the way to the Indianapolis airport, where hundreds of curiosity seekers waited to see the famed Gun Girl handed over to the Texas sheriff. Isabelle screeched and fought the law enforcement officers nonstop as they plucked her out of the car, forced her across the tarmac, and shoved her into the private, four-seater airplane. According to the *Tipton Daily Tribune*, as the plane taxied down the runway for takeoff, even the swoosh of the propellers couldn't muffle her wails.

A few hours later, Elwood's Gun Girl again stewed in her distant Odessa jail cell, unable to carry out the murderous threats she had hurled to her Tipton County captors. Sheriff Hobbs was relieved. Under no circumstances, he said, did he want that woman back in his jail. Hobbs, along with residents of Madison and Tipton Counties, released a collective sigh of relief and settled back into their mundane, daily lives.

BULLETIN!

When the Tuesday, November 12, 1940, *Elwood Call-Leader* rolled off the press, it broke the paper's five-month embargo on Gun Girl news. A late-breaking, four-inch article had been stripped onto the lower right side of page one, and readers might have overlooked it had it not been headlined "BULLETIN!"

The first sentence—"Isabelle Messmer, Elwood's far-famed Gun Girl, has escaped again from Ector County Jail"—revealed the dreaded news, and all over the city, readers groaned. From Texas to Indiana, Gun Girl fans and embarrassed law enforcement officials watched and waited.

In early January 1941, an Anderson newspaper ran an unsourced and unconfirmed report about a Gun Girl sighting on New Year's Day. The story generated excitement and newspaper sales, but Elwood police deemed it a "hoax." According to the story, Isabelle and a pilot friend landed a plane at the Hobbs airport and hiked the five miles to Elwood, where she briefly reunited with her mother. The story ratcheted up the excitement with suggestions that minutes after Isabelle and her friend flew off into the wild blue yonder, the FBI supposedly swooped in, hot on her tail.

Two months passed before the next Gun Girl sighting. This one on March 17 placed her at the Muncie bus station looking for a ride to Elwood. Although Elwood-area police went on high alert, maintaining a round-the-clock vigil, no one reported a trace of Isabelle.

Imprudent Proposition

A month later, on April 22, Isabelle got caught after making sexual advances to the wrong man outside a San Francisco hotel. The man was a plainclothes police officer. She told him her name was Jean Lamar, but her fingerprints revealed otherwise.

When another police officer found a revolver in her purse, Isabelle confessed she had intended to kill the arresting officer but didn't because "he was just so nice."

Isabelle spent the night in the San Francisco jail, not cheerfully. By the next day, when the Texas authorities arrived to take her back to Odessa, she calmly admitted, "I don't mind going back to Texas. I'm kind of glad it's all over. I've been living like a rat in a hole."

The long, sixteen-hundred-mile road trip back to Texas calmed Isabelle and gave her time to think things over. Six months on the lam had changed the Gun Girl, tempered her innate rancor, softened her gangster demeanor, sweetened her temperament, and opened her heart to new possibilities.

"The Gentleman," a snarky daily column appearing in the *Odessa American*, wrote on April 30, 1941: "Well! Well! Isabelle, belle of the ball and chain, is due back in town. . . . We can't wait to see what all the excitement's about, but the national press services are awaiting her arrival as anxiously as they used to watch for the stork at the imperial palace."

When her car pulled up in front of the Ector County courthouse on May 1, 1941, to the press corps' surprise, Isabelle stepped out of the car neatly dressed in a purple-checked skirt, a tailored white blouse with peaked shoulders, white shoes, and a broad, serene smile that exuded her newfound peace. She was still smiling when she stepped into the solitary jail cell reserved for her.

As the door clinked shut behind her, a reporter asked if she had given up trying to escape and reconciled the punishment awaiting her.

Isabelle immediately replied, "Yes, I'm going to pay my debt to society and get this three-year sentence behind me. When I get out, I want to start all over, get a job, and live an ordinary life."

Epilogue

Isabelle was transferred to the penitentiary in Huntsville, Texas, four weeks later. Her three-year sentence was reduced by half, and a small article in the December 22, 1942, *Arizona Republic* of Phoenix reported that she had been returned to Clinton, New Jersey, in October to complete her sentence at the women's reformatory. After that, except for one retrospective article in the April 19, 1947, *Tipton Daily Tribune* about her 1940 capture at the Ritz Theater, historians are hard-pressed to find her name in another newspaper.

That's likely the way she wanted it. She'd had her fill of headline-making when she entered that Texas penitentiary in the spring of 1941.

Today, a few longtime Elwood residents still remember their Gun Girl—"this bright young woman, this mite of a girl with the rolling eyes and a sense of humor." Her name sparks a wistful smile. To some, Isabelle

Messmer was nothing more than an outlaw. To others, she represented an exciting lifestyle free of restraints, rules, and expectations—albeit not without foolish risks, dangers, and hurtful consequences. It must not be overlooked that she took a life, and there is nothing admirable in that.

What is admirable, people say, is that Isabelle ultimately grew up, admitted that the "big-time excitement" she craved wasn't all it was cracked up to be, accepted her punishment, and lived a most spectacular "ordinary life."

PART VIII
UNSOLVED BUT UNFORGOTTEN

19

MURDER MOST FOUL

NOBLESVILLE, 1901

The night an assassin's bullet claimed the life of John Seay, he had never been happier. His heart was overflowing with love for the beautiful Noblesville socialite Carrie Phillips, and she loved him too. He had courted her since October and, from the first, he'd had but one thought on his mind. She already had accepted his marriage proposal. Christmas, only three days away, would be the perfect occasion to make their engagement official by asking Carrie's father for his permission—a mere formality, of course. Their family and friends all expected them to marry.

Between one and two o'clock the morning of December 22, 1901, Seay, who was assistant head miller at the Noblesville Milling Company, finished his nightly inspection rounds and, as was his custom, slipped away to the quiet, back stairwell for a moment alone. Seating himself on the fourth step of the second-floor landing, he pulled out a pocket knife and began to trim his nails.

A cold chill prickled shimmied down Seay's spine. Indiana had been trapped in a deep freeze for days, and that night, the mercury dropped to its lowest point of the year—well past ten below. He turned up the collar on his wool jacket and glanced upward at the window over his shoulder. It was shut, but apparently the brittle outside air had found a way in

John Seay was murdered by a bullet to the back of his head during the early morning hours of December 22, 1901, as he took a work break from his shift at the Noblesville Mill. *Photo courtesy Hoosier State Chronicles; originally published June 10, 1902, by the* Indianapolis News.

through the cracks around the wooden frame. As he returned to his nail grooming, thoughts of Carrie likely filled his head—her lilting laugh, her fetching smile, her eyes . . . those sparkling, hazel eyes that had melted his soul.

Perhaps his intense focus on the love of his life is what caused the scraping sound at the window to escape his attention. A second later, a shotgun blast blew a wide hole in the glass and an earsplitting explosion ripped through the stairwell. The force of the shot drove a lethal wad of bird shot into the back of Seay's neck and propelled his body forward, down the three steps, and onto the floor. Death was instantaneous for John Seay. He never knew what hit him.

Seay, twenty-seven, was a native of Richmond, Virginia. He had moved to Noblesville seven years earlier, drawn there by the promise of a future at the flour mill. Humble and reserved, he was well liked and popular; his affability and gentle personality had earned him many friends. Before his murder, no one imagined he'd had an enemy in the world. But after, one man—a self-obsessed, failing businessman named William Fodrea—stood out as a likely suspect.

Even though Fodrea and Seay had never formally met, the two were bound by a force more powerful than life and death. They both loved Carrie Phillips.

Suspect Arrested

Night patrolman J. L. Carey had been patrolling the train depot when the shot rang out. The moment he heard it, he rushed across the street to the mill and set to work, searching for the source of the gunfire. A mill worker named Frank Bond spotted Carey and shouted, "This way." Carey followed Bond into the stairwell, and there he found Seay's blood-soaked body lying faceup. Carey sent a messenger to the police station, and soon three more law enforcement officers—Town Marshal Owen, Deputy Sheriff Everett Bray, and Patrolman Stephenson—joined him at the crime scene. Together, the men looked for clues, bandied about likely motives, and mulled over possible suspects.

Noblesville in 1901 was a bustling but still relatively small community, and residents were well acquainted with one another. They kept tabs on their neighbors—across the street or across town—and what they were up to. There were few secrets. Who was sleeping with whom, blossoming romances, lovers' quarrels, and even jealous suitors were all fair game for local gossipmongers. So when John Seay turned up dead—the back of his neck ripped apart by a load of bird shot—the first responders considered only one suspect: Seay's rival, William Fodrea.

Fodrea was the moody, melancholy, twenty-nine-year-old son of the former county recorder. After serving as deputy recorder during his father's administration, Fodrea opened a laundry. Entrepreneurship, he quickly learned, was not his forte, and he had been wringing the last few drops of life out of his foundering business for months.

The officers hotfooted it to the Fodrea home in Lincoln Park, several blocks north of the mill. Arriving around 3:00 a.m., they found a wired Fodrea, who had not yet been to bed. In fact, he was still wearing his street clothes and had returned only some fifteen minutes before.

"Where were you, Will?" the police asked.

"Downtown," Fodrea answered, explaining that he'd gone out around eleven o'clock.

The police probed deeper. "And what exactly were you doing all that time?"

"Sitting on the courthouse steps," Fodrea said, "trying to figure out a way to raise the money to pay the mortgage on my laundry."

The officers weren't buying it. No one in their right mind would spend three hours loitering downtown in the middle of the night, while the mercury plummeted to below zero.

"Sorry, Will," Carey said. "We've got to take you in."

Fodrea shrugged. "I suppose when you get me downtown, you'll tell me what you want with me."

"You know what we want with you, as well as we do," the officer said. Fodrea made no reply.

Jilted

After the police took Fodrea to jail, they paid an early morning visit to the Phillips home on East Harrison Street. Upon hearing the news of Seay's death, Carrie Phillips's knees buckled. She would have collapsed if not for her mother, Olive, who helped her to a chair in the parlor.

"It was Fodrea," Carrie said between gasps. Blinking back tears, she went on as the police gathered around her. "He was insanely jealous."

They had been casually acquainted for years, she explained, but early that year, Fodrea began to call weekly. The friendship started innocently enough, and Carrie never encouraged his affections. By spring, in Fodrea's estimation, the friendship had turned to love, even though Carrie still viewed him as merely a friend. Within a few months, Fodrea's attachment to her turned to obsession, and by late August, she felt compelled to insist that he stay away.

"I broke it off," Carrie said.

"What did he say?" asked one of the officers.

Carrie shrugged and shook her head. "He began to follow me and lurk around the neighborhood. He was once discovered hiding under the veranda. It was awful." She dabbed her eyes with a hankie. "He made me feel terribly uncomfortable."

Carrie's mother recalled the night a few weeks earlier when an angry Fodrea vowed to never give up Carrie, to never step aside so another man could have what was his. Fodrea had knocked at the door looking for Carrie, said Olive. When she informed him that her daughter was out with a young man, he pulled a notebook and pencil from his pocket and demanded the name of Carrie's new suitor.

"I wish now that I hadn't told him," Olive said, blinking.

The deputy stepped forward, eager for her to continue. "What did you tell him?"

"That Carrie's new beau was John Seay." Olive's face grew taut, her eyes moistened, and she raised a hand to her mouth.

"Go on," the deputy pressed. "What happened next?"

"He wrote it down," she said, "and when he looked up at me, something had changed. I could see it in his eyes. I could feel it. The man was filled with rage."

"Did he make a threat?" Town Marshal Owen asked.

"Not exactly," Olive said. "Only that he would attend to him later. And then he left."

Carrie jumped in, adding that Fodrea recently had said if she refused to keep his company, he would likely spend the remainder of his days in the penitentiary.

That was all the officers needed to hear. On Monday, December 23, the day following Seay's murder, prosecutor J. W. Beals went to the jail and questioned Fodrea relentlessly. The newspapers called it a "sweatbox examination," but Fodrea remained cool. He insisted he had nothing to do with Seay's murder, although the prosecutor noted, "The young man does not deny his infatuation for the girl, but he denies killing John Seay. If nothing more develops, conviction is out of the question, and he will be released."

The notion that police might set Fodrea free didn't set well with some in the community, and rumors of a lynching began to swell. As a precaution, the sheriff posted guards around the jail, and whispers of the threat by lawless vigilantes faded and died.

Seay Goes Home

The next day, Christmas Eve, the train transporting John Seay's body rolled into Richmond, Virginia, accompanied by J. F. Jackson and John Atkins of Noblesville. They were met by a delegation of Masons and Pythians.

"Mr. Seay was one of the most popular and beloved young men in Noblesville," Atkins told the Richmond *Times* reporter, "and the murder was one of the most dastardly I ever heard of."

Jackson added, "If the crowd could have had its way, there would have been one less man in Noblesville."

Meanwhile, back in Noblesville, two boys had found a double-barreled shotgun, minus the stock, beneath a pile of brush in the woods near Crownland Cemetery, not far from Fodrea's home. The barrel appeared to be new, and only the right chamber had been discharged. A wad that had

Will Fodrea was the primary suspect in the shooting death of John Seay. Fodrea was charged and tried, but he was found not guilty. *Photo courtesy Hoosier State Chronicles; originally published June 10, 1902, by the* Indianapolis News.

been found at the crime scene fit the weapon. It was a substantial piece of evidence, but the police couldn't tie it to Fodrea. It, like everything else that pointed to Fodrea, was not clear-cut.

Police determined that no such gun had been sold in Noblesville. However, it could be ordered from the latest Lyon Brothers of Chicago catalog, which Fodrea possessed. Was it a coincidence? Police wanted desperately to prove the shotgun belonged to Fodrea, but fingerprinting as a criminal investigation tool had not yet been adopted in the United States. Even after questioning every gun dealer in Hamilton and surrounding counties, investigators were never able to tie the shotgun to Fodrea.

With Fodrea locked up and no new developments in the case to report, the press lost interest. Not a word about the case appeared in print again until March 11, 1902, the day after the grand jury returned its indictment, charging Fodrea with murder in the first degree. Deputy Sheriff Bray served Fodrea with an arrest warrant, even though he had been confined to his jail cell since December 22. To the disappointment of the scandal-starved public, Fodrea accepted the warrant with an eye roll and a sigh, showing the same lack of interest he had displayed during his initial arrest. Since suspects charged with first-degree murder were not entitled to bail, Fodrea would remain locked up until the next court session. That wouldn't be until June.

Order in the Court

A suppressed murmur swept through the Hamilton County courtroom on the morning of June 9, 1902, when William Fodrea confidently breezed in. A pair of deputies flanked him, and his beautiful sister, Leota, followed. Fodrea was nicely dressed in a neat, well-fitting, dark suit. Although he was pale and drawn, thanks to his long confinement in jail, his appearance and demeanor made striking statements of good taste and self-assurance. He and Leota took their places at the defense table and conferred with his attorneys. They paid no attention to the gawking onlookers who packed the courtroom. Even Carrie Phillips, striking in her emerald green dress, could not divert spectators' eyes from Fodrea.

"Looking at him," the *Hamilton County Democrat* wrote, "one would figure him as about the last man on earth to commit such a heinous crime."

On calling order in the court, circuit court judge John F. Neal invited members of the press to the bench for an impromptu confab. Reporters, surprised by the unusual request, gathered before the judge. Neal offered no apology and sternly reminded the press corps of their responsibility to report only the facts of the trial and stressed that only those who checked their biases regarding Fodrea's guilt or innocence at the door would be welcome in his courtroom. Although short of censoring the press, Neal warned the reporters that because of the division of sentiment over the guilt or innocence of Fodrea, sensationalized stories that inflamed or excited the public would not be tolerated.

In his opening remarks, prosecuting attorney Ralph Kane laid out a graphic depiction of Seay's final moments and the grisly aftermath of his assassination. While Kane addressed the enthralled courtroom, Carrie Phillips pressed her hankie to her eyes and wept softly. Fodrea, on the other hand, gazed around the room and appeared unaffected by the oratory.

Testimony kicked off the afternoon. The prosecuting attorney grilled a string of witnesses—the man who found Seay's body, the doctor who examined it, a witness who claimed he'd seen Fodrea skulking around the mill shortly before the shooting, the head miller who refused to hire Fodrea, and the Hamilton County jail inmate who swore Fodrea identified the type of gun that fired the lethal shot. One by one, each witness helped the prosecution build an airtight, although circumstantial, case to seal Fodrea's guilt.

Carrie Phillips was the young woman who was loved by both John Seay and his accused killer, Will Fodrea. *Photo courtesy Hoosier State Chronicles; originally published June 11, 1902, by the* Indianapolis News.

On day two of the trial, the prosecuting attorney called his star witness. Carrie Phillips rose from her front-row seat. She was the picture of understated good taste in her starched black taffeta skirt that rustled with each step, a white shirtwaist blouse edged in black, and a white hat topped with black plumes. Spectators craned their necks to watch the young woman slowly make her way to the stand.

Seating herself in the witness chair, Carrie radiated confidence as she answered prosecuting attorney Kane's questions. She told the court she had known Fodrea casually for four years, and late last spring, he began calling for her once a week. It didn't take long, she said, until he wanted more from her than she was willing to give. Carrie had told Fodrea time and again to no avail that she wasn't interested. She finally put a stop to it in early fall.

Carrie's shoulders slumped, and she lowered her eyes. The onlookers' whispers ceased, and the room grew still and tense. A bristling beat passed, and Kane stepped toward the witness, closing the gap between them to an arm's length. In a low voice, he nudged her on.

"Miss Phillips," he said, "please tell the court how you put a stop to it."

Carrie's gaze met Kane's. She nodded once. "I told him I could not go with him any longer." Her tone had grown unapologetic, deliberate. "But you know Will. He seemed not to understand and insisted I tell him my reason."

"And you gave it to him, I presume," Kane said.

"Yes," Carrie answered, pressing her lips into a hard line.

"What was the reason you gave?"

"I said I simply didn't want to be with him. I didn't care for him and never would. I told him emphatically to stay away from me."

The humiliating dismissal could not have been clearer. However, Fodrea refused to accept the obvious. The second week of October, he again knocked on the Phillips's front door, and Carried had repeated her repudiation.

"He told me I would see the time when I would be sorry that I did not go with him," she said, "and I would regret that I had treated him as I have. He declared many times that if he could not have me, no one else could."

In the cross-examination, the defense attorney asked Carrie when she had become acquainted with John Seay.

"October 6," she replied.

On day three of the trial, the defense attorney, W. S. Christian, made his opening statement, announcing that the defendant, William Fodrea, would not testify on his own behalf. "The defense," said Christian, "will show that the defendant has an unblemished reputation, and that alone would overcome all the proof submitted by the state."

Christian called four witnesses who, one after the other, dismantled the testimony that had been so carefully laid out by the prosecution. Effective as Christian's witnesses had been, it was the testimony of Fodrea's younger sister, Leota, on day four that turned the tide in his favor.

"When the white face—with its big, staring eyes and frail little form—faced the great crowd in the courtroom," the June 13, 1902, edition of the *Indianapolis News* reported, "there was an unusual scene. . . . The eyes of two or three of the jurors became moist, and women hid their faces behind their fans. Even the attorney for the state was misty about the eyes as the witness, in her childish, prattling way, told how she and Will played together as children, how he used to run away to a machine shop and work, and how she would go with him. . . . She told of the dolls he made her, the mechanical toys he constructed, and the engines he built."

Everyone in the room seemed to realize that the delicate, devoted sister was pleading for her brother, and it appeared that her testimony had produced the desired effect.

Before the defense rested, it called Fodrea's father, Levi, to the stand. Levi testified that his son was home the night of the assassination and not sitting on the courthouse steps, as his son had previously told police.

Levi Fodrea, the final witness, stepped off the stand, and both sides—the prosecution and the defense—made their closing arguments. At three o'clock, Judge Neal turned the case over to the jury.

What the jury would decide was anybody's guess. Both sides were confident. The prosecution team, declaring that the defense was weak, felt they had made a good case; while the defense insisted the state's evidence was insufficient to erase the presumption of their client's innocence. Not in twenty years, the *Indianapolis News* proclaimed, had there been a case in the Hamilton Circuit Court that attracted so much attention.

Verdict

The jury deliberated just one hour. After four ballots, the jury reached its eagerly awaited verdict.

The scene in the courtroom sizzled. Spectators' emotions were as hot as the sunbaked air that pressed in on them. Judge Neal cautioned the spectators to keep their voices down and to remain civil. A buzz of muffled chatter persisted, but when the jury foreman handed the verdict to Judge Neal, silence befell the room.

The judge unfolded the paper and studied the words written neatly across it. Raising an eyebrow, he handed the paper to the clerk, who read it to the anxious audience. "We the jury," he said, "find the defendant not guilty."

A collective gasp seemed to suck the oxygen out of the room. Fodrea, revealing no emotion, looked at his mother. She grasped his hand and smiled. Once Fodrea fully digested what he had just heard, he rose from the defense table and approached the twelve men of the jury, shaking their hands and speaking quietly with them. Leota, absent for the reading of the verdict, entered the courtroom and rushed to her brother to embrace him. The Fodrea family then escorted William home. Six months had passed since he'd last walked through his front door.

Summing up the trial and the outcome, the *Indianapolis Journal* reported, "Thus ends the second act in the most mysterious tragedy that ever occurred in Hamilton County." The *Hamilton County Democrat* wrote, "That so heinous a crime should be committed and go unpunished is to be regretted. It is a great disgrace to the county."

Epilogue

The police who worked the Seay murder case had only one suspect and believed Fodrea was a shoo-in for a guilty verdict. When their suspect was acquitted, no other suspect was ever considered. Although William Fodrea lacked a solid alibi for the night of John Seay's murder, he did have his family's sterling reputation to his credit and a jury that may have overplayed the reasonable doubt card.

What became of Fodrea? Was the shame of a murder trial enough to permanently sully his reputation? To ruin the rest of his life? To shame him into permanent hiding?

A year after the trial, according to the *Fort Wayne Sentinel*, Fodrea invented a canning machine, and in 1908, he and a partner astonished Noblesville crowds with their homemade automobile, dubbed "Beetle Flyer." Fodrea left Noblesville a year later and settled in Little Rock, Arkansas, where he and his wife, Minnie, remained for the rest of their lives. Over the years, he received many patents for his mechanical inventions. He died May 16, 1951.

20

THE STRANGE DEATH OF GARNET GINN

PORTLAND, 1950

Portland, Indiana, school superintendent Donald S. Weller had a bad feeling on that Tuesday morning in late February 1950. Garnet Ginn, his highly regarded home economics teacher, was missing. She had not called in, nor was she answering her phone. None of her friends had seen or heard from her since their sorority meeting the night before. Shrugging off her responsibilities at school was not her style.

By 11:00 a.m., Weller was certain something was terribly wrong. He drove to Garnet's apartment at 199 East Arch Street, and, seeking answers, he knocked on her door. When he got no response, he went around the corner to the two-car garage at 318 North Harrison, where Garnet rented a space for her 1949 Pontiac. Hoping to find a clue, Weller wasn't sure what would be worse—finding her parked car or finding an empty spot.

Weller entered the dark garage and shone a flashlight through the driver-side window of Garnet's car. The open purse and a powder puff on the front seat piqued his curiosity, prompting him to walk around the back of the vehicle to the passenger side. He flashed his light beam on the cement floor and was drawn to a large object in the shadows a few inches beyond the light's penumbra. He swept the beam upward to illuminate the entire area, and paralyzing reality began falling into place.

Garnet Ginn's body was found February 28, 1950, in her garage. At first, investigators deemed her death a suicide, but today Portland police are certain she was murdered and believe they have identified her killer. *Photo courtesy Jay County Historical Museum.*

When the light settled on a woman's face—mouth agape, sightless eyes fixed upward—Weller recoiled in horror. He had found his missing teacher.

Garnet, who stood five-foot-eight and weighed 135 pounds, was wedged in a fourteen-inch space between her automobile and the wall. Perched on her left knee, she was suspended in an upright position by a taut, narrow strap—one end tied to the car door's handle, the other looped around her neck.

Weller dropped his flashlight and rushed to the neighbor's house to phone the police.

Till We Meet Again

Thirty-three-year-old Garnet Ginn was born in Fulton County in 1916 into a family of educators. She earned her own teaching degree in 1940 from Ball State Teachers College. In 1943, after a brief teaching stint in Albany, Indiana, she moved twenty-five miles east to Portland and taught high school home economics.

Garnet was a popular teacher, well liked by students and faculty. Outside the school, she made friends easily. One of her neighbors, Addie Sonafrank, described Garnet as "a high type girl. Very careful of her actions and very precise." While Garnet was known for her sunny disposition and upbeat, positive outlook on life, she was never frivolous. She kept her social life a private matter, dating only occasionally and never flaunting her male friends for public scrutiny at the risk of uncharitable scuttlebutt. She took herself and her place in the community seriously and never turned a blind eye to the influence a high school teacher wielded.

On the evening of February 27, Garnet attended a Psi Iota Xi party with her sorority sisters at the Jay County Country Club. One of the sorority members later reported that during a songfest at the party, Garnet had requested two numbers—"God Be with You Till We Meet Again" and "Goodbye, Sweetheart"—and sang along joyfully. Another said Garnet had been in good spirits all day.

When the meeting ended around 10:30 p.m., Garnet gave one of the women a lift home and continued on. She lived only two blocks up the street. None of her friends reported seeing or hearing from her after that. If someone knew what happened next, it was never spoken of.

Garnet's funeral was held three days later, on Thursday, March 2, at the Portland Methodist Church. Burial was the next afternoon in the Akron Independent Order of Odd Fellows Cemetery in Fulton County.

Suicide or Murder?

The day following the discovery of Garnet's body, Wednesday, March 1, newspapers throughout Indiana reported her death in prominent front-page stories. Although light on details, the reports stated that Jay County coroner Donald Spahr would withhold his verdict until the police completed their investigations. Conversely, the papers also reported that Portland police chief Clyde Kegerreis had already dismissed the possibility of murder. He even ruled out foul play.

Why or how the lead law enforcement official on Garnet's case could make such a statement was puzzling, particularly so early in the investigation, while the circumstances of her death were so precarious.

The next day, the *Muncie Evening Press* reported that the coroner had settled on strangulation as the cause of death. The story went on to note that he claimed the body bore no marks or signs of violence, which is why, he said, he believed Garnet took her own life. Although Spahr stopped short of calling his opinion "official," his dismissal of murder was as puzzling as Kegerreis's.

Without explanation, by Friday, March 3, local and state police had all but closed the book on the case, declaring Garnet Ginn's death "most likely" a suicide. That news was the last about Garnet for the next five weeks.

Perhaps the investigation would have stopped there had it not been for the actions of her family.

Pleas to Press

On Friday, April 14, several Indiana newspapers published a front-page story announcing the findings of a secret autopsy performed by the Indiana State Police on the exhumed remains of Garnet Ginn. The stories explained that within days following Garnet's March 2 funeral, her frustrated parents—Gail and Estil Ginn of Mount Summit—had contacted the *Indianapolis Star* complaining about the Portland authorities' "slipshod" investigation. They asked for the *Star*'s help in clearing the stigma of suicide that had stained Garnet's memory and thus removing the Portland police–imposed barrier to identifying and bringing her killer to justice.

As far as the family was concerned, suicide didn't fit. They said Garnet never complained and was almost always cheerful and upbeat. She had last been back to Mount Summit to visit her parents in mid-February and had been in high spirits then. "I feel that I am really in a position to enjoy myself now," she had told her mother. "I have my car, I am getting my master's degree, and I am sitting on top of the world."

When the Ginn family first approached the *Indianapolis Star*, the paper's editor agreed that the circumstances seemed to point to murder. He urged the family to reach out to the Indiana State Police to request an autopsy on their daughter's remains.

That's exactly what the family did. On April 12, Garnet's body was exhumed from its Fulton County grave and transported to Indianapolis General Hospital, where a staff pathologist performed the autopsy.

The autopsy reportedly found that Garnet had been struck seven times over the head with a blunt weapon. She also had been choked, and both her knees were bruised and the left was badly cut. For the family, the findings confirmed what they had been certain of: Garnet Ginn had been murdered.

Contaminated and Trampled Crime Scene

Almost as astonishing as the autopsy results were the reports that the day Garnet's body was discovered, curious bystanders, mortuary employees, and even police had contaminated the crime scene before the arrival of the Jay County coroner. In addition, according to the *Muncie Star*, the undertaker had already removed the body from the crime scene, preventing Spahr from making a thorough examination of the body.

The Ginn family had also given Indiana State Police chief technician Charles A. Davis the clothing Garnet had been wearing the night she died, so he could evaluate it for trace evidence. The clothing examination showed that Garnet's fur coat was ripped and dirt covered its back; the backs of her gloves were dirty, and the palms were stained with blood; the underarm seams of her blouse were ripped, its neck soiled, and part of the collar was torn loose; the knee of her left stocking was in shreds; and her shoes were freshly scuffed.

Davis later journeyed to the parents' home in Mount Summit to examine their daughter's automobile. He discovered blood on the rear fenders and along the passenger side leading to the door handle. Davis concluded that Garnet was likely attacked on the driver side as she stepped out.

The *Indianapolis News* asked Spahr for a comment about the autopsy results, but he declined until he made "further investigation." Speaking in his own defense, Spahr claimed he had talked with the family about an autopsy back in early March. But they turned it down, he said. Whether his claim was substantiated by the family was never reported.

Portland chief of police Clyde Kegerreis, who had told the *Indianapolis News* in March that Garnet's death was likely a suicide, could not be reached for comment prior to the release of the April 14 story. The *Indianapolis News* did, however, reach Jay County prosecutor Keith Fraser before the story went to press, but he declined to comment until he read the autopsy report.

The *Indianapolis Star*'s intervention opened the Portland community's eyes and begged the question: Were the local authorities simply incompetent, or had they deliberately stymied the investigation? And if they had, what was their motive?

The same day, Arthur E. Graham, editor of Portland's weekly paper, the *Graphic*, released a special edition filled with stories about the case.

Frustrated at the pace of the investigation and eager for answers, Graham announced that the *Graphic* was offering a $500 reward for information leading to the arrest and conviction of the murderer.

Developments Finally Unfurl

The *Muncie Evening Press* reported that the night of Garnet's death, Mrs. Raymond Willert Smith, who lived next door to Garnet's garage, heard a scream shortly before 11:00 p.m. "It was late . . . and we heard her come in," Smith said. "My husband and I got up and went to see what was the matter."

When a cat darted across the driveway, Smith figured she'd been mistaken about the scream. However, she did see a figure moving inside the garage but assumed it was Garnet. She also noticed Garnet's headlights were still burning. At 6:30 the next morning, when Smith's husband drove his car out of the garage, which they shared with Garnet, her headlights were off.

Garnet's billfold and driver's license were missing from the scene of the crime. A change purse in her handbag, sitting open on the front seat, contained only a dime. According to Mrs. Robert Jones, who had attended the February 27 sorority meeting, Garnet had offered to buy soft drinks for her sorority sisters that night at the country club. Debit and credit cards were unheard of in 1950; thus, Garnet's offer suggested that she had far more than ten cents on her that evening.

According to the *Muncie Star*, investigators didn't know whether robbery was the motive or the billfold was taken to conceal the real motive.

Following the autopsy, the family spoke with the state police and pushed for a full investigation. The police were already on top of it. Major Robert A. O'Neal, executive officer of the state police, immediately ordered a "full scale" investigation and placed Detective Sergeant Frank Jessup of the Pendleton post in charge.

The Saturday, April 15, *Muncie Star* reported that two men were being sought for questioning. One of the men lived in Portland and the other in Lafayette. Both reportedly had known Garnet for some time, both had dated her, and both were prominent in their communities.

The information broke the previous day, shortly after Indiana State Police launched their full-scale investigation, questioning everyone who had been with Garnet in the hours before her death and others who had known her during the seven years she had taught at Portland High School. The investigators traced her movements on her last day—from 7:30 a.m., when she arrived at the school, until approximately 10:30 p.m., when she dropped off her sorority sister and headed for home.

The *Muncie Star* revealed more new information in its Sunday, April 16, edition. According to the state police, about two weeks before her death, Garnet had told a close friend that one of the men under surveillance surprised her one evening in her garage. Speaking on anonymity, the friend told the newspaper that Garnet had walked to her garage, intending to drive to a meeting, and found the man waiting for her and ready to go for a ride. Garnet had denied she was going anywhere and puttered around her car, engaging the man in small talk until he finally left. According to the friend, the man had "forced his attentions" on Garnet several times before.

The state police would not reveal the identity of the man in question.

Threats and Rewards

The next day, Monday, April 17, the *Palladium-Item* of Richmond reported that Merle Burdg, a veteran writer at the *Graphic* in Portland, had received a threatening telephone call regarding the Ginn case. Burdg claimed that an unidentified man phoned her on April 6 and told her to "lay off that murder case." At that time, Garnet's body had not yet been autopsied, and the Portland authorities still asserted that the death was a suicide.

Burdg also revealed that she had rushed to Garnet's garage after learning she had been found dead. Shortly after Burdg's arrival, she noticed a deep heel print in the dirt floor about twelve inches from the driver-side door of Garnet's automobile. "I pointed this out to Portland Chief of Police Clyde Kegerreis and other police officers," Burdg said, "but they just laughed it off." The imprint of the heel was so deep, Burdg said, it seemed that whomever it belonged to had lost his balance "and his entire weight fell on that foot, or he might have been carrying a heavy load."

The next day, Tuesday, April 18, the *Indianapolis Star* announced that it was offering a $1,000 reward for evidence leading to the arrest of Garnet Ginn's killer. Jay County sheriff Clarence Bishop also offered a $200 reward. These, added to the *Graphic*'s previously announced $500 reward, brought the total bounty to $1,700.

The article in the *Muncie Star* mentioned that police had found bloodstains on the headlight switch in Garnet's car. Could the bloody light switch have indicated that her killer turned off the lights? The paper speculated that the bloody light switch proved that Garnet had been seized before she could turn off the lights. Perhaps the scream her neighbor heard had occurred as Garnet was being abducted and dragged from her car by the intruder, whose heel print had been embedded in the dirt floor. The paper theorized that Garnet was likely choked as she was dragged from the car. If that's what happened, she may have sustained some of the blows in this struggle. The blood spatters on both sides of the car, the back, and inside, suggest that some of the blood may have belonged to her killer.

Thus, the *Indianapolis Star*'s appeal to the public for leads pointing to suspects included these words: "The murderer probably had a bloody nose the night of Feb. 27 or a bite on his hands or face."

Mayoral Mitigation

Responding to the recent barrage of news reports about the Portland police department's failure to zero in on obvious clues, Portland's mayor Albert Abramson felt obliged to issue a public statement. In it, he dismissed the charges that the Portland police "bungled" the investigation as "grossly exaggerated." And while Abramson praised the state police for their work on the case, he did not explain how the criticism of his police force was unfounded.

Public reaction to Abramson's statement probably wasn't what he had hoped for. The next day, Tuesday, April 18, the *Elwood Call-Leader* printed a page-two opinion piece that argued, "Any police chief who overlooks as many murder clues as the Portland police overlooked in the murder of Miss Garnet Ginn, and then takes the easy way out by passing the murder off as a suicide, should be fired."

The piece called the chief and his men lazy for ignoring the obvious evidence that Garnet's body, clothing, and automobile bore the signs of a struggle. It credited the *Indianapolis Star* for assisting Garnet's parents in obtaining permission for the exhumation and the autopsy. As the *Call-Leader* noted, both were measures the local authorities should have pursued. "When, and if, there is a conviction," the article continued, "the Portland police should hide its face. Members of the department might try digging ditches or mowing lawns or take up some other vocation that does not require a little extra effort to do a job as it should be done."

Case Is a Dead Duck

As days passed, the larger city news agencies tried to keep the Garnet Ginn story front and center, but with no new developments, the stories grew shorter and more infrequent. The Purdue suspect was cleared, while the other—the high-profile Portland resident—was reportedly still under observation. Two new suspects were hinted at, but the state police wouldn't comment, and nothing ever came of the allegations. Garnet's missing wallet was never found, and no other witnesses came forward.

A May 11 *Muncie Evening Press* editorial addressed a reader who had called, asking whether the papers had tired of the Ginn case and simply dropped their coverage of it. The writer assured the reader that the newspapers remained highly interested, but when there was nothing new to report, and as long as the state police maintained its stock statement, "It's still being worked on," there was little the news reporters could do to keep the story alive.

"Will there be new developments soon?" asked the *Muncie Evening Press* editorial. "This writer is beginning to have his doubts. Evidence doesn't get any easier to find as time goes on. And, despite the old saying, 'murder doesn't always come out.'"

A few days later, papers reported that Jay County coroner Donald Spahr had filed his official verdict in the Ginn case, listing "death by strangulation" as the cause of death. What he didn't mention, however, was the manner. Was it suicide or murder? Spahr still wouldn't say.

According to Spahr, the injuries to Garnet's scalp and knees were insufficient to deduce foul play. He also dismissed strangulation at the hands of an assailant because the hyoid bone in her neck hadn't been broken. The grotesque positioning of Garnet's body, the blood on and in the car, the rips in her clothing, the heel print in the dirt, the reports that Garnet had been accosted in her garage just a few days before her death, and the scream heard by the next-door neighbor the night of Garnet's death apparently were insufficient to persuade Spahr that his official decision was wrong.

Perhaps it was the *Muncie Evening Press*'s editorial of June 15 that best summarized public opinion of the coroner's official verdict. "What is the matter with the police in this case?" the editorial asked. "Well, in the first place, the Portland police don't think there was anything wrong, and they seemed to be caught flat-footed in an error that lots of people would call plain stupid. They still seem to prefer to close the case as a mystery." Quoting the editor of the *Graphic,* Portland's newspaper, the *Muncie Evening Press* editorial concluded, "The case is pretty much a dead duck."

Renewed Interest Brings New Tip

Fast forward to November 28, 2018. Dozens of Portland community residents gathered for a downtown meeting with Portland police officials to discuss the Garnet Ginn case. Some of the attendees had lived in the city when the strange death occurred. A woman who had been a Portland High School student back then recalled Garnet as her favorite teacher. Another who had been a child in 1950 vividly remembered the gossip about who might have committed the murder.

Current Portland police investigator Todd Wickey wanted answers and wondered whether modern technology or new leads might provide breakthroughs. Unfortunately, all of the evidence—original case notes, blood, fingerprints, clothing, the autopsy report—disappeared long ago, forcing Wickey to build his case on faded memories and newspaper reports.

But three months later, Wickey got lucky. He received a credible tip naming a person of interest. The alleged suspect was a man, long deceased, with ties to Garnet Ginn. The scenario described by the tipster made sense to Wickey and convinced him that the new person of interest actually could be Garnet's killer. However, because there was no physical evidence to prove the man's guilt, Wickey chose not to disclose his suspect's name.

Some of the Portland residents expressed disappointment at the outcome, while others were relieved that the new information exonerated individuals long rumored to be suspects. Ultimately, perhaps the *Graphic*'s editor, Arthur E. Graham, had it right after all when he wrote, "The case is pretty much a dead duck."

BIBLIOGRAPHY

The newspaper stories noted here are listed in the order they appeared in print.

Chapter 1—The Mysterious Death of Belle Shenkenberger

"Mrs. Shenkenberger Passes Away after Illness of About Four Weeks." *Daily Crescent* (Frankfort, IN). August 27, 1898.

"Death of Mrs. Shenkenberger the Result of Slow Poisoning; Her Mother-in-Law Under Arrest, Charged with the Crime." *Daily Crescent* (Frankfort, IN). September 1, 1898.

"Now in Jail: Charged with Murder of Her Son's Wife." *Frankfort Banner*. September 3, 1898.

"Found Plenty of Arsenic; Probable Guilt." *Frankfort Crescent*. September 9, 1898.

"Dr. Hurty's Report: Seventeen and Eight-Tenths Grains of Arsenic Found in Mrs. Shenkenberger's Stomach." *Frankfort Crescent*. September 16, 1898.

"Plea of Abatement Filed: Mrs. Shenkenberger's Attorneys Take Exceptions to Miss Palmer's Presence." *Frankfort Crescent*. September 23, 1898.

"The Poisoning Case; Mrs. Shenkenberger's Trial for Alleged Murder." *Frankfort Crescent*. November 25, 1898.

"On Trial for Murder: Sarah A. Shenkenberger Is Called to Face a Clinton County Jury." *Frankfort Banner*. November 26, 1898.

"The Shenkenberger Case; Evidence on Both Sides All in and Arguments Begin Today." *Frankfort Crescent*. December 2, 1898.

"Guilty as Charged." *Frankfort Crescent*. December 9, 1898.

"Not Granted a New Trial: Court Sentences Mrs. Shenkenberger to Prison for Life This Morning." *Frankfort Crescent*. December 23, 1898.

"To Prison for Life; Mrs. Shenkenberger Hears the Sentence Unmoved." *Frankfort Crescent*. December 30, 1898.

"Christmas Dawn Teems with Joy for Aged Woman; Pardon for Mrs. Shenkenberger Comes from Gov. Ralston." *Frankfort Crescent News*. December 23, 1913.

Chapter 2—The Liberation of Nora Coleman

"Mrs. Ward Coleman of Jackson Twp. Slays with Shotgun." *Angola Herald*. February 8, 1918.
"Murderess Picks out Coffin for Victim." *Fort Wayne Journal-Gazette*. February 8, 1918.
"Woman Admits Killing Mother, Justifies Crime." *Indianapolis Star*. February 8, 1918.
"Woman Makes Confession." *Fort Wayne News and Sentinel*. February 8, 1918.
"Confesses Murder: Mrs. Nora Coleman Talks Freely of Crime." *Steuben Republican*. February 13, 1918.
"Insanity Will Be Mrs. Ward Coleman's Defense." *Fort Wayne News and Sentinel*. February 14, 1918.
"Hope to Show Accused's Ancestors Acted Queerly." *Fort Wayne News and Sentinel*. February 26, 1918.
"Claims Insanity." *Steuben Republican*. February 27, 1918.
"Sister of Murdered Woman on the Stand." *Fort Wayne News and Sentinel*. February 27, 1918.
"Seek to Prove Woman Murderess Is Insane." *Huntington Press*. February 28, 1918.
"Dr. Says Mrs. Coleman Has Low Blood Pressure." *Fort Wayne News and Sentinel*. February 28, 1918.
"Woman Insane, Doctors Assert." *Indianapolis Star*. March 1, 1918.
"Mrs. Coleman Indifferent." *Indianapolis News*. March 2, 1918.
"Angola Jury Acquits Woman of Matricide." *Muncie Sunday Star*. March 3, 1918.
"Mrs. Coleman Goes to the Asylum." *Indianapolis Sunday Star*. March 3, 1918.
"Miss Nora Coleman Found to Be Insane." *Indianapolis News*. March 4, 1918.
"Mrs. Coleman Is Not Guilty." *Steuben Republican*. March 6, 1918.
"Court Refuses to Free Woman Who Slew Her Mother." *Garrett Clipper*. May 19, 1924.
"Nora Coleman Given Freedom." *Angola Herald*. March 22, 1929.
"Nora Coleman in Custody." *Steuben Republican*. September 11, 1929.
"Nora Coleman Given Liberty." *Steuben Republican*. September 18, 1929.
"Nora Coleman Sues for Divorce." *Angola Herald*. February 26, 1932.
"Death Notice." *Angola Herald*. September 25, 1957.

Book

Lombardo, Paul A. *Three Generations, No Imbeciles: Eugenics, the Supreme Court, and Buck v. Bell*. Baltimore: Johns Hopkins University Press, 2008.

Chapter 3—"Sweet Dreams, Mother"

"Mrs. Wm. M. Blake Murdered." *Anderson Morning Herald*. March 22, 1908.
"A Murderer Captured Here." *Fort Wayne News*. March 23, 1908.
"Earth Gently Closed One Chapter, Iron Grasp of Law Opened Another in Blake Tragedy." *Anderson Morning Herald*. March 24, 1908.
"Looks upon Dead Face of the Mother, Whom He Had Slain, Grover Blake Collapses." *Fort Wayne Journal-Gazette*. March 24, 1908.
"Inquest May Deny Story of Blake; Testimony Favorable to Reynolds' Effort to Prove Alibi." *Anderson Morning Herald*. March 26, 1908.

"Indictments against Grover Blake and Orzo Reynolds." *Anderson Morning Herald*. April 4, 1908.
"Insanity as Defense of Blake." *Anderson Morning Herald*. April 8, 1908.
"Self-Confessed Murderer to Be Arraigned in Court Today." *Anderson Morning Herald*. April 9, 1908.
"'Judge Was Easy,' Grover Blake, Self-Confessed Murderer, Said after Being Sentenced for Life." *Anderson Morning Herald*. April 10, 1908.
"Grover Blake Warns against Loose Habits." *Muncie Sunday Star*. April 12, 1908.
"Grover Blake to Prison Monday." *Anderson Morning Herald*. April 12, 1908.
"The Week's Events." *Elwood Free Press*. April 16, 1908.
"Effort to Have Grover Blake Transferred from Prison." *Fort Wayne Sentinel*. September 29, 1909.
"Father Asks Pardon Board to Free Son." *Indianapolis Star*. March 28, 1913.
"Another Parole Move for Grover Blake." *Anderson Herald*. July 22, 1913.
"Grover Blake Asks to Be Pardoned." *Huntington Herald*. June 20, 1914.
"Board of Parole Turns Down Appeal by Slayer of His Mother." *Fort Wayne Sentinel*. June 23, 1914.
"Grover Blake Seeks Pardon." *Indianapolis Star*. November 19, 1918.
"Body of Grover Blake Expected Here Today." *Anderson Herald*. February 11, 1920.

Chapter 4—Dan Snider and the Strychnine Solution

"Suspicion of Murder at Tipton." *Indianapolis Journal*. October 28, 1876.
"History of the Snyder [sic] Case." *Tipton Advocate*. September 2, 1881.
"Snyder [sic] Pardoned." *Indianapolis Journal*. November 2, 1893.
"It Was Our Dan." *Tipton Advocate*. June 21, 1895.
"Mrs. Dan Snyder [sic] Fatally Burned." *Tipton Daily Tribune*. March 23, 1920.
"Death Recalls Local Tragedy of Years Ago; Daniel Snyder [sic] Killed at Russiaville Thursday." *Tipton Daily Tribune*. June 7, 1929.

Legal Depositions

Georgia Evans, November 2, 1876
Dr. M. V. B. Vickrey, November 2, 1876
C. C. Bowlin, November 16, 1876
Dr. H. G. Evans, November 2 and November 16, 1876
Dr. J. M. Grove, November 16, 1876
Cassius King, November 16, 1876
John S. Mount, November 16, 1876
Mrs. John Mount, November 16, 1876
John Snider, November 16, 1876

Chapter 5—The Case of the Drowsy Uxoricide

"Kills Wife Who Left Him, Shoots Himself in Head." *Indianapolis News*. June 5, 1911.
"Wife Murderer Indicted; Cicero Man Tells Coroner He Remembers Nothing of Crime." *Indianapolis Star*. June 17, 1911.
"Slayer of Wife Escapes Jail." *Indianapolis Star*. September 23, 1911.

"Hiatt Is Brought Back to Jail by Relatives." *Indianapolis News*. September 23, 1911.
"Hiatt Returns to His Cell." *Indianapolis Sunday Star*. September 24, 1911.
"Insanity Is Defense Made by Attorneys for Hiatt." *Indianapolis Star*. October 17, 1911.
"Hiatt Case Goes to Jury." *Indianapolis News*. October 25, 1911.
"Jury in Hiatt Murder Trial Fails to Agree; Discharged after 55 Hours Deliberation." *Indianapolis News*. October 28, 1911.
"Mrs. Voss Tells Court of Daughter's Murder; Harry Hiatt Sleeps during Recital of Crime." *Indianapolis News*. January 16, 1912.
"Hiatt Defense Rests." *Indianapolis Star*. January 23, 1912.
"Hiatt Testimony Ends." *Indianapolis Star*. January 25, 1912.
"Hiatt Gets Life Term; 16-Day Trial Ends in Conviction of Wife Murderer." *Indianapolis Sunday Star*. January 28, 1912.
"6 Long-Term Felons Seek Board's Help." *Hammond Times*. November 18, 1936.
"Harry E. Hiatt, Arcadia, Succumbs." *Tipton Daily Tribune*. December 22, 1959.

Records from Indiana State Prison

Case History, February 2, 1922–December 19, 1945
Discharge from Parole, signed by Indiana governor Ralph F. Gates, December 19, 1945

Chapter 6—Death on Maish Road

"Woman Found Dead in Auto." *Frankfort Morning Times*. February 2, 1932.
"Grand Jury Is Called to Investigate Death." *Frankfort Morning Times*. February 3, 1932.
"Investigation of Grand Jury Is Not Complete; Dead Woman's Mother Comes to This City." *Frankfort Morning Times*. February 4, 1932.
"Gladden Is Indicted for First Degree Murder. *Frankfort Morning Times*. February 7, 1932.
"Gladden's First Inning in Court Is Feb. 20th." *Frankfort Morning Times*. February 9, 1932.
"Gladden Withdraws Petition for Writ of Habeas Corpus." *Frankfort Morning Times*. February 26, 1932.
"Seek to Quash Five Counts in Gladden Case." *Frankfort Morning Times*. March 6, 1932.
"Gladden's Murder Trial Will Begin Monday." *Frankfort Morning Times*. April 10, 1932.
"Fail to Get Gladden Jury on the First Day; Mother of Dead Woman Creates Scene in Room after Court Adjourns." *Frankfort Morning Times*. April 12, 1932.
"Six State Witnesses Heard in Gladden Case." *Frankfort Morning Times*. April 13, 1932.
"Gladden Had $11,000 Insurance on His Wife." *Frankfort Morning Times*. April 14, 1932.
"Illicit Love Affair Charged by State." *Frankfort Morning Times*. April 15, 1932.
"Gladden Unmoved by Wife's Death, Police Say." *Frankfort Morning Times*. April 16, 1932.

"Gladden Trial Marked by Dramatic Scene." *Frankfort Morning Times*. April 18, 1932.

"Chittick Testifies Carbon Monoxide Gas Caused Death of Mrs. Gladden." *Frankfort Morning Times*. April 20, 1932.

"State Rests in Gladden Murder Trial; Dead Woman's Mother on Witness Stand." *Frankfort Morning Times*. April 21, 1932.

"Gladden May Go on Witness Stand." *Frankfort Morning Times*. April 22, 1932.

"Gladden on Witness Stand Nearly Five Hours." *Frankfort Morning Times*. April 26, 1932.

"Gladden Case Will Go to the Jury Today." *Frankfort Morning Times*. April 27, 1932.

"Gladden Guilty of First Degree Murder." *Frankfort Morning Times*. April 28, 1932.

"Gladden Is Taken to Michigan City Prison." *Frankfort Morning Times*. April 29, 1932.

"May Seek New Trial." *Kokomo Tribune*. February 15, 1933.

"'Lifer' Gladden Nears Parole." *Frankfort Morning Times*. February 11, 1966.

Magazine

John N. Makris, "The Mysterious Land of Nod," *Mechanix Illustrated*, March 1954.

Chapter 7—Chirka and Rasico

"Present Bill to Establish Electric Chair in Indiana." *Indianapolis Star*. January 15, 1913.

"Hangman Will Lose His Job." *Fort Wayne Sentinel*. January 30, 1913.

"Murders Wife in Front of Children." *Lake County Times* (Munster, IN). May 15, 1913.

"Chirka Is Not a Bit Sorry." *Lake County Times* (Munster, IN). May 17, 1913.

"Slays Wife and Baby in Terre Haute Home." *Muncie Sunday Star*. September 14, 1913.

"Talks Glibly about Murdering His Wife." *Indianapolis News*. September 15, 1913.

"Electric Chair Is Sought by Rasico; Says He Will Not Go to Prison." *Princeton Clarion-News*. September 17, 1913.

"Doomed to Death by Jury." *Lake County Times* (Munster, IN). September 18, 1913.

"Pair of Indiana Murderers Are to Die in Chair." *Muncie Sunday Star*. September 21, 1913.

"Rasico Sentenced to Die in Electric Chair." *Indianapolis News*. September 22, 1913.

"State Needs an Electric Chair." *Daily Republican* (Rushville, IN). September 22, 1913.

"Governor Will Pay for Electric Chair." *Muncie Morning Star*. October 3, 1913.

"Chirka's Friends to Appeal to Governor." *Lake County Times* (Munster, IN). October 31, 1913.

"Murderers Await Execution." *Times-Tribune* (Alexandria, IN). December 3, 1913.

"Meade Believes Chirka Is Crazy." *Lake County Times* (Munster, IN). December 4, 1913.
"Governor Sets Feb. 20 as Date for Executions." *Indianapolis Star*. January 8, 1914.
"Will Chirka Burn?" *Lake County Times* (Munster, IN). February 7, 1914.
"Gov. Ralston Will Not Commute Wife-Murderers' Death Sentences." *Fort Wayne Sentinel*. February 13, 1914.
"Governor Rules Two Uxoricides Must Die Feb. 20." *Indianapolis Star*. February 13, 1914.
"Rasico and Chirka Are Electrocuted." *Princeton Clarion-News*. February 20, 1914.
"Two Convicts Meet Death in Electric Chair." *Muncie Evening Press*. February 20, 1914.
"A History of Executions in Indiana." *Indianapolis Star*. December 11, 2019.

Chapter 8—Manhunt for the In-Law Outlaws

"Posse in Pursuit of Deputy's Slayer." *Indianapolis Sunday Star*. April 1, 1906.
"Exciting Manhunt in Indiana Wilds." *Indianapolis Star*. April 2, 1906.
"Roby and Haycock Caught by Posse." *Indianapolis Star*. April 3, 1906.
"Mob Thwarted by Posse from Paoli." *Indianapolis News*. April 3, 1906.
"Killed Deputy Sheriff." *Indianapolis Star*. April 4, 1906.
"Governor to Be Asked to Protect Two Prisoners When They Are Tried for Murder." *Evening Herald* (Huntington, IN). April 10, 1906.
"Orange County Grand Jury at Work." *Indianapolis Star*. April 13, 1906.
"Deputy's Slayers Arraigned." *Fort Wayne Sentinel*. April 16, 1906.
"Prisoners Returned to Paoli with Much Secrecy." *Courier-Journal* (Louisville, KY). April 16, 1906.
"Roby and Haycock Sentenced for Life." *Indianapolis Star*. April 17, 1906.
"Roby and Haycock Off for Prison." *Indianapolis News*. April 17, 1906.
"Fifty Prisoners Ask Board to Free Them; Petitions for Release Recall Six Indiana Murders." *Indianapolis News*. March 27, 1911.
"Says Fatal Shots Were Fired by John Roby." *Muncie Morning Star*. December 12, 1913.
"Ralston Grants Lifer Freedom." *Indianapolis Star*. October 20, 1915.
"Roby Case Plea Is Heard." *Indianapolis News*. June 28, 1917.
"2 Life Termers Get Clemency; John Roby and Elbert Meredith in for Murder, Paroled." *Indianapolis Star*. July 7, 1922.

Chapter 9—The Black Sheep of Goldsmith

"Frankfort Policeman Is Slain in Gun Battle with Clyde Jones." *Frankfort Morning Times*. October 13, 1929.
"Clyde Jones, Killer of Officer Is Taken." *Tipton Daily Tribune*. October 14, 1929.
"Slayer of Policeman Is Held in County Jail." *Frankfort Morning Times*. October 14, 1929.
"Police Locate More Evidence against Jones." *Frankfort Morning Times*. October 17, 1929.
"Clyde Jones, Chas. Cudahy Are Indicted." *Frankfort Times*. October 20, 1929.

"Clyde Jones Arraigned in Circuit Court." *Frankfort Times*. November 23, 1929.
"Jones Pleads Not Guilty to Murder." *Frankfort Times*. November 28, 1929.
"Clyde Jones Case Venued to Boone County; Will Be Tried Before Judge J. W. Hornaday." *Frankfort Times*. November 30, 1929.
"Killer Faces Trial for Life." *Greenfield Daily Reporter*. January 20, 1930.
"George Zook Is First Witness in Jones Trial." *Frankfort Times*. January 22, 1930.
"Nine Men Testify for State in Clyde Jones Trial on Third Day." *Frankfort Times*. January 23, 1930.
"Gun Is Explained." *Tipton Daily Tribune*. January 23, 1930.
"Two State Witnesses Testify Jones Had Threatened Officers Zook and Webster." *Frankfort Times*. January 24, 1930.
"Murder Trial at Lebanon Nearing Close." *Frankfort Morning Times*. January 25, 1930.
"Jones Trial to Close Monday." *Tipton Daily Tribune*. January 25, 1930.
"Jury Deliberating Fate of Clyde Jones." *Frankfort Times*. January 28, 1930.
"Clyde Jones Found Guilty of Slaying." *Tipton Daily Tribune*. January 28, 1930.
"Jones Convicted of First Degree Murder; Will Receive His Sentence on Saturday." *Frankfort Morning Times*. January 29, 1930.
"Jones Given Life Term in Penitentiary." *Tipton Daily Tribune*. February 1, 1930.
"Clyde Jones Given Life Sentence; Judge Denies Motion Made for New Trial." *Frankfort Morning Times*. February 2, 1930.
"Jones Starts Term; Former Goldsmith Man Convicted of Murder Taken to Prison." *Tipton Daily Tribune*. February 4, 1930.
"George W. Zook, Former Officer Here, Commits Suicide." *Lafayette Journal and Courier*. August 16, 1930.
"Clyde Jones Seeks Release." *Tipton Daily Tribune*. December 12, 1935.
"Clyde H. Jones" (Obituary). *Tipton County Tribune*. November 2, 2000.

Records from Indiana State Prison

Case History, May 12, 1930–September 15, 1950
Commutation of Sentence and Parole, signed by Indiana governor Ralph F. Gates, March 12, 1945
Discharge from Parole, signed by Indiana governor Henry F. Schricker, September 14, 1950

Chapter 10—He Was Her Man, but He Done Her Wrong

"Frankie, Leland Were Lovers; He Done Her Wrong, Is Shot." *Waukesha (WI) Daily Freeman*. March 20, 1950.
"'Frankie' Loves 'Johnny,' So She Shoots Him." *Indianapolis News*. March 20, 1950.
"Grand Jury Convenes Friday in Miller Case." *Frankfort Morning Times*. March 21, 1950.
"Grand Jury May Reach Verdict Today." *Frankfort Morning Times*. March 24, 1950.
"Frankie Miller Is Indicted." *Frankfort Morning Times*. March 25, 1950.

"Frankie Miller Pleads Not Guilty to First Degree Murder." *Frankfort Morning Times*. April 5, 1950.

"Trial of Frankie Miller Will Open in Circuit Court Monday." *Frankfort Morning Times*. May 21, 1950.

"Frankie's Life Not at Stake; Extreme Penalty Is Waived by Prosecutor Tom Robison." *Frankfort Morning Times*. May 23, 1950.

"State's Evidence in Case Presented; Jury Hears Frankie Quoted, 'I Killed Him, I'm Glad of It'." *Frankfort Morning Times*. May 25, 1950.

"Frankie Faces Girl Holliday Chose Night He Was Killed." *Frankfort Morning Times*. May 26, 1950.

"Defense Takes Over at Trial." *Frankfort Morning Times*. May 27, 1950.

"Frankie to Tell Own Story; To Take Stand Wednesday." *Frankfort Morning Times*. May 30, 1950.

"Jury Will Get Case Today." *Frankfort Morning Times*. June 1, 1950.

"Frankie Bares Her Story to Jury." *Dixon (IL) Evening Telegraph*. June 2, 1950.

"Frankie Convicted of Manslaughter." *Frankfort Morning Times*. June 2, 1950.

"Frankie Miller Is Sentenced to Women's Prison." *Frankfort Morning Times*. June 6, 1950.

"Frankie Miller Goes to Prison." *Kokomo Tribune*. June 6, 1950.

"Robert Starr Is Victim of Heart Attack; Veteran Newsman Collapses, Dies in Few Minutes." *Frankfort Morning Times*. June 10, 1950.

"Marriage Licenses." *Kokomo Tribune*. December 1952.

"Obituaries." *Kokomo Tribune*. May 1993.

Sidebar: Legendary Clinton County Attorney Frank S. Pryor

"Frank S. Pryor, Noted Frankfort Attorney Dies." *Frankfort Times*. February 16, 1981.

Chapter 11—Fairy's Grim Tale of Murder on LaFountain

"Mrs. Fairy M'Clain-Miller Murdered by Worley Osborne [sic]." *Kokomo Daily Tribune*. April 8, 1908.

"Woman's Slayer Eludes Pursuers." *Muncie Morning Star*. April 9, 1908.

"Helped by Man in Buggy, Worley Osborne [sic] Got Away Wednesday Night." *Kokomo Daily Tribune*. April 10, 1908.

"Reward of $1,000 Provided by the County Council for Arrest and Conviction of the Murderer of Fairy McClain Miller." *Kokomo Daily Tribune*. April 14, 1908.

"Osborn Makes Full Confession of Guilt." *Kokomo Daily Tribune*. April 18, 1908.

"Slayer Lured to Net by Thought of Home." *Indianapolis Star*. April 18, 1908.

"Kokomo Murderer Caught by Police." *Muncie Morning Star*. April 18, 1908.

"Osborn to Be Up Thursday; Judge Elliott Sets Time for Murderer's Hearing." *Kokomo Daily Tribune*. April 20, 1908.

"'Blubber' Is Taken." *Lake County Times* (Munster, IN). April 20, 1908.

"Osborn's Plea Is Withdrawn." *Kokomo Daily Tribune*. April 23, 1908.

"Osborn Renews Plea of Murder in Second Degree." *Kokomo Daily Tribune*. April 24, 1908.

"Slayer Osborn Is Sentenced." *Kokomo Daily Tribune*. April 25, 1908.

"Life Sentence Given Osborn, the Kokomo Murderer." *Elwood Call Leader.* April 25, 1908.

"Osborn's Last Day in Jail; Sends for Reporter and Makes Statement; Says He Is Thankful." *Kokomo Daily Tribune.* April 28, 1908.

"Osborn Off for Prison; Big Crowd at Train." *Kokomo Daily Tribune.* April 29, 1908.

"Application of Howard Lifer Heard by Parole." *Kokomo Daily Tribune.* December 5, 1919.

"Michigan City Lifer Is Paroled by Death." *Fort Wayne News and Sentinel.* July 26, 1920.

Chapter 12—Murder on Anderson and Main

"Elwood Disgraced by a Foul Murder: Frederick Kaiser Shot and Killed by A. J. Baker." *Daily Record* (Elwood, IN). September 4, 1903.

"Elwood Murder Result of Domestic Trouble." *Indianapolis News.* September 4, 1903.

"Baker Case Now Being Investigated by Grand Jury." *Daily Record* (Elwood, IN). October 7, 1903.

"Baker Indicted." *Daily Record* (Elwood, IN). October 23, 1903.

"He Wants Out." *Daily Record* (Elwood, IN). October 28, 1903.

"A. J. Baker Is Arraigned." *Indianapolis News.* January 19, 1904.

"Show Feeling against Baker." *Anderson Morning Herald.* January 22, 1904.

"Baker Will Go on Witness Stand." *Daily Record* (Elwood, IN). January 23, 1904.

"Kaiser Made Many Threats." *Anderson Morning Herald.* January 24, 1904.

"Baker Unshaken by Cross Examination." *Anderson Morning Herald.* January 27, 1904.

"Lawyers Are Arguing Baker Case; Will Go to Jury Late This Afternoon." *Daily Record* (Elwood, IN). January 27, 1904.

"In the Hands of the Jury." *Anderson Morning Herald.* January 28, 1904.

"Rumors of Tampering with the Jury in Baker Case Are Circulating." *Daily Record* (Elwood, IN). January 29, 1904.

"Jury Will Be Called upon to Tell the Court Why They Cannot Agree." *Daily Record* (Elwood, IN). January 30, 1904.

"Hung the Jury to Save Baker from Sentence." *Muncie Morning Star.* January 31, 1904.

"Baker Will Be Tried Here; Will Not Ask for Change of Venue." *Daily Record* (Elwood, IN). February 2, 1904.

"Baker Trial Will Go to Another County." *Daily Record* (Elwood, IN). February 24, 1904.

"Will Plead Guilty to Manslaughter." *Daily Record* (Elwood, IN). April 5, 1904.

"Baker's Means Are Almost Exhausted." *Daily Record* (Elwood, IN). June 6, 1904.

"Baker's Trial Goes Over in Hamilton County Court." *Elwood Call Leader.* June 8, 1904.

"Baker Has Been Prisoner in County Jail for One Year." *Elwood Call Leader.* September 3, 1904.

"Baker's Trial May Be Venued to Madison County." *Elwood Call-Leader.* September 19, 1904.

"A. J. Baker Taken to the Jail at Noblesville." *Elwood Call Leader*. November 19, 1904.
"Jury Empanelled and Baker Trial Is Now Underway." *Daily Record* (Elwood, IN). November 21, 1904.
"Second Trial Under Way." *Indianapolis News*. November 23, 1904.
"Baker Gets Liberty; Jury in Hamilton County Finds the Accused Not Guilty; Verdict Was No Surprise Here." *Elwood Call Leader*. November 28, 1904.
"Is Bitter Against State's Attorney." *Muncie Morning Star*. December 1, 1904.
"A. J. Baker Located at Indianapolis." *Daily Record* (Elwood, IN). January 21, 1905.
"Andrew J. Baker, 88, Dies." *Indianapolis News*. April 22, 1929.

Chapter 13—The Strawtown Murders

"Unwelcome Suitor Ends Two Lives." *Indianapolis News*. October 4, 1907.
"Lynching Talk Near Noblesville." *Fort Wayne News*. October 4, 1907.
"Father and Son Are Murdered." *Hamilton County Ledger* (Noblesville, IN). October 8, 1907.
"Citizens Murdered." *Enterprise* (Noblesville, IN). October 11, 1907.
"Hensley Indicted; Grand Jury Charges Him with Murder in the First Degree." *Hamilton County Ledger* (Noblesville, IN). October 18, 1907.
"Trial Will Be Held in March." *Indianapolis News*. January 18, 1908.
"Hensley on Trial." *Hamilton County Ledger* (Noblesville, IN). March 3, 1908.
"Sweetheart Tells of Double Murder." *Indianapolis News*. March 4, 1908.
"Evidence in the Hensley Murder Trial About Finished; State Rested Wednesday." *Hamilton County Ledger* (Noblesville, IN). March 6, 1908.
"Manslaughter Is Hensley Verdict." *Muncie Sunday Star*. March 8, 1908.
"Hensley Guilty; Convicted of the Crime of Manslaughter in the McClintock Case." *Hamilton County Ledger* (Noblesville, IN). March 10, 1908.
"Convict Will Be Tried on a Charge of Murder; James W. Hensley, Now Serving Indeterminate Sentence, Is Charged with Killing Enoch McClintock." *Indianapolis News*. April 27, 1910.
"Hensley Again on Trial, Enters Self-Defense Plea." *Indianapolis Star*. May 3, 1910.
"Murder Trial Jury Fails to Agree on Punishment." *Indianapolis Star*. May 8, 1910.
"Slayer of Walker McClintock and E. McClintock Returned to Prison." *Indianapolis News*. May 9, 1910.
"Repudiates Her Testimony, Miss Mary McClintock Complicates Matters in Hensley Murder Case." *Indianapolis News*. May 10, 1910.
"Motion to Free a Murderer of Charge." *Huntington Herald*. April 15, 1912.
"Four Murderers Granted Pardons as Were a Bunch of Thieves and Cutthroats." *Fort Wayne Daily News*. December 23, 1912.
"James Hensley Released." *Indianapolis News*. January 8, 1913.

Chapter 14—Murder Unbecoming a Hero

"A Man Shot by an Army Officer." *New York Tribune*. November 19, 1869.
"Tragedy at Kokomo, Ind.: Joseph Vanhorn Killed, Lt. Daugherty Avenges His Sister's Honor." *Chicago Tribune*. November 22, 1869.

"Fatal Affray: An Army Officer Kills the Slanderer of His Sister." *Huntington Herald.* November 24, 1869.
"Private Vengeance." *New York Daily Tribune.* November 26, 1869.
"Slandering Women." *Daily Milwaukee (WI) News.* November 30, 1869.
"Editor's Journal: Letter to the Editor from Mrs. Sarah Van Horn." *Kokomo Journal.* January 21, 1870.
"State vs. Daugherty." *Kokomo Journal.* May 27, 1870.
"The Daugherty Case: Immense Piles of Affidavits; The Case Goes to Tipton." *Kokomo Tribune.* June 2, 1870.
"Notice." *Kokomo Journal.* October 14, 1870.
"Lieutenant Daugherty." *Kokomo Tribune.* October 20, 1870.
"Daugherty-Van Horn Trial." *Kokomo Tribune.* November 10, 1870.
"Lieutenant Will Daugherty Acquitted." *Indianapolis News.* November 10, 1870.
"Indiana Items." *Indianapolis News.* November 11, 1870.
"More Insanity: Daugherty-Van Horn Murder Case." *New York Herald.* November 14, 1870.
"The Daugherty Trial." *Kokomo Tribune.* November 17, 1870.
"The Daugherty Case." *Waterloo (IN) Press.* November 24, 1870.
"Retired Army Officer, Age 81, Dead." *Indianapolis News.* February 4, 1922.
"Kokomo Saloons Served Turkey for Free Lunch." *Kokomo Tribune.* November 27, 1929.

Book

Dunn, Jacob Piatt. *Indiana and Indianans: A History of Aboriginal and Territorial Indiana and the Century of Statehood.* Chicago and New York: American Historical Society, 1919.

Chapter 15—The Awful Crime of Jesse McClure

"Atrocious Crime of an Elwood Man." *Daily Record* (Elwood, IN). October 26, 1903.
"Shot His Two Babies in Revenge. *Indianapolis News.* October 26, 1903.
"Awful Crime of Jesse McClure Near Point Isabel." *Kokomo Daily Tribune.* October 26, 1903.
"Read Stories of Crime: Jesse McClure Gloated Over the Annals of Murder." *Kokomo Daily Tribune.* October 27, 1903.
"Murderer McClure Is in the Tipton Jail and the Grand Jury Will Convene Monday—Funeral of One Victim." *Daily Record* (Elwood, IN). October 27, 1903.
"The Hurry Up to Be Given Murderer Jesse McClure." *Kokomo Daily Tribune.* October 28, 1903.
"Has Begun to Weaken: Murderer McClure Now Wants to See His Wife." *Kokomo Daily Tribune.* October 29, 1903.
"McClure Finally Shows Signs of Penitence; Five Physicians Make Another Examination and Declare the Prisoner Sane." *Daily Record* (Elwood, IN). October 30, 1903.
"McClure's Bearing Does Not Indicate Insanity." *Daily Record* (Elwood, IN). October 31, 1903.

"Courtroom Packed at Tipton Opening of Murderer McClure's Trial." *Kokomo Daily Tribune*. November 23, 1903.
"May Save His Neck by Convincing the Jury He Is Crazy." *Kokomo Daily Tribune*. November 25, 1903.
"Saves Neck but Must Go to Prison for Rest of His Days; Verdict No Surprise." *Kokomo Daily Tribune*. November 28, 1903.
"McClure Receives His Sentence to Prison and Will Be Taken to Penitentiary Tomorrow." *Daily Record* (Elwood, IN). December 1, 1903.
"Child Slayer Mad." *Elwood Call Leader*. August 5, 1905.
"Child Killer Has Gone Insane." *Muncie Sunday Star*. August 6, 1905.
"Jesse McClure Is Dying at Michigan City." *Logansport Reporter*. August 8, 1905.
"Died in Penitentiary." *Seymour Daily Republican*. January 14, 1907.
"Jesse McClure Dead." *Elwood Call Leader*. January 14, 1907.
"Tipton Murderer Is Dead." *Daily News-Democrat* (Huntington, IN). January 14, 1907.

Chapter 16—Massacre on Laughery Creek

"Find 5 Slain on Indiana Farm." *Hammond Times*. May 19, 1941.
"'Hot Suspect' Held in Killings." *Muncie Morning Star*. May 19, 1941.
"Kin, Quizzed Here, Denies Slaying Part." *Indianapolis News*. May 19, 1941.
"Suspect Admits Killing 5 of Kin." *Indianapolis News*. May 20, 1941.
"Brutal Slaying of Five Confessed by Auroran after Being Grilled for 60 Hours at Lawrenceburg." *Cincinnati Enquirer*. May 21, 1941.
"Murderer of Family of Five Confesses." *Lawrenceburg Register*. May 22, 1941.
"Quintuple Murder Mystery Solved." *Lawrenceburg Press*. May 23, 1941.
"First Degree Murder Mass Killer Verdict." *Lawrenceburg Press*. May 30, 1941.
"Alleged Slayer Pleads Innocent in Death of 5." *Indianapolis News*. June 18, 1941.
"New Dearborn Judge's First Case to Concern Mass Slaying in Aurora." *Indianapolis Star*. October 12, 1941.
"Neighbor of Slain Family Describes Finding Bodies to Dearborn Jury." *Indianapolis Star*. October 16, 1941.
"Will Prove He Did Not Kill Any of Quintet, Indiana Jurors Are Told." *Cincinnati Enquirer*. October 16, 1941.
"Carter Fails in Plans to Escape." *Lawrenceburg Press*. October 17, 1941.
"Liquor, Women Sought by Carter on Night after Agrue Killings, Graves Says." *Cincinnati Enquirer*. October 19, 1941.
"Murder Case: Defendant Denies That He Killed Family of Five." *Tipton Daily Tribune*. October 21, 1941.
"Aurora Man Charged with Murder of Family of 5 Names Friend as Slayer." *Indianapolis Star*. October 21, 1941.
"Carter Sentenced to Death." *Cincinnati Enquirer*. October 22, 1941.
"Carter Paves Way to Present Appeal." *Muncie Evening Press*. November 15, 1941.
"Governor Scans Execution Case, Says He Won't Halt Sentence without New Evidence." *Indianapolis Star*. February 7, 1942.
"Carter Dies in Electric Chair." *Muncie Evening Press*. February 10, 1942.
"Private Rites Held for 'Dink' Carter." *Lawrenceburg Press*. February 13, 1942.
"Dearborn County Gets Bill for $50 for Execution of Virginius Carter." *Indianapolis Star*. February 15, 1942.

Newsletter article

"Son-in-Law 'Dink' Carter Confesses to Killing Family." *Doorway to History*, Newsletter of the Dearborn County Historical Society. May–June 2011.

Chapter 17—The Legend of Kokomo Mayor H. C. Cole

"Killed While Stealing; Dr. H. C. Cole, Mayor Kokomo, Shot by a Sheriff's Posse." *Indianapolis News*. September 20, 1881.
"Horrible Tragedy: Mayor Cole Shot Dead while Committing Felony." *Kokomo Dispatch*. September 22, 1881.
"An Ex-Mayor Killed as a Thief." *New York Times*. September 24, 1881.
"Slayers of Mayor Cole Discharged." *Daily Evening Republican* (Columbus, IN). November 1, 1881.
"Indiana." *Fort Wayne Daily Gazette*. November 18, 1881.
Mayor Cole Killed Night Garfield Died." *Kokomo Daily Tribune*. October 30, 1925.
"Mayor Cole Killed Here 50 Years Ago." *Kokomo Tribune*. September 19, 1931.
"Some Anecdotes about Unusual Kokomoans." *Kokomo Tribune*. October 30, 1950.
"Famed Actress Rooted in Kokomo." *Kokomo Tribune*. December 20, 1990.
"Mills Were Part of the Daily Grind in Kokomo." *Kokomo Tribune*. October 13, 1991.
"Letters: Story Behind Mayor's Death, by Bill McKibben and Jeff Hatton." *Kokomo Tribune*. March 31, 1994.

Sidebar: The Mollihan Gang

"Many Murders Laid at His Door." *Daily Democrat* (Huntington, IN). July 16, 1894.
"Notorious Tough Captured." *Huntington Herald*. July 17, 1894.
"Its Work Recalled. Record of the Mollihan Gang at Kokomo, Ind." *Chicago Daily Tribune*. July 30, 1894.
"Back to Old Haunts." *Tipton Daily Tribune*. September 9, 1912.
"Many Murders Still Wrapped in Mysteries." *Kokomo Tribune*. December 1, 1937.

Books

Booher, Ned. *Kokomo: A Pictorial History*. St. Louis, MO: G. Bradley, 1990.
Pershing, M. W. *History of Tipton County, Indiana: Her People, Industries and Institutions*. Indianapolis, IN: B. F. Bowen, 1914.

Chapter 18—Gun Girl

"Local Girl Held in Pennsylvania; Miss Isabelle Messmer Battles Pittsburgh Police after Arrest on Gun Charge." *Elwood Call Leader*. October 20, 1933.
"Two-Fisted Elwood Gun Girl Paroled, Must Quit State." *Indianapolis Star*. December 12, 1933.
"Elwood Girl Is Given Freedom; Messmer Classified as 'Psychopathic Personality' at Washington." *Elwood Call Leader*. August 15, 1934.
"Elwood Too Slow; Messmer Girl Back Home but Won't Stay Long." *Tipton Daily Tribune*. August 23, 1934.

"Elwood Girl Is Sent to Prison." *Elwood Call Leader.* February 25, 1938.

"Police-Kicking Girl Is Sought: Isabelle Messmer Flees Reformatory with Pal." *Pittsburgh Post-Gazette.* January 23, 1939.

"Isabelle Now Claims She Shot and Killed a Man." *Elwood Call-Leader.* October 9, 1939.

"Isabelle Messmer Shuns the Limelight of the News, Turns a Moody 'Gal' and Won't Talk." *Elwood Call-Leader.* October 10, 1939.

"Texas Extradites Hoosier Gun Girl; Isabelle Messmer Faces Charge of Slaying Ballplayer." *Indianapolis Sunday Star.* October 15, 1939.

"Isabelle Messmer Claims Confession to Be Ruse to Prevent Her Return to New Jersey." *Elwood Call-Leader.* October 18, 1939.

"Gun Girl Goes on Trial This Week." *Elwood Call-Leader.* December 11, 1939.

"Self-Defense Is Isabelle's Claim." *Elwood Call-Leader.* March 26, 1940.

"Gun Girl Convicted of Murder." *Elwood Call-Leader.* March 27, 1940.

"Two-Gun Girl Breaks Prison in Texas Town." *Pittsburgh Post-Gazette.* April 9, 1940.

"Notorious Elwood Gun Girl Arrested in Lobby of Ritz Theater Held in Tipton Jail." *Tipton Daily Tribune.* May 30, 1940.

"Texas Sheriff Will Come to Tipton to Get Escaped Gun Girl." *Tipton Daily Tribune.* May 31, 1940.

"Crazed Gun Girl Starts a Long Trip; Isabelle Messmer Caused Much Commotion When Taken from Jail on Her Way to Texas." *Tipton Daily Tribune.* June 4, 1940.

"Bulletin." *Elwood Call-Leader.* November 12, 1940.

"Isabelle's Back in Clink for Good (We Hope!)." *Elwood Call-Leader.* April 23, 1941.

"Kicking Around the Basin." *Odessa (TX) American.* April 30, 1941.

"Messmer Says She Wants to Be a Good Girl and Start All Over." *Odessa (TX) American.* May 2, 1941.

"Woman Felon Gets New Term." *Arizona Republic* (Phoenix, AZ). December 22, 1942.

"Crime Doesn't Pay but Keeps Kenny Wines Busy." *Tipton Daily Tribune.* April 19, 1947,

Chapter 19—Murder Most Foul

"Foully Shot: Load of Buckshot Crashed Through Window; John Seay Victim of Unknown Assassin." *Indianapolis News.* December 23, 1901.

"Work of an Assassin." *Hamilton County Ledger* (Noblesville, IN). December 24, 1901.

"Jealousy Was Cause of It All; John Seay Was Shot by a Young Rival." *Times* (Richmond, VA). December 25, 1901.

"An Awful Murder Shocks Public." *Hamilton County Democrat* (Noblesville, IN). December 27, 1901.

"Gun Barrel Uncovered; Part of Weapon Used in Killing John E. Seay." *Indianapolis News.* December 27, 1901.

"Mystery of the John Seay Assassination." *Indianapolis News.* January 7, 1902.

"Fodrea Is Indicted." *Daily Record* (Elwood, IN). March 11, 1902.

"Seay Murder Trial on at Noblesville; William Fodrea Is Charged with Assassinating J. E. Seay." *Indianapolis News*. June 9, 1902.

"Fodrea Case Now Underway." *Indianapolis News*. June 10, 1902.

"State's Best Day in Fodrea Case; Miss Carrie Phillips the Star Witness in the Noblesville Murder Trial." *Indianapolis News*. June 11, 1902.

"William Fodrea Not on the Stand; Will Not Testify in His Own Behalf." *Indianapolis News*. June 12, 1902.

"Argument Begun in the Fodrea Case; Testimony Closed and Lawyers Began to Talk; Sister on the Stand." *Indianapolis News*. June 13, 1902.

"Fodrea Is Acquitted." *Indianapolis Journal*. June 15, 1902.

"Jury Declares Fodrea Innocent." *Fort Wayne Weekly Journal Gazette*. June 19, 1902.

"Fodrea Finds Freedom at Hands of Jury." *Hamilton County Democrat* (Noblesville, IN). June 20, 1902.

"New Canning Machine." *Fort Wayne Sentinel*. July 2, 1903.

"Astonish Crowds with Homemade Auto." *Indianapolis Star*. July 13, 1908.

Chapter 20: The Strange Death of Garnet Ginn

"Find Portland Teacher Dead; Hanged on Car." *Muncie Star*. March 1, 1950.

"Believe Woman Took Own Life." *Muncie Evening Press*. March 2, 1950.

"Teacher Ended Own Life, Police Believe." *Muncie Star*. March 3, 1950.

"Added Evidence Is Uncovered in Portland Killing." *Indianapolis Star*. April 14, 1950.

"Autopsy Proves Teacher Didn't End Own Life." *Muncie Evening Press*. April 14, 1950.

"Ginn Was Murdered." *Extra: The Graphic* (Portland, IN). April 14, 1950.

"Lack of Police Probe in Death of Teacher Hit." *Indianapolis News*. April 14, 1950.

"Portland Teacher Murdered." *Muncie Star*. April 14, 1950.

"Added Evidence Is Uncovered in Portland Killing." *Muncie Star*. April 15, 1950.

"Murder Suspect Accosted Her in Portland Garage." *Muncie Star*. April 16, 1950.

"Writer Tells of Threats in Portland Case." *Palladium-Item* (Richmond, IN). April 17, 1950

"Star Offers $1,000 for Murderer." *Indianapolis Star*. April 18, 1950.

"Newspaper and Sheriff Add to Fund." *Muncie Star*. April 18, 1950.

"Editorial: Portland's Police Chief Should Be Fired." *Elwood Call-Leader*. April 18, 1950.

"In the Press of Things: Murder Case Not Dropped." *Muncie Evening Press*. May 11, 1950.

"Mystery Still Surrounds Death of Portland Teacher." *Muncie Star*. May 14, 1950.

"Ginn Death Is Unsolved." *Terre Haute Tribune-Star*. May 14, 1950.

"In the Press of Things: Portland Case Unsolved." *Muncie Evening Press*. June 15, 1950.

"Portland Feminine Reporter Has Hopes Teacher Slayer Will Crack." *Muncie Evening Press*. October 16, 1951.

JANIS THORNTON is the Indiana-based author of the true crime book *Too Good a Girl*; two cozy mysteries, *Dust Bunnies & Dead Bodies* and *Dead Air & Double Dare*; and a stand-alone mystery, *Love, Lies, and Azure Eyes*. In addition, she has produced three pictorial-history books in the Images of America series for Tipton County, Frankfort, and Elwood, all in Indiana. She is a member of the national Sisters in Crime organization and its Indianapolis chapter, the Authors Guild, Indiana Writers Center, and the Tipton County (Indiana) Historical Society. You many visit her online at www.janis-thornton.com and facebook.com/janisthorntonauthor, and follow her on Twitter @JanisThornton.